HERESY AND THE IDEAL

BOOKS BY DAVID BAKER

POETRY

The Truth about Small Towns   1998
After the Reunion   1994
Sweet Home, Saturday Night   1991
Haunts   1985
Laws of the Land   1981

CRITICISM

Heresy and the Ideal: On Contemporary Poetry   2000
Meter in English: A Critical Engagement   1996

HERESY
and the
IDEAL

On
Contemporary
Poetry

DAVID BAKER

The University of Arkansas Press
Fayetteville
2000

LIBRARY OF CONGRESS CATALOGING-IN-PUBLICATION DATA

Baker, David, 1954–
    Heresy and the ideal : on contemporary poetry / David Baker.
        p.   cm.
    ISBN 1-55728-602-7 (alk. paper) —ISBN 1-55728-603-5 (pbk. : alk. paper)
    1. American poetry—20th century—History and criticism. I. Title.

PS325 .B35 2000
811'.5409—dc21   99-057806

for Ann and Katie

Genius, perhaps, is making anything
worth the world's stealing. Remembering Spender's
"I think continually of those who were truly great,"
I soap my face, brush teeth, lay head

on down-filled pillow wrapped in white cotton,
and lie in a bed with four posters—
not three, not five,
as the quatrain here is an unimprovable discovery.

—JANE HIRSHFIELD

ACKNOWLEDGMENTS

These works first appeared in the following publications, to whose editors I extend my gratitude:

American Book Review: "The Crux of The Matter: David Wojahn"

The Denver Quarterly: "The Romance of Betrayal: David St. John"

The Gettysburg Review: "On Explication"

The Kenyon Review: "Against Mastery: Adrienne Rich and Philip Levine"; "Framed in Words"; "Heresy and the American Ideal: On T. R. Hummer"; "Hieroglyphs of Erasure: Albert Goldbarth"; "Kinds of Knowing"; "Line by Line"; "Probable Reason, Possible Joy"; "The Push of Reading"

The Missouri Review: "Still-Hildreth Sanatorium, 1936"

Poetry: "Culture, Inclusion, Craft"; "On Restraint"; "Plainness and Sufficiency"; "Romantic Melancholy, Romantic Excess"; "Smarts"

The Southern Review: "To Advantage Dressed: Miller Williams among the Naked Poets"

Passages from "Heresy and the American Ideal: On T. R. Hummer" also appeared in earlier form in "A Fullness of Heart," my review of T. R. Hummer's *The Angelic Orders,* published in *New England Review/Bread Loaf Quarterly.*

I am also grateful to the following for permission to use extended quotations from the copyrighted works of these poets:

Robert Bly, *Eating the Honey of Words: New and Selected Poems* (HarperCollins, 1999). Copyright © 1999. Reprinted by permission of the publisher.

Eavan Boland, *Outside History: Selected Poems 1980–1990* (W. W. Norton, 1990). Copyright © 1990. Reprinted by permission of the publisher.

Henri Coulette, *The Collected Poems of Henri Coulette* (University of Arkansas Press, 1990). Copyright © 1990. Reprinted by permission of the publisher.

CONTENTS

INTRODUCTION

Today is a chilly, sunny day in April as I start these introductory remarks to *Heresy and the Ideal*. The first flowers are fading already, little clumps of crocus in debris, white daffodils along the sidewalk. The maple leaves have unfisted and are starting to shine.

April in America is National Poetry Month. Last week I gave a benefit reading, from my own poems, at a large chain bookstore in Columbus, Ohio. It had seemed one of the less odious chain stores, interested in literature and culture, and I was glad to be asked to take part in the event. When I arrived, the manager met me at the door and pointed me back to the porta-podium, which waited in a cleared area near the large coffee bar and cafe. There were a dozen tables, mostly empty, and a few people reading newspapers or books.

I read my poems for about forty-five minutes, and people came and went, listening with eagerness, sometimes, or with curiosity or bemusement. Some sat and stayed, attending hard, though the cash registers whirred and doors opened and closed and conversations bubbled around us. Sometimes they clapped, quietly, or asked questions.

"Where are your books?" was one question, and when we looked to the manager for direction, she made a sad face. "We don't carry David's books here," she said. We all shared an embarrassed group laugh. "If the national buyer doesn't pick a book for all the stores," she explained, "then we don't carry it. None of the stores carries it. It's all or nothing." There were two poetry shelves in the store, with a few dozen volumes: Dickinson, Whitman, Milton; several brightly-colored books with covers depicting sea shores and sunshine; a few popular anthologies; and half-a-dozen contemporary poets, including the year's best-selling poet, Jewel, a teenage pop-music celebrity. I imagined that offering, in that exact presentation—the books like little bags of french fries in their slots—at every one of the chain's stores.

April is National Poetry Month. It is also National Lawn and Garden Month, Alcohol Awareness Month, Fresh Florida Tomato Month—I'm not making this up—Holy Humor Month, Sports Eye Safety Month, and so on. It is a shame that poetry is relegated to the status of a public-relations event.

It is a shame that any of these activities or concerns is a public-relations or sales event. But a joke, a tomato, a black eye, a poem are all equivalent commodities in the devouring market.

The store manager's predicament was an example of the problem. She couldn't carry my books because my books weren't likely to sell enough copies to make it worth the shelf space. So that day no one found my books. I was there as a good-will publicity stunt, as corporate entertainment, like the New Age guitarist tuning up in the coffee bar to play all afternoon or like the puppeteer who regularly entertains kids in the children's book and toy section. After all, why give up space to a book of poetry, which might sell a thousand or two copies in a year across the nation, when you can stock a book that will sell many thousands, even hundreds of thousands, of copies? Octavio Paz accurately describes this circumstance: "The literary trade today is motivated by purely economic considerations. The value of a book, thus, is the number of people who purchase it."

Poets operate within an economy that places little value on their works, and thus on their work. Poetry brings no return on the monetary investment. The major book companies are headed by people whose expertise is advertising, finance, management, and international relations, not literature, and whose motivation is sales. Here is Paz again: "The best-seller, be it a novel or a book on current affairs, appears on the scene like a meteor: everyone rushes to buy it, but in a short time it disappears forever. Best-sellers are not works of literature, they are merchandise. What distinguishes a literary work from a book that is merely entertaining or informative is the fact that the latter is meant literally to be consumed by its readers, whereas the former has the ability to come back to life." Lewis Hyde rightly avers that art functions not as an element of the consumer market but as a component within a gift economy.

The marketplace has always been an unfriendly site for poetry. But the contemporary academy is not very enthusiastic about the art, either. For the past two decades the literary professorate has disengaged itself from the literary text as a whole. I have colleagues who don't read literature anymore, although they read earnestly about theories of literature. A poet friend recently told of a reading she gave, at a college well known for its writers and English department. "There were two hundred students, listening and asking questions, and one member of the English department, and she was my host," said my friend, shaking her head. The academy has never been especially nurturing to the art, but at least, at its best, it has been a critical audience.

During the past twenty years the university has experienced a kind of explosion. Its greatest efforts have been to widen its own scope and nature, and among the central developments are these: critical attention to the rhetoric of popular culture and the mass media; a worthy embrace and guidance of growing cultural diversity; and expansive investigations (and deconstructions) of the very notion of genres, departments, and intellectual disciplines. At its best the English department has opened for interrogation its own canonical presumptions and has produced an era of new voices, genres, and projects. At its worst its fascination with theory—and with theory's technically bland language—has blinded its ability to appreciate, to evaluate, and to savor. Issues of aesthetics have given way to issues of cultural politics, but as Paz clarifies, the project of political criticism just isn't adequately equipped to describe the full experience of a work of art: "Reading a poem in this way [deconstructing its political significance only] is like studying botany by scrutinizing a Corot or Monet landscape." While a reasonable mind might indeed see the interrelationship of aesthetics and politics, too many contemporary scholars have hardened the discourse into an either/or dialectic. The price is obvious and high. In his editor's comment in a recent issue of *New Literary History,* Herbert F. Tucker notes that "the often politically urgent critique of historical and cultural meanings has a way of approaching literature as if it were information, of regarding a text's formal literariness as if it were a code to be broken and discarded in favor of the message it bears."

Part of the anxiety that drives the rhetoric of the contemporary academy derives from a corporate rigor not unlike that of the chain bookstore. The need to develop new fields, and thus new teaching and research positions, is part of the compulsion to compete in a powerfully competitive economy. Issues of academic publishing and tenure are, as well, issues of politics and power. One paradox is that this is all happening at a time when the American professorate senses that the worth of its opinions is being diminished, in the public eye, to the point of obsolescence. The public seldom turns to the professor for intellectual or moral guidance; hence, the professor hardens opinion into panicked certainty, in a last-ditch attempt to influence and convert the few listening. There is certainly nothing like negative capability in today's scholarly discourse. The American academy is running the risk of turning into a chain bookstore, with each book in its small place, driven by a corporate bottom line and a manic appeal to the public. Ironically, the academy's fascination with popular culture has produced a rhetoric of extreme exclusion, a language which few but the well-trained can share.

But people no longer read poetry for the same reasons they turned to it in earlier times. Poetry doesn't have the same audience because poetry doesn't serve the same purposes it did in the nineteenth or the fifteenth century. The advent of rapid publishing and the growth of literacy have produced an abundance of genres, forms of writing for every need and interest. We have short, long, sudden, flash, children's, airline, literary, erotic, minimalist, and interactive fiction. We have many more kinds of writing to convey many more kinds of information and experience—to say nothing of video, film, varieties of music, and other expressions. But poetry has a smaller corner in the larger market, and poets strain to identify its purpose. What is the purpose of poetry? Who is it for? How does it mean and continue to mean? These questions should be central to every poet and reader of poetry. They are also in my mind as I prepare to usher into the world a book about contemporary poetry. Who may read this book, and why? Where will they find it? What do they desire to know?

I have wanted to make a few remarks about the context for poetry in the current reality, and about the contexts for a practical criticism of poetry. Even with the complaints I have mentioned above, poetry seems healthy, resilient, relevant, and available. People who read poetry know where to find it—mail-order and internet outlets, the flourishing (yet always imperiled) small presses, the essential literary bookstores, the poetry readings and writers' conferences all over the country, libraries and schools and cultural centers. If most of the big book companies are abandoning the art, then small presses and some university publishers are trying to fill the void. As a subculture, poetry seems to thrive, partly in and partly out of the academy, the marketplace, the popular media, and the collective discourse.

In fact, some of the contemporary problems facing poetry are not merely contemporary. They are the abiding circumstance of an art which is neither especially democratic nor municipal. "The American public . . . does not care for, nor understand, serious poetry. Moreover, the special audience for poetry even among those who have gone through college is incredibly small . . . nowhere else in the world is [poetry] so thoroughly exiled as in America." So wrote Oscar Williams in the introduction to his great *A Little Treasury of American Poetry,* which was first published in 1948. More than half a century later, his reasons for the predicament of poetry are still accurate: "The American emphasis upon material welfare and mechanical gadgets, the reverence for the mysteries of science, the journalistic corruption of language in popular periodicals and upon the radio, the never-lifting oppression of economic anxiety and extrovert ideals, together with much else, make the simplest kind of escape entertainment, in the reality of their day's living, not only of more attraction, but actually of more value to the majority than so demanding an exercise as the reading of serious poetry." Only the radio dates his remarks.

Poetry is more resilient than one might think. Contemporary poets have confronted, even embraced, some of the problems above and turned them into the challenge of subject matter and method. The infusion of poetry with science and technology has marked the work of A. R. Ammons and Alice Fulton. The application of popular culture, with its linguistic and imaginative "corruption," provides Albert Goldbarth some of his most brilliant inspiration. Philip Levine has made his art by exposing the damages of the modern production line, as Adrienne Rich has made hers from a vivid indictment of the oppressive practices of power and politics. The Language poets, among many others, are busy adapting the form and actual presentation of poetry for the computer and the worldwide web. And poets continue to sing, lament, think, and praise, as they have for millennia.

If university English professors are busy theorizing about literature, many of their students seem more compelled to try to write it. After World War II the American university embraced—well, accepted—the literary writer, and in turn the writer brought a wide new discipline, creative writing, into the ivied halls. Indeed, college students are more interested in poetry and creative writing than ever before, and writing classes are plentiful, the programs rich and diverse. Accusations that poetry has subsequently become more insular, restrictive, or complacent are simply wrong. A college teaching position is virtually the only thing that poets as various as Susan Howe, Edward Hirsch, and June Jordan might be said to share. Some say that poets shouldn't be in college teaching positions. But where should they be? Where should sculptors and literary critics and physicists be, if not teaching the young the knowledge and methods of arts and sciences? In the writing class, students know that the literary text is a text in process. As a most practical expression of reader-response theory, the writing workshop is a forum for negotiation and creation and flexibility, where the text is not merely an instrument used to prove or disprove a professor's political position.

Heresy and the Ideal is a collection of many of the essays and essay-reviews which I have written and published throughout the 1990s. It is a discussion of the work of more than fifty contemporary poets. Herbert F. Tucker's solution to some of the issues he identified in his comment in *New Literary History* is part of my own impulse for assembling the present volume: "It seems time we broke up the habits of a decade and renewed our attention to the interrogation of the literary medium and, concurrently, of the critical medium of the interrogation." I aspire for *Heresy and the Ideal* to be a type of practical criticism, and I have taken as my guide and model some of the great critical books of the past three decades, especially Richard Howard's masterpiece, *Alone with America;* Helen Vendler's *Part of Nature, Part of Us, The Music of What Happens,* and *Soul Says;* as well as other works by Laurence Lieberman, Marjorie Perloff, Carol Muske, and Mary Kinzie. Like them, each in their way, I have hoped to represent many—though certainly not all—of the modes and tastes and concerns of the poetry of our time and language. I cannot imagine another period when so many fine poets were writing and publishing, nor has any other era seen such an explosive opening-up of voices—of minority writers, women writers, experimental writers, spoken-word artists, performance poets, traditionalists, lyric and narrative and speculative poets, writers of every political and cultural cadre. I can imagine fifty entirely different, yet equally engaging, poets in another book like this; that's how abundant our time is.

By the term practical criticism, I mean a criticism devoid as possible of exclusionary jargon, a criticism that pays persistent attention to the individual poem and book of poems. I write for readers of poetry as a kind of critical advance scout. Louise Glück's recent poem "Nest" says it well: "in my life, I was trying to be / a witness not a theorist. // The place you begin doesn't determine / the place you end." Just so, this is an enterprise whose biggest reward is as likely to be surprise as it is substantiation. "We cannot be content to like poems merely at random, and to pay them the compliment of no more than a passing glance; we cannot be content to take from a great poem only what we were expecting from it, as though it were simply a confirmation of something we already knew. The great poem has the power to enrich and extend us, to make us something more than we were before," according to C. B. Cox and A. E. Dyson in their old but useful textbook, *The Practical Criticism of Poetry.*

It is also true that practical criticism can be a code for the New Criticism, where everything but absolute attention to the text is jettisoned as irrelevant or misleading. (Of course we seem to live in a literary period when everything is included *except* textual engagement!) I recall the exasperated words of one of my critic-heroes, Randall Jarrell: "Personally, I believe that it would be profitable for critics to show less concern with poets, periods, society (big-scale extensive criticism) and more concern with the poems themselves (intensive criticism)." Certainly poems don't exist by themselves, but rather within the complex matrices of culture, and readerly intention, and social pressure, and yes, politics. But poems do exist as poems and not as advertisements, or sermons, or planks in a candidate's platform. So says Paz: "States fall, churches break apart or petrify, ideologies vanish—but poetry remains."

In the late 1980s I began to write about new books by contemporary poets, thanks to the invitations of several editors who solicited my work as critic and reviewer. In some cases I have written as I have pleased, as in my work on T. R. Hummer. In other cases editors have asked me to write on specific poets and/or specific books; Michael Burns started this project by first commissioning a long essay on the work of Miller Williams. Sometimes editors have given me a short list of preferred and available books—this is how *Poetry* arranges its critical reviews—and I have chosen from (and added to or negotiated) that list. *Heresy and the Ideal* is shaped by my own interests as well as by the editors who have aided and advised me.

It is important to me that the present book feels, at least in part, assigned—that it reflects a wide and diverse reading in contemporary poetry, as books have come to me by invitation or commission. Many of the following pieces are constructed as that hybrid form, the essay-review. What better way to consider a poet's purposes and achievements than through the review of individual volumes? Each book of poetry is a discrete and important method of delivery, for here the poet shapes and orders work into a very deliberate formal and thematic package. I have tried to make something deeper of this work, too. I have tried to reflect the range of recent poetry and turn that diversity toward my own aesthetic statements and judgments. Here each piece stands as an essay, based on the books at hand, but with a coherent set of theses and arguments of my own development.

There are few books about the present period of contemporary American poetry. True, there are many how-to-write-poetry books, plenty of theoretical analyses of the poetics of Postmodernism, and more than enough memoirs. But there are hundreds of new books of poems published each year, with many dozen significant prizes and awards for that work, and little actual assessment of that work. I hope that *Heresy and the Ideal* can take its place for readers as a critical introduction to the work of many individual poets as well as a document monitoring poetry at the end of the millennium. I have tried to blend the tactics of explanation, analysis, and evaluation, hoping to clarify a poet's work and methods more often than to complain or condemn. Even still, some of the work here indicates my disappointment with the poetry at hand. This may stem from the happenstance of the book reviewed. I am critical of Sharon Olds's *The Wellspring,* though her earlier *The Dead and the Living* stands in my mind as one of the most influential poetry volumes of the past two decades. Likewise, Mark Doty's 1991 volume, *Bethlehem in Broad Daylight,* disappoints my judgment, but two years later he published his finest work, *My Alexandria.* I try to explicate the strengths and limitations of all the poets at hand.

I hope to represent another particular interest in these essays, too. Much of my graduate schooling, and subsequently much of my teaching, has been in American and Romantic literatures. *Heresy and the Ideal* finds its critical center—its theory—based on my sense of Romantic poetics, especially on how contemporary poets have applied, altered, or rejected certain Romantic principles. The heart of the lyric poem is fundamentally Romantic, as much of America's social and political heritage is Romantic. But while a concern with Romantic poetics undergirds this book, I have not wanted to make everything comply to this set of precepts. I admire the Romantic legacy behind the work of Charles Wright and A. R. Ammons, for instance, but also appreciate the Neoclassical bases of Henri Coulette, the baroque formulations of Alice Fulton and Wayne Koestenbaum, the social satires of Billy Collins. I have employed the Romantic trope as a means by which to lay out a continuum of discussions: to measure the tension between passion and reason (or intuition and logic) in contemporary poetry, between the problems of literary transcendence and the obligations of social engagement; and to gauge a range of rhetorical styles, from stark plainness to the most enriched eloquence.

My first section, with essays on T. R. Hummer and Miller Williams, sets out much of the critical range of the whole book. Hummer is a latter-day Romantic, skeptical of but still compelled by transcendental figures and stances, using the rhetoric and tropes of Platonism and the nineteenth-century American Romantics while also constructing a radical critique of them. He seems to justify Elisa New's claim that "an American is one who believes his soul's poetry must first be invented, then discovered," though his desire to realize the Romantic origin is inevitably frustrated by his self-conscious sense of belatedness. No poets from the generation of the early 1950s write with more intellectual expanse or demanding curiosity than Hummer and, perhaps, Jorie Graham. Unlike Hummer, Miller Williams is a decided realist, a colloquial Southern descendent of the Neoclassicists, and I read his poetry by examining how he operates counter to the Romantic tradition embodied by the Deep Imagists of the 1960s and 1970s. In subject, rhetoric, and sensibility, Williams rejects the premise of the transcendental plain style in favor of a language of social aptitude and worldly engagement. Each in their way, then, these two poets provide a heretical stance against the Romantic premise of the ideal.

The book's next three sections present a variety of essay-reviews arranged to focus on other related topics. In Part Two, "Culture, Inclusion,

Craft," the essays' concerns are often focussed on cultural diversity, or the poetics of inclusion, and on the many things this implies—from narrative to political and philosophical inclusions—and on the poetic techniques of addition and removal. The next section, "Kinds of Knowing," is about different manners of intellectualization—how poets think, how poetry may carry an overtly discursive or scholarly aesthetic, how the lyric itself may be a kind of thinking. I am interested in related issues of style and tactics, again, to determine how poets formulate their brand of thought and passion. Part Four, "Probable Reason, Possible Joy," measures the tension between reason (the apex of Neoclassical aesthetics) and joy or awe (a destination of Romantic lyrics), as between other related dichotomies, such as melancholy and excess, or restraint and abundance. It is important that all of these features are neither good nor bad in themselves; rather, I hope to show how some poets succeed and some are troubled by the practice of each trope. The book's final section, "Heiroglyphics of Erasure," is a series of shorter essay-reviews on individual poets. Here the figure of erasure—of loss and mourning, and of the vanishing point of language at the point of transcendence—runs through the whole section.

Another of my special concentrations throughout *Heresy and the Ideal* is with the generation of poets born in the late 1940s through the mid-1950s. This is a vibrant generation, to be sure, comparable to the excellent generation of poets born in the late 1920s. Many of the books and poets addressed here are representative of this group. I have felt less compelled to write about poets who are already the subject of considerable study. John Ashbery, for one example, is frequently nominated as our greatest living poet, though I don't share that opinion. I regret not finding space for W. S. Merwin, on whose work my master's thesis focussed more than twenty years ago, and whose work may last longer than anyone else's from our age written in English. And I look forward to opportunities to write about other poets, like Marilyn Hacker, Carl Phillips, Frank Bidart, C. D. Wright, and John Koethe. I look forward to expanding the critical circle started here.

It has been gratifying to hear from many people as these essays have appeared over the past decade in journals and books. Friends and strangers have passed along questions, criticism, recommendations, and sometimes extensive commentary. They have added greatly to my understanding of poetry and to my conviction that this manner of attention to our poetry is essential. The conversations I have had with other poets and critics have been too many to recount here. I owe further gratitude to the editors who first solicited these essays. They have helped in many ways: by inviting my work; by suggesting or assigning particular volumes for discussion; by careful supervision, prudent advice, and tolerance. For their editorial custody of the present work, I wish to thank David H. Lynn and Marilyn Hacker of *The Kenyon Review,* Joseph Parisi and Stephen Young of *Poetry,* Rochelle Ratner of *American Book Review,* Donald Revell of *The Denver Quarterly,* Peter Stitt of *The Gettysburg Review,* Greg Michalson of *The Missouri Review,* and James Olney of *The Southern Review.* Robert Pack and Jay Parini invited me to compose "On Explication" for their *Introspections: American Poets on One of Their Own Poems* (Middlebury / New England, 1997), and Michael Burns encouraged me to write an essay on Miller Williams for his *Miller Williams and the Poetry of the Particular* (University of Missouri Press, 1991). Finally, I wish to express my love and my gratitude for her unfailing critical intelligence to Ann Townsend, who tended every word in this book and its author.

I began these comments with concern for the contemporary audience for poetry, for the plight of the book of poetry in the marketplace, and for the plight of poetry within an academic environment driven (and riven) by theory. Though I have referred to him often, I must conclude with the exacting wisdom of Octavio Paz: "Hence it is not so important that a work is read in the beginning by only a few. The preservation of the collective memory by a group, even a small one, is a true tablet of salvation for the entire community."

PART ONE

Heresy and the American Ideal

Heresy and the American Ideal: On T. R. Hummer

I.

Any significant poetic based on Romantic aesthetics must contain the impulse for, and then must enact, an overthrow of some sort. That is to say, the heart of Romanticism beats most rapidly and vividly when rebellion is its design. America is an especially appropriate field for such principles to be engineered, given this country's history, its foundation on the precepts of insurgence and renewal. Samuel Willard's 1694 election sermon, "The Character of a Good Ruler"—itself an early but typical example of American zeal produced at the blending of politics and faith—anticipates by nearly a century the most astonishing paradox upon which the Declaration of Independence resides. Willard's assertion that "A People are not made for Rulers, But Rulers for a People" invites the subsequent framers of the Declaration to determine that

> [W]hen a long train of abuses and usurpations . . . evinces a design to reduce [the people] under absolute despotism, it is their right, it is their duty to throw off such government, and to provide new guards for their future security. Such has been the patient sufferance of these colonies; and such is now the necessity which constrains them to *expunge* their former system of government.

The paradox is the imperative, inscribed *within the system,* for an overthrow of this or any other system at the point where it fails to act in the best interests of the general populace. But such a paradox is consistent with the logic of Romanticism. Expunging tyranny is the doubled desire to improve the future by remembering the past, especially if the past originates in the immaculate society of Eden. As Octavio Paz formulates it: "Revolution is an eminently historical act that nonetheless negates history. The new time that it ushers in is a restoration of original time."

The father of American literary rebellion, Ralph Waldo Emerson, translates this collective Romanticism into the romance of the individual. In his famous essay of 1839, "Self-Reliance," he argues that merely to conform to social standards is to betray the self and the self's potential for natural, and thereby spiritual, fulfillment: "Society everywhere is in conspiracy against the manhood of every one of its members." In essentially writerly terms, Emerson formulates that to be oneself and to realize one's own "great potential" is "to be misunderstood." To be misunderstood is both a trope for and the realization of self-reliance and creative originality—the Romantic manifestations of the highly personalized "state" of grace itself. To be self-reliant in the Emersonian sense is thus, in Harold Bloom's phrase, "to be empowered by eloquence and vision." Emerson's eminently more practical compatriot, Thoreau, extends such encouragements for rebellion and rejection to include not only social institutions and standards of behavior but even his furniture; faced with three dirty paperweights, for instance, Thoreau handily expunges the villains with the simple solution of "[throwing] them out the window in disgust!" This literal throwing-out enacts the basic Romantic imperative for transformation. Romanticism must contain revolution.

This is one of the fundamental figures handed from Emerson to our current, if post-apocalyptic, Romantic critic, Harold Bloom. Bloom's aesthetics of transformation, his depiction of a "strong poet" and of that strong poet's agonistic, embattled relationship with the past, mark an appropriate way to consider one of this country's most speculative and most demanding poets, T. R. Hummer. Indeed, both Bloom and Hummer pronounce a rigorously Romantic ideology—so thoroughly, in fact, that one authenticates and illuminates the other. Hummer inherits and Bloom describes the longstanding imperative of American individualism to rebel against forebears, and Bloom's own compelling theory of agonist strength describes the manner and effect of such an overthrow. "Poetry . . . is conflict and crisis," he succinctly states. What strong poetry conflicts with, in Bloom's theory, is prior strong poetry. This critical relationship describes Bloom's theory of agon, where one voice or stance attempts intentionally to revise or unintentionally to repress another voice or stance:

> Poetry crisis . . . is always a crisis in which a quotation or quotations from another poem or poems are being repressed. The overcoming of crisis . . . is never a true overcoming but is always an out-talking of a rival poem.

The successful out-talking of one poem by another, in essence the revising of one poetic vision by another, is what Bloom calls a transumption:

> All strong poets, whether Dante or Milton or Blake, must ruin the sacred truths to fable and old song, precisely because the essential condition for poetic strength is that the new song, one's own, always must be a song of one's self. . . . Every sacred truth not one's own becomes a fable, an old song that requires corrective revision.

In this single formulation, echoing not only Emerson but also Marvell (with irony) and Whitman, Bloom iterates the major precepts of the ideal of American Romanticism: rebellion, overthrow-as-corrective, originality, sacredness, essentiality, and determined individualism.

These may seem rather grand gestures by which to begin a consideration of a relatively young poet—still in his late forties—yet I believe T. R. Hummer to be both purposefully and successfully carrying out Bloom's fierce, revisionary Romanticism. In a period notable for its poetry's modesty and self-containment, its polite self-satisfaction, Hummer is an ambitious, even ferocious aspirant to the membership of strong poets. His intention seems to be nothing less than to identify, confront, and revise the ideals of American Romanticism and transcendentalism. While his entanglement with these ideals is complex, and while his criticism of them is stern, often veering to disbelief, his project nonetheless places him directly and paradoxically in the mainstream of Romanticism itself. By rebelling against an essentially rebellious schema—perhaps in the way that the Declaration of Independence contains within itself the imperative for its own amendment or overthrow—Hummer reaffirms some of Romanticism's most basic precepts while revising others into currency.

Even the titles of Hummer's six volumes of poetry indicate his purposeful falling away from the more sentimental graces of a transcendental poetic: *Translation of Light* (1976), *The Angelic Orders* (1982), *The Passion of the Right-Angled Man* (1984), *Lower-Class Heresy* (1987), *The 18,000-Ton Olympic Dream* (1990), and *Walt Whitman in Hell* (1996). The obvious bearings signified in the titles point to Hummer's early embrace of a rather ethereal and derivative poetic and to his increasingly earthy, fallen, ironic, or unwieldy Romanticism. His progress is transcendental in reverse— "subscendental," he calls his own strategy in one poem—from the sublime toward the parodic, from the outer and upper toward the inner and sunken, from the stance of the highly serious believer to that of the supremely bleak comedian as the letter T. He is both rebel and heretic—a skeptic toward the politics and faith embedded in American culture and a revisionist of the Romantic ideal.

2.

Bloom makes it clear that transumption requires containment. The strong poet must occupy or possess the past in order to throw it over (for even Bloom's "repression" of a strong past indicates possession or containment). Hummer's first major collection, *The Angelic Orders,* is especially important for its conventional accomplishment, its establishment of an order of belief which will serve to represent the subject of Hummer's later revisions. Already in *The Angelic Orders* Hummer's work is distinctively voiced, formally masterful, and driven by a desire for narrative clarity, these three qualities being the primary advances over his first, limited-edition volume, *Translation of Light.* This first small book is generally negligible, an apprentice's workshop, whose primary influences may be Lorca and Bly and whose typical stance represents a mild, pastoral transcendentalism. But it is worth noting here the characteristics of the starting point of Hummer's work: reliance on the deep image, a sentimental attitude toward nature and the sublime, a rather vague lyricism, and an unshaped voice. Published six years later, *The Angelic Orders* announces the presence of a talented and probing, if still in some ways conventional, young poet.

The poems of *The Angelic Orders* evince a remarkable growth away from the deep image toward the more vernacular and narrative tradition of Southern poetry. Written during Hummer's doctoral studies at the University of Utah, where he worked under the guidance of Dave Smith, these poems reject the Lorca/Bly model in favor of James Dickey, James Whitehead, Smith himself, and especially Robert Penn Warren. We might usefully arrange the poems of *The Angelic Order* into three types in order to examine their range and focus. The most popular, widely anthologized poems here are a group of ten sonnets gathered as the volume's second section. Under the title "Carrier," these poems are based on Hummer's father's occupation as a rural mail deliverer. They trace the speaker-carrier's interactions with his patrons as he recounts the sometimes mundane, sometimes sensational details of his work life. A second grouping of poems from *The Angelic Orders* evolves out of the traditional structure of the mailman sonnets. Tight, narrative, formally coherent, these poems often employ charming characterizations mixed with unusual or dramatic episodes from rural life, like latter-day eclogues. Finally, his most ambitious (but sometimes less successful) poems are longer and considerably more speculative or rhetorical. This third category pushes toward the philosophical eloquence or grandeur of Warren, where we find issues of time, history, truth—themes "writ large"—directly confronted.

Eden seems a good place to begin. Typical of the Carrier poems is "The Rural Carrier Discovers That Love Is Everywhere":

> A registered letter for the Jensens. I walk down their drive
> Through the gate of their thick-hedged yard, and by God
>   there they are,
> On a blanket in the grass, asleep, buck-naked, honeymooners
> Not married a month. I smile, turn to leave,
> But can't help looking back. Lord, they're a pretty sight,
> Both of them, tangled up in each other, easy in their skin—
> It's their own front yard, after all, perfectly closed in
> By privet hedge and country. Maybe they were here all night.
>
> I want to believe they'd do that, not thinking of me
> Or anyone but themselves, alone in the world

Of the yard with its clipped grass and fresh-picked fruit trees.
Whatever this letter says can wait. To hell with the mail.
I slip through the gate, silent as I came, and leave them
Alone. There's no one they need to hear from.

Like a few others in this volume the Carrier poems are a hybrid variety of sonnet, taking considerable influence from James Whitehead's *Local Men*. Here the lines are lengthened to as many as sixteen syllables and seven or eight stresses, brimming over, and thus suited to the narrative fullness of the poems. The mixed rhyme scheme—in this poem a near-Petrarchan octave and Shakespearean sestet—is both subtle and flexible. Hummer is further proficient at linking his end rhymes to interior sounds. In the last three lines only, notice "from" turning back to "them" as well as to "came"; "mail" remembers, with enjoyable irony, its precedent "hell," as though "hell" itself had evolved out of "world." The drone of "Alone" connects with "no one" and perhaps to the *n* in "need" and the *om* in the terminal "from." The musical effects are rich and sonorous. All the conventional rhetorical twists of the sonnet are effectively deployed as well.

But this hardly accounts for the pleasure of the scene itself. The clear, linear narratives of *The Angelic Orders* demark the considerable distance travelled from the generic, abstractive lyrics of Hummer's apprentice work. "The Rural Carrier Discovers That Love Is Everywhere" is especially tender, a scene of lovemaking that resists interruption by the carrier's routine visit. The domestic setting of the poem also establishes the primary metaphor of the poem, that of Adam and Eve in the privacy of their garden, the newlyweds, as viewed by the first visitant of a soon-encroaching world. The Southern narrative is rich in this tradition: the South often depicts itself as a latter-day Christian garden tainted by the intruding serpent of the North, thus reenacting the earlier Puritan and New England allegory of much the same impulse. If the poem appeals to the Southern sentiment, it appeals as well as to the formalist aesthetic with its coherent speaker (here issuing a dramatic monologue), chronological narrative, and evolved sonnet form. Like the other Carrier sonnets this poem is deeply rooted in the virtues of Romanticism: the valorization of innocence and privacy, the rustic or pastoral setting far from the commercial world, a plainness of speech (recall Wordsworth's "man speaking to men"), a common experience or working-class perspective, and the self-reliance of the lover.

The poem yields many pleasures. It is also about pleasures—both innocent and guilty. First, the newlyweds themselves have experienced their sensual or carnal pleasure and are still "tangled up in each other" and innocently asleep, immune to the disruptions of the world. Second, the rural carrier seems both touched and pleased ("I smile") by his inadvertent discovery. His language is gentle and lyrical, and his carriage is protective; he "slip[s] through the gate" in order to protect this private Eden. But his pleasure is redoubled by a more complex rhetoric of pun and double entendre. He "can't help looking back," and in just this way, the language turns back on itself. He clearly enjoys the Biblical applications of his description. The "clipped grass and fresh-picked fruit trees" suggest, for instance, a tamed wilderness and the bitten apple. He likes the gentle epithets, which operate as double entendres. "By God" and "To hell" are colloquial emphatics, gentle local curses, but they are also accurate and specific to the allegory. Adam and Eve are given their lives *by God,* who provides their further benefits of ease, nourishment, and grace. Yet the mail, the news of the world— the serpent of knowledge—seems certain to send them *to Hell,* destroying the self-contained pleasures of their garden. The final element of the carrier's pleasure is explicitly erotic, for his voyeurism results in the suggestion of his sexual release. He is, at last, "silent as [he] came." This phrase indicates his quiet carriage but also his fulfillment.

As readers we look down on the whole scene from above, knowing all, as we gaze over the shoulder of the carrier himself. The newlyweds are still innocent, and yet they are exposed to us. Their situation is beautiful but perilous: after sex but before the fall. Incapable of language, they exist in a pre-state of ourselves—our better, earlier personae. But we retain the position of power, envying the present, pitying the inevitable future. This is Hummer's deepest metanarrative, here and throughout the body of his poetry: the solitary lover-speaker is compelled, and condemned, to watch other real lovers from afar, his passion borrowed, his pleasure a usurpation. Overlooking passion becomes his primary form of cognition, understanding, and grief. The voyeuristic occasion is the site of argument and rhetoric; it is the origin of speech.

A fundamental tactic of the Carrier poems is the use of the father's perspective or voice. As in the Christian allegory, the presence of the father is a double irony. The Edenic yard with its fruit trees is the province of God-the-Father. But here the carrier substitutes for God in a kind of a personal metonymy. Bearing language, he brings the news of the world, and this language will prompt the lovers' fall from innocence and self-containment. As the carrier substitutes for God, so the poet substitutes for his father. The poet's work replaces the father's voice or proximity, in an allegory more Oedipal than Biblical. The son replaces the father and enjoys, if inadvertently, the erotic favor of the woman-lover. The transference of power is complex and fascinating, as though one myth were out-talking another in an agon of archetypes.

The second variety of poems in *The Angelic Orders* extends the narrative and formal coherence of the Carrier sonnets. This group, which includes "Elijah Edwards Meets the Angel out on Star Route #1," "The Naming," "Calf," "Calton Busby Makes a White-Oak Casket," and several others, typically features local characters and neighbors, whose actions are narrated with colloquial, dramatic clarity. Miller Williams, the younger James Dickey, and Robert Morgan may be among the immediate forebears of this category of Hummer's work. Here, in poems like "The Naming," the language is crisp, and the occasions emerge from the experiences of farm life. If the Carrier sonnet foresees the dooming knowledge that the news of the world will convey, then "The Naming" brings that foresight into realization.

"The Naming" is a two-fold narrative—one sonnet in each of two numbered sections—and again features a powerful father as an agent of sexual experience and worldly aptitude. The first of its two sonnet-sections is a scene of instruction and occurs, appropriately, in "the boys' room at Macon Elementary," where the young speaker sees an obscenity written on the wall "in black Ink." He doesn't recognize "the small neat word I thought / Was a name like other names / Scrawled there, a name like Jack or Buck," but senses a danger attached to it:

> Whoever
> Belonged to a name like that
> Couldn't be spoken of lightly.

He'd drive fast, smoke,
Carry a quick bright knife.

The tight, consonantal language makes a music of internal rhymes and sharp, short sounds, like thrusts. The suggestive language is so deftly constructed that not only do "Jack" and "Buck" indicate the forbidden word the speaker fails to recognize, but so do the hints of "black," "Ink," "spoken," "smoke," and others. Even the final, phallic image of the "quick bright knife" is consonantal as well as conclusive.

Hummer, however, moves this poem past the limited capacity of the Carrier sonnets, as he provides the dramatic counterpoint, in part two, of a second, separate scene. The innocent Adam has been awakened, and now he must learn his task of assigning names. The collision of dramatic events produces the tension of this poem. The speaker's understanding derives from his witnessing, then trying to articulate, the new words and acts he encounters:

They brought the bull over in the back
Of a black truck. Lord, he was big.
The heifer in the pen smelled him and lowed
Loud enough to let him
Know it was time. He came down
Quick and ready. From the top
Rail of the corral, I saw him rear,
Saw the red flesh swollen bigger than my arm

Go in. They bellowed and rocked
In the hoof-marked mud of the pen,
And when they were done, my father
Turned and looked at me hard.
I couldn't say what I had seen. But in the spring
They gave the calf my name.

The sexual act referred to in part one is carried out in part two. Here again Hummer's careful enjambment of lines contributes a doubleness of meaning ("He came down / Quick and ready. From the top"). The speaker still does not fully understand what he has seen; after all, he still can't *say* it, and saying is the point of knowing for Hummer. Again, the father is compelled to "turn and look," prefiguring the speaker's anguish, more Orphic here than the "looking back" suggested in "The Rural Carrier Discovers That Love Is Everywhere." The father's turning back suggests the trope of deliberation and vision, of thinking and seeing. The father possesses the further capacity to convert that vision into words—he understands—by naming the calf in the spring, whereas the young speaker is still passive, receiving impressions as he receives language.

The basic Romantic formula, where innocence is wordless and experience is articulate, carries into Hummer's other poems from this second category. Perhaps the most masterful poem in the book, "Where You Go When She Sleeps," demonstrates his finest, most subtle achievement. *The Angelic Orders* is a poetic *bildungsroman,* tracing the development of the central speaker, and as this poem is the book's final piece, "Where You Go" shows the speaker's considerable growth and maturation, both in his language and his experience. Composed of a single, incredibly complex sentence, the poem's very syntax enacts its narrative. Here Hummer has learned not only to complicate his poems by providing more than one narrative episode but also to interweave the narratives rather than present them in sequence. "Where You Go" consists of twenty-nine extremely long lines (up to eighteen syllables and nine stresses), two separate scenes—and two Romantic clichés.

The two scenes are related, are in fact connected, by the coincidence of their images. The framing narrative, with which the poem begins and ends, is a further development of the erotic narrative which underscores the whole book. Here we find the speaker holding his lover's head in his lap while she sleeps; looking down, the man watches his lover dream ("her eyelids jerk, but she is not troubled, it is a dream / That does not include you") and seems swept into "her hair falling richly on [his] hands, shining like metal." Her hair is a color he cannot name, "as though it has just come into existence." The unnameable instigates a further, alternate scene, as the speaker himself starts to daydream of a young farmboy who falls into his father's grain silo and dies of asphyxiation. Once more the father serves as an agent of forbidden knowledge and sexual awakening; his occupation and the fecundity of his yield, after all, doom his innocent son. The swirl of syntax seems dizzying but clarifying, as well:

> And you are like the boy you heard of once who fell
> Into a silo full of oats, the silo emptying from below, oats
> At the top swirling in a gold whirlpool, a bright eddy of grain, the boy,
> You imagine, leaning over the edge to see it. . . .

The boy ignores "his father's warning," looks down, and in his vertigo falls "in a gold sea, spun deep in the heart of the silo, / And when they find him, his mouth, his throat, his lungs / Full of the gold that took him, he lies still, not seeing the world. . . ." The connective images of gold, hair, and oats and the long-breathed syntax complete their spiral as the speaker emerges from his vision, stunned:

> . . . you touch that unnameable
> Color in her hair and you are gone into what is not fear or joy
> But a whirling of sunlight and water and air full of shining dust
> That takes you, a dream that is not of you but will let you
> Into itself if you love enough, and will not, will never let you go.

The powerful, solemn rhetoric of this poem is enhanced by its ironic playfulness. In addition to the enjoyable sinuousness of the syntax, this poem is founded on two Romantic clichés. Hummer literalizes the banal expression *falling in love* by the actual, fatal fall that the boy experiences. His fall is his death, as the speaker's own figurative fall erases his capability with language. The speaker's fall takes him down to the other world of dream and vision and finally to the hell of knowing his fate. His lover has *taken his breath away.* Just so, the boy's asphyxiation mimics the speaker's speechlessness. His language is extinguished by the overpowering, yet sleeping, lover; he is struck dumb by "unnameable" passion—or, more precisely, by his acute awareness of the depth and self-erasing destination of his passion. Hummer has travelled far from the innocent viewing of "The Rural Carrier Discovers That Love Is Everywhere." His speaker has experienced work, sex, loss, and love, but further, he has seen deeply into the perilous heart of these passions, where a self might be lost, where language fails.

The final category of poems in *The Angelic Orders* consists of longer, speculative works. These are Hummer's most ambitious and his most uneven poems and include such pieces as "Weight," "Snowlines," "Something about How Time Works," and "A Refusal to Mourn the Death of the World by Fire." One point of interest here is the way poems from this group prefigure —though they don't exactly anticipate—the direction of his later books away from the normative, linear narrative, the Romantic sublime, and the regional poetic. Sometimes these poems go astray, as Hummer's grasp exceeds his skill. Even the ambition expressed in the titles of some of them indicates their unwieldiness. Like Robert Penn Warren, Hummer wants to drive these poems past the narrative into the philosophical, addressing in direct fashion issues of time, history, religion, passion. But in "A Refusal to Mourn the Death of the World by Fire," for instance, his large gesturing becomes quickly melodramatic: "I held my bottle up, looked through, saw everything / Amber, color of flame, and thought *This is what God sees.*" In "The Names Love Takes Away," familiar for its trope in which passion erases language, Hummer's desire to confront vital issues results in the insipid or the fuzzy:

> The loneliness of men and women
> Cannot be measured in years.
> You will have to talk about lives
> Not wasted, but spent without this:
> A moment, in a park, under arc lights,
> In wind, with leaves trembling, gusted.
> I touch you. It changes.
> I know what I am saying.

These opening lines seem too rhetorical, their halting syntax less dramatic than full of self-announcement or self-importance. In later lines his admirable intellectual desire for an abstract idea (God? passion? fate?) yields the imprecise rather than the universal: "There was something then to return to / That was not us, that loved us / Not for ourselves, but because it made us / And could not forgive us our lives."

The relative shortcoming of some of these poems is temporary. Like Warren, never shy of the grandiose or abstractive, or like Rilke, from whose

Duino Elegies Hummer derives the title of this book, Hummer intends to confront big matters. In *Duino* Rilke defines fate as "to be facing each other / and nothing but each other / and to be doing it forever." In Hummer's lexicon such fate is the "circumstance" against which our "passion" collides. The confrontation of these primal elements provides Hummer's poetry with its classical magnitude. While many contemporary poets seem satisfied with small ironies—sarcasm of voice, the wistfulness caused by small personal losses, saying one thing while implying another—Hummer's poetry finds its strength at the point at which "absolutely incommensurate realities collide and cannot be resolved," to use Bloom's own definition of sublime irony.

"Flight" is one of the strong examples of this category in *The Angelic Orders*. At 115 lines this longer poem confronts the dual nature of irony, interweaving fate and desire, or "circumstance" and "passion," to find that even memory is transformed by the power of passion. The distance of "fifteen years / and half [his] life ago" enables Hummer's speaker, now fully mature, to understand a time from his youth when, lost and startled by an owl's cry, he ran far through a shadowy woods and stumbled, breaking his glasses against an old headstone. His "vision" shattered, thus handicapped but at least no longer lost, the youth recognizes the burial ground he visited as a child:

> I know I am on the edge
> Of the old graveyard I came to
> Once with my father to read
> Epitaphs of people not our kin,
> Forgotten names, dead histories—
>
> But human enough, now
> To tell me which way is which.

He climbs a hill above the province of the dead—again, a position of visionary strength—only to view the secret passion of the living. A young woman and man "not much older than I am" lie near a gravestone, "locked in [illicit] passion." Unlike the Carrier sonnet, here the speaker witnesses a private moment of passion *in progress* and so seems more fully complicit in the event.

Despite his fear of the past (the dead), he observes the momentary resurrection that the living in their passion may find. The young woman

> throws
>
> Her arms back, beating
> The air like wings. She lifts
> From the stone. Her back arches so high
> She is not touching anywhere
> but her heels and the back of her head,
> He rising with her, both of them hanging
> At the peak of their flight
> Impossibly long. . . .

The ecstasy of the lovers' action is prolonged by the length of this last sentence, which continues beyond my quotation; the whole, halting movement is punctuated frequently, as by quick breaths; the lines are enjambed to enhance the sense of hanging, suspension between one life and another. The various incidents—being lost and scared, finding the familiar but foreboding graveyard, discovering the saving passion of lovers—combine to provide the speaker's renewed sense of location and identity. With his "one good eye" he sees, beyond the graveyard hill, the lights of his father's house and knows he has found his way home. More important, from the additional vantage point of the present, the adult speaker understands also

> I have been here
> Long enough to see
> As well as I can, half my life ago,
> One way of being alive,
> One way of rising
> Out of darkness. . . .

To remember and to articulate the past are the first steps toward containing it and addressing the present. Many of the poems of *The Angelic Orders* involve such inheritance, as Hummer willingly accepts the past's burden—familial, regional, aesthetic. The strong poet must occupy the past before he can correct it.

3.

Published only two years after *The Angelic Orders, The Passion of the Right-Angled Man* is a pronounced step forward. This volume provides the largest number of conventionally appealing poems, as Hummer perfects his normative rhetoric. Many of these poems enact the regional sublime and the traditional Romantic narrative, with its intact, singular speaker, which Hummer developed in *The Angelic Orders.* Here too he successfully begins to investigate and dismantle the conventions of his earlier work. *Lower-Class Heresy,* three years later, even more fully engages the revolution of the Romantic, exploiting features of literary satire and of social and aesthetic critique. Warren-like, Hummer is learning to blend his lyric voice and narrative gift with a poetic anxiety and strength that transcends—or subscends—the personal.

The anxiety of historical inheritance provides the opening tension of *The Passion of the Right-Angled Man.* The first poems indicate this anxiety in a number of ways. "Coming Back, False Dawn" reanimates the powerful paradigm of "Flight," where again the solitary speaker is thrust into a potentially dangerous nature. He is "half drunk, stumbling, driven / By a woman's body." Yet he is older, and the scene is rendered with more acute distress, than anywhere in the prior volume. In an act of self-citation his speaker yearns "to see past passion, past circumstance." These poems show a further erotic initiation, too, as in "The Age before Passion." This love poem is set again, significantly, in a father's field but provides its characters only an indistinct, and thereby frustrating, vision of future lovers. Hummer's regional idiom resounds in "Any Time, What May Hit You," where "The foreman whacks him hard / In the back of the head and calls him / *Dumbass* because he is lost / In the dream of the woman he touched / last night. . . ." In other words, these first poems evince Hummer's desire to readdress and rewrite the fundamental tactics of his earlier works.

Yet, as I noted, the sense of anxiety or agitation is severe here. These love poems are gripped by a growing violence, which indicates the lover's frustration but also points to Hummer's dissatisfaction with or sense of the insufficiency of his poetic. "The Beating" depicts a scene of instruction at a school playground, where one boy—"not half-bright"—carves his would-be girlfriend's name on a tree, is seen and taunted, and in turn beats the group of boys who tease him. The title is a double entendre on the beating he gives them, for he also wins the race to an adult-like passion:

It wasn't fear

That defeated us. It was surprise

That it mattered so much what we'd done.

How could we know? He'd been one of us all our lives,

So close it was hard to see how he'd beat us

This once: he was already man enough to think he loved a woman.

This poem is conventional for Hummer in some ways: its rural setting, vivid characterizations, linear narrative, and Southern idiom. But it also shows Hummer's inventive evolution away from his norm. If violence is a trope of this anxiety, as I believe, then the form is its vehicle. The poem is composed in five-line stanzas with an isolated terminal line. Hummer's rhyme scheme is ABxAB, with an unrhymed middle line in each stanza. The quality of the rhymes, however, is more than subtle. Barely a rhyme at all, if not for the pattern established in earlier stanzas, "surprise" and "us" in the stanza above seem more a dismantling of rhyme, an antagonism with the notion of ideal form. It rhymes, begrudgingly, only through the context of its form and resists all rhyme in its middle line. In other words, each five-line stanza contains within it, as though buried, a rhymed quatrain. The line length of the poem is ragged, unsettled, as though further resisting itself. It's as if the poem does not fit itself, as if its size is insufficient to contain the internal pressure. Maybe this is a paradigm of an adolescent growth spurt. Maybe Hummer is finding need for a longer form.

Longer form indeed: "The Beating," at twenty-six lines, maintains the precise rhetorical proportions of a sonnet. If we recall the importance of the sonnet in *The Angelic Orders*, we might see this as another example of Hummer's use and anxious adaptation of his own past. The first fifteen lines of this poem establish the narrative of Clifton Cockerell's actions and of the boys taunting him. As we enter the fourth stanza, quoted above, the rhetorical emphasis shifts from description to explanation, as the speaker in hindsight now can comprehend the "half-bright" boy's quicker maturation. He begins to summarize from the particulars of the initial narrative. The numbers are immaculate: this shift coincides exactly with the sonnet's turn between its octave and sestet. Eight is to fourteen as fifteen is to twenty-six. The poem's last stanza moves the poem out of its narrative and its subsequent analysis into a larger assessment for our application:

> So he came down on us sudden, boys,
> All of us, and he gave us a taste of the hurt
> We'd live to know another way: how love
> Can be wrong and still be the only boy
> That's real: how, when we come to it,
>
> We stand amazed but take the blow, transfigured, idiot.

The last four lines duplicate again—both in proportion and in rhetorical purpose—the couplet of a conventional Elizabethan sonnet. Even the final rhyme of "idiot" recaptures both "it" and "hurt." Hummer is working to adapt elements of one form into another, larger one, enacting an agon of both form and rhetoric. The violence which attends this adaption is both dramatically appealing and psychologically wrenching.

The crisis is a crisis of vision. The title poem, "The Passion of the Right-Angled Man," presents Hummer's widening sense of distress in vivid form. In a single stanza of thirty very long lines—with as many as twenty-eight syllables, nine or ten primary accents—Hummer traces again the running lover, driven by love to climb a TV signal tower in his desperation: "Halfway up, he sees it is morning, sees / Clouds turn neon red with florescence of dawn / And suddenly he is sober." The poem rhymes in alternating lines, ABAB, but again the quality of the rhyming is severely partial. What began as a drunk's dare, an act of performance for his watching friends, turns life-threatening for the character, yet he finds himself compelled, though sober, to continue his climb—even as the rhyming pattern, once started, must go on. He hears a sad love song playing in a car below, "some poor fool in love / With someone gone," and realizes the inevitable fate of his passion: "he'll go home too, alone, / To the room where he suffers those dreams of her."

It is a poem of flight and of delicate, impermanent balance. Hummer's speaker is driven to keep climbing, as though to restore the sanitary, heightened vision of earlier poems. He strains for a view from above. Such a perspective—oddly canted, risen—would presume to do three things. It would protect him from real involvement (and heart-break) with the lover. It would prevent his mortification before his friends. And it would restore another fundamental relationship with the figure of God-the-father, as with his own original vision: "he wants to pray to someone / He doesn't believe in anymore." Recall that, for Hummer, to overlook passion is the origin of speech. He wants up and yet is drawn down, to the Hell of the world.

Throughout *The Passion of the Right-Angled Man* Hummer is learning to make his longer poems more vivid. In "Correspondence: Faded Love" he converts the abstractive themes of his earlier long poems into characterizations. That is, his characters and their narrative circumstances now dramatize the theses that left his earlier long poems rhetorically blurred. "Correspondence: Faded Love" begins a series of historical inquiries that Hummer expands in subsequent books. This long, sequential poem interweaves a present scene—the speaker on a blinding-white winter day in Oklahoma, desolate, lonely for a lover never to come—with a partly excavated and partly imagined series of love letters between "George Woodward, my uncle / Four times great / And a hundred-some years removed" and "Nannie Carlisle, who is forever / Silent, her letters in return / Lost." The epistolary vehicle figures prominently in the narrative, suggesting again the agency of the carrier-father who brings language, the world's news.

The language itself—the collision of its presences and absences—provides the critical center of the poem. Crisp and unfolded, George's letters are a tactile presence as the speaker addresses—with resigned sadness—Warren's dictum in *Audubon* to "Tell me a story of deep delight" in these plaintive lines:

> I want to tell you a story.
> The truth is, there is no story,
> There is only the wanting to tell.
> The truth is, there is only
>
> Me, watching the window to see
> How long it will take the light

To vanish altogether.
The truth: the light is all there is.

Absent, though, are Nannie's lost words and thereby an essential part of the historical past, the integral Southern and familial inheritance on which Hummer has elsewhere relied. Nannie is gone, and her absence echoes within the speaker's own circumstance—his grief at an unreachable lover—throughout the book. Hummer further emphasizes the horror of absence by three additional elements. First, the snow storm produces an increasing erasure of the landscape, a whiteout of detail, until, as above, "the light is all there is." Second, Hummer's rhetorical style is plainer, stripped down, especially as compared to his tendency elsewhere for density or rhetorical flourish:

> Imagine
> Yourself nowhere.
> Imagine a place that is not a place,
> Light that is not light
>
> But memory, trying to make something be there.
> Imagine you love a face
> You'd swear you've never seen.
> That is what distance is, that
>
> Trying to imagine.

The place that is not a place is, of course, the snowed-over landscape. It is also the site where memory and language are rubbed out. The plainness of this passage shows an absenting of idiom. It verifies as well Hummer's third element of erasure: the fading farther, into impossibility, of the "real" lover behind so many of his poems. Even though Hummer reaches further back into history's cache, as though to locate a sufficient paradigm by which to frame his present circumstance, his speaker still seems fated to grief. But the poem, grounded in drama, avoids the melodrama of some earlier, longer works. Driven by narrative—by narratives fused into narratives—it does not succumb to the grandiose or vague.

Published three years after *The Passion of the Right-Angled Man,*

Lower-Class Heresy is the work of an even more able and innovative poet. This volume bridges the normative earlier work and the radically original poetry of *The 18,000-Ton* Olympic Dream and *Walt Whitman in Hell*. Here we see Hummer in the midst of revolutionary anxiety, where he addresses — in order to out-talk, as Bloom might say, or to critique—not only his own past but many primary elements of the Romantic tradition. His demeanor is considerably more complex, as he exploits elements of the comedic and the satirical, employing pun and allusion to pierce the subjects of his deepening critique. He pushes beyond the regionalism of his earlier work, too, toward wider fields of setting, subject, and idiom. The love story is suppressed now, and in its place a more public, socio-political entanglement proceeds. In other words, the love poem—forlorn and lonely—evolves into the speculative complaint, as the principal motivation behind Hummer's poetic anxiety shifts from romance to Romanticism.

The speaker-hero is coming down to earth, as though reversing the impulse of the Romantic lyric. Paul DeMan describes the Romantic bearing as

> the movement by means of which the poetic imagination tears itself
> away . . . from the terrestrial nature and moves toward this "other
> nature" . . . associated with the diaphanous, limpid, and immaterial
> quality of a light that dwells nearer to the skies.

Hummer's "The Second Story" revises the scheme of his own earlier poems where the risen speaker observes the lovemaking of others. Now, driven outside "by a dream / Not frightening," he "looks up at the house" where a wealthy couple is making love. His inferior trajectory means he can no longer witness the love of others, though he overhears their lovemaking, "her low voice [rising] / Toward a classic soprano." He feels neither envy nor desire: "I know I have missed my chance, they are beyond me, / Too far gone for any word / I could shout ever to bring them down." Instead, he regards their heightened, impossible status not so much in terms of love but rather in terms of class difference and economic privilege ("these are the second homes / Of the rich"). The law which governs the spiritual is love, so Shelley asserts. But Hummer's lover no longer gazes down from the graceful proximity of the angelic orders, no longer "believes" in the spirit-life of the lover. In *Lower-Class Heresy* Hummer's project is to learn to embrace the fallen body. That is his Romantic heresy. He faces, as he writes in "The Moon and Constellations," "the one great law of the physical, / The body, which appropriates everything."

With an acceptance of the bodily comes a more practical solution to things. In earlier poems the precarious attitude of the lover from on high produced a kind of vertigo, a spinning drunkenness. It seemed a condition of his stricken Romanticism to be disconcerted, dangerously dizzy. In "The Inner Ear," however, Hummer demystifies his speaker's condition. With the added distance of the third-person narrative, the poem gives a bodily and genetic, rather than spiritual, cause for falling: "He thinks it incredibly strange / That the spinning he feels in the world is not in the world // But in the dust inside his head." His doctor's report of an infected inner ear leads the main character into understanding a sudden, whirling cacophony of other missteps and misapprehensions: the memory of a young girl's misspoken church recitation ("'Consider,' she read aloud, 'The lilies of the field. They do not sow, / Neither do they rape'"); his wife's relief at his condition ("'I thought it was your heart'"); and his own misperception. Each scene is related to the others by the shame (and relief) of a mistake. Hummer literalizes with irony Emerson's trope that to be "heroic" is "to be misunderstood." The dark comedy of this poem does not derive from the idiomatic pleasure of the regional, as in earlier poems, but rather from skeptical disbelief.

Throughout *Lower-Class Heresy* Hummer directly challenges other conventions of the Romantic. Its promises—to transcend the turmoil of the social, to recapture the primitive or original clarity of experience, to merge spiritually with the natural or supernatural, to govern the soul by the laws of love—are found suspect, failed, or at best, misleading. Even his titles indicate Hummer's revisionary rebellion against Romantic precepts: "The Subscendentalists," "The Undersoul," "The Afterworld," "The Immoralities: Drunk All Afternoon," "The Unpoetic." That is, he turns his attention to a substantial critique of those Romantic properties which promise spiritual fulfillment. Romantic impressionism is only possible if one takes off one's glasses.

The centerpiece of this splendid book is four long poems under the section title "Dogma." Two of them, "The Ideal" and "The Real," illustrate the rigor and range of Hummer's Romantic agon in this volume.

Though entitled "The Ideal," the first of the two is about trickery and sham, a deconstruction of the American promise of perfection. Of course, the trope of trick and satire maintains its Romantic impetus, as William Carlos Williams professes in his prologue to *Kora in Hell:* "There is nothing in literature but change and change is mockery." The framing narrative of the poem finds the speaker in Cooperstown, New York, the land of "Those people who haunted my people / With the Shadow of hatred" and residence of P. T. Barnum's great lucrative hoax, the Cardiff Giant. Over the poem's 181 lines a swirl of references fuses the "Yankees'" gullibility, who "plowed it up / Like a freak potato [and] fell to their knees," with his grandmother's skeptical realism *("Just because it's written down / In black and white don't make it so").* Likewise, the Northerners' fancy barns with "gingerbread at their eaves / And widow's walks" contradict the speaker's own practical knowledge: "These are not barns to me / But the idea of barn, unreal / And perfect, unattainable // To any farmer I ever knew." The rhetoric of the Platonic ideal underscores Hummer's critique. From the Yankees' precedent Puritan heritage (Edwards and Winthrop in particular) to the speaker's own past (his grandmother, his agrarian upbringing), Hummer casts the shadow of doubt on all varieties of inherited truth. "It is a problem in pure faith," he complains, as even he recalls his revered grandmother's unbelievable utterance: *"Nobody a thousand miles away // Can tell us how to run things. / Our niggers know their place."* The sham he detects becomes the source of personal as well as national shame.

The culpability of American idealism is Hummer's new subject, as his poems out-talk Emersonian Platonism. The central figure at the end of this poem—the long shadow of doubt—is juxtaposed with American idealism and hope: "We want to be larger than something. / We want to be more than ourselves. / It is dark. I turn my headlights on. // The shadows they cast span fields." The parodic figure of the shadow becomes not merely ironic but terrifying in the next poem, "The Real," where the allegory of Plato's shadow is an overt subject.

Initiating with another scene of instruction at school, "The Real" is a based on a series of misspoken or misheard varieties of the word "Platonic." A field-trip lesson provides the speaker's first exposure to Plato, who was "older than Jesus." Faulty history is akin to faulty theology:

Jesus I knew about,
Since he was an obvious American

Institution. Jesus and I
Came to an understanding early on.
When I was seven, my eyes went bad,

Nearsighted, and I prayed for vision.
What I got was glasses.

The practical explanation for his skewed vision—bad eyes, like the infected organ of "Inner Ear"—is both comedic and damning. This first misapprehension in turn leads to the several other scenes and problems of the poem:

By the time I was twelve, I'd confused
Plato and *Pluto* and *plutonium.*
It was 1962. We were going through

The Cuban missile crisis
When a girl in my science class
Started screaming: *There's going to be*

A war, we're all going to die.
The teacher calmed her down
And we prayed together, but I
Would not close my eyes.

We'd seen films of Hiroshima
And diagrams of nuclear explosives.
We knew about chain reactions and fallout shelters.

We knew that when the fireball comes
You look away. Maybe that girl's fear
Was what made me want to kiss her.
No, she said, *let's be platonic.*

I didn't know that soap-opera word.
I thought it meant dead. It worked.

It's hard to overstate the many delights and puns in these crisp lines. The speaker's insistence on not closing his eyes confirms his growing realism while it also exposes the faulty advice of the Cold War. The incongruity of prayer in the science class, the commingling of a fatal strike with the suddenly erotic, the replacement of one misunderstanding with another, all point to Hummer's gift: the concurrence of satiric critique, linguistic play, and ideological revision. The poem's final image, suggesting not only the Platonic shadow but also the damages (both natural and human-made) of Pompeii and Hiroshima, seems considerably more murderous than promising:

> We were dying blind, turning into permanent shadows
>
> Caught in some meaningless moment
>
> Of what we prayed was not
>
> The only life: burned childlike
>
> Out of ourselves at any given instant
>
> Of grace: touched by the fire, etched white
>
> Against a pure black wall.

Poem after poem in *Lower-Class Heresy* interrogates the misleading promise of history, inheritance, and faith. The fields of his study range from the aesthetic and philosophical (as above) to the erotic ("Inner Ear") to the tyrannies of class and economic imbalance. "Course of Empire," whose title points to Bernard De Voto's history of nationalist expansion, *The Course of Empire,* shows Hummer's hero once again on the road, alone. Yet even this Emersonian vision of self-reliance is a falsehood, for the speaker has broken down on his new frontier of self-dependence and must seek help: "We're beyond irony now. We've come to destiny, manifest." The poem shows Hummer's deepening critique of the national premise, his lengthening distance from the origin of hope. The "shadows cast" in the previous poems are mere words now, his curse against both faith and circumstance: "*Goddamn, Goddamn,* the only thing / We ever define as fate in the land of the free, / Cast out now in perfect impersonal thanks, / for nothing, dying."

4.

The dream of Romantic Platonism is transcendence. Its doom, as Hummer now argues, is the body, "which appropriates everything." The substantial weight of that body, the burden of the real, increases manyfold in Hummer's two latest books. In some ways his 1990 volume, *The 18,000-Ton* Olympic Dream, is his most challenging, due partly to the considerable severity of both voice and vision. The heavy pressure of Hummer's new poetic preempts some of the kinds of enjoyment we might have felt in his earlier work, as he embarks on an odyssey of disillusionment—away from transcendence, away from his native American South, and away from some of the conventional techniques of his earlier work—into the wider worldly arena. His travels take him to England as well as to the American West and New England, and his anxious demand for largeness, for visionary scope, results in his struggle to find a style capable of great socio-political, geographical, and historical range.

"The 18,000-Ton *Olympic Dream*," the book's first poem, opens with an image of the Romantic "light" described by DeMan as "diaphanous, limpid, and immaterial . . . that dwells nearer to the skies," but Hummer immediately ironizes the Romantic potential: "*Ex nihilo,* / that's how it begins. / Light as consciousness." This particular, initiating light is produced by the artificial means of a lighthouse and is further synthesized by the cinematic self-reflection of a TV camera. Hummer's *Olympic Dream* is, after all, not an epic god-wish but an oil tanker recently sunk, and the speaker watches the news report of the disaster from his hotel lobby in England. The literalization of the epic—the allusion to Mount Olympus; the real, sea-crossing ship; the heroic journey of the speaker—is another form of Hummer's dismantling of the Romantic dream. The poem proceeds in a complaint against power-politics and Romantic ideals, as the great figures of American and English Romanticism, Emerson and Wordsworth, are both satirized. "Man Thinking is the breached body of the West's / *Olympic Dream*," the speaker claims, even as he begins to suffer from *"Wordsworth's Revenge . . . Emetic motion regurgitated intranquilly"*—that is, the nausea of "strange food, / strange water." The body, the real circumstance of the self, produces an existential disease from which the speaker now suffers.

The tone of this poem—and this book—moves beyond the plaintive. As Hummer widens the field of his critique, his voice turns past grievance to distrust, disappointment, even anger. He concedes that even the "whole miserable show" of the televised newscast might be authorized as

> One more lie
>> from me, one son of a bitch
> In a universe at the mercy of sons of bitches
> With bodyguards or mandates
> Or Presidential Bibles, or Truth half baked
> Like a bastard file in MacFarlane's sickeningly sweet
> Key-shaped cake,
>> to which the whole third world
> Replies, in the words of the prophet, *America,*
> *Go fuck yourself with your atom bomb.*

The image of nuclear destruction again provides a figure for Hummer's powerful, ultimate critique. His self-reflective rhetoric becomes a trope for analysis, for study and complaint. But it often now indicates more discouragement with the self than pride, as even the self becomes a model of disenchantment rather than a model for belief or emulation.

I think it is not unreasonable to argue that the severity of Hummer's complaint derives, at least originally, from the double disappointments of romantic love and Romanticism. Both are, to him, false promises, where the attainment of the "other"—the lover or the transcending self-into-god—is an impossible dream. The seventeen dense, difficult poems that comprise the first part of this book are rich with the range of his dejection and rage. Affection, after all, has become "a heart attack in the country." The "origin of revelation" concludes now in "the breakdown of the syntax of prayer." Courtly love turns into "a desperate holding on," and pastoral landscapes dry up into "The salt of the lost American / Sea that might have drowned Manifest Destiny if the continental plates / Had given the slow bump and grind of their tactical shifting a rhythm politically correct." Here, in "Salt Flats Crossing: Homage to Vachel Lindsay," even the prospect of naturalist typology has devolved into the mere commercial, "the radical slogans of the natural world." Indeed, if nature may still be read as a symbol of the spirit, as Emerson says, its message is damning: "I saw a streak of light in the sky like the middle finger of God." Hummer extends the metaphor in "Spring Comes to Mid-Ohio in a Holy Shower of Stars":

> . . . then another
> Finger gestured godlike halfway down from the zenith, another, another,
> And the sky burned with the print of a whole left hand.
> That's the way the past works:
>> brilliance, and a slap in the face.

The growing violence I identified in the love poems of *The Passion of the Right-Angled Man* has become a mortifying infliction of pain, as the obscene gesture of God's curse turns into a physical, light-struck assault.

If *Lower-Class Heresy* was Hummer's enacting of an ideological war between skepticism and Platonic idealism, then this book is a description of the battlefield, its debris, its corpses strewn with abandon. Hummer finds little to praise, much to mourn, and more to condemn. The fascinating drama of *Heresy* derived, in part, from our watching as Hummer chose his allegiances and formed his new tastes. Like Matthew Brady's photograph of Civil War battlefields, *The 18,000-Ton Olympic Dream* feels post-apocalyptic, with a touch of propaganda amidst the gritty, realistic details. The strength of these poems is their passion. But they are sometimes opaque as well, held static, as Hummer's convictions are unrelieved by humor, ambiguity, or uncertainty.

"Bluegrass Wasteland" is Hummer's longest poem to date, and makes up the final forty pages of *The 18,000-Ton* Olympic Dream. Here Hummer combines the severity of the book's shorter poems with a further intensi-fied curiosity about his own method. Though it is long, at just over one thousand lines, the poem reads with the dexterity of prose fiction. Its crisp triplet stanzas prefigure a similar construction in Hummer's later "Walt Whitman in Hell," as both poems borrow something of the formal pace of Dante's terza rima. Hummer is simply not interested in replicating the pleasures of an intense lyric; he is more expository, didactic. When the poem occasionally thickens from its rhetorical steerage, like some of the longer poems in *The Angelic Orders,* that is because this poem is its own subject, a literally intimate account of "technique."

"Bluegrass Wasteland" is a breakdown of Hummer's metanarrative. A breakdown is a bluegrass song, dense and melancholic, but it is also a collapse and an analysis. The story—here, a pair of lovers in Mount Vernon, Ohio, observed in illicit passion by a hidden speaker—provides a vehicle into the poem's deeper subject. This is Hummer's last such love poem, after all, and he inspects his impulses with an autopsist's precision:

> Are you starting to get a feel for how the voice
> Echoes? How *echo* here means motion in space *and* time?
> It travels the way a lover's mumbled word crawls. . . .
>
> The theory is, such motion is transcendence and thus salvation.
>
> That's how it is with voices. The man, the voice can say,
> Remembers, hears, anything at all the moment the woman lays
> The satin whisper of her panties against his leg. . . .

The overlooking of passion was once the origin of speech for Hummer. Now the continuity of his speech depends both on overseeing others and, more centrally, on overhearing the self while creating the scene of looking. Hummer's intensity is revelatory—that is, directed not just towards understanding but towards exposure. His rigor is not unlike what Bloom describes in his account of Shakespeare's great characterization:

> I myself always am struck by the varied and perpetual ways in which
> Hamlet keeps *overhearing himself speak.* This is not just a question of
> rhetoricity or word consciousness; it is the essence of Shakespeare's
> greatest originalities in the representation of character, of thinking,
> and of personality. [Hamlet] changes with every self-overhearing.

This poem's deepest subject is technique itself. "Comme ça," the speaker's grandmother used to say, in teaching the youngster how to eat gumbo: *"And she'd play-eat hers with a fork. / It was French, but it wasn't intellectual. / It was a joke. It was technique. It was rhetoric insofar / As it was persuasion."* Her instruction to "do it this way" is picked up and respoken by the female lover, as she guides her partner in ways to provide her increased enjoyment, leading eventually to orgasm: "She steps closer to him // And he takes her left nipple into his mouth. / His tongue moves, and she speaks, she moans, and it means / *Yes. Do it that way. Do it this way.*" The techniques of pleasure—consuming food, gratifying an erotic companion—are examined further in Hummer's exploration of aesthetic and poetic style. As the poem proceeds, as the lovers undress, as the surrounding history of the town and of the speaker unfolds, Hummer reveals the many "illusions" which combine to make a work of art. From the initiating *"cinematic illusion . . . where language rises / against the reader's imagination like images on film"* to the final *"passionate illusion,"* he discusses, even while he carries out, the act of poetic creation. The intellectualization of pleasure has become, for Hummer, pleasure itself, as the several illusions—the intimate illusion; the heretic illusion; the objective, blank verse, wonder, syncronicity, and déjà-vu illusions—provide his opportunity to overhear his own evolving act of making. Rarely have readers of contemporary poetry been occasioned with such a thorough, captivating account of poetic creation. Even in the end, as the lovers consummate their passion, Hummer exposes the mechanism and artifice of the work itself:

> He touches her with the absolute authority
> The body, revealed, reveals. History, mythology,
> Biology, the art of the family
>
> Suspend as the man and woman move together.
> And that might be all, that might be the end of the story
> If the voice chose to let you forget
>
> The truth: that this is the workplace, that you are here
> To witness everything, beginning to end,
> And since you have given yourself up
>
> To this, *the passionate illusion,* you can only go into the body
> Of the act, into the reality of consequence,
> Into the life of that slice of the natural world
>
> We choose to call *Mt. Vernon, Ohio,*
> Within which and outside of which
> Everything that happens here happens.

Hummer's voice authors its own authority. It demands our awareness of the "truth" and "consequences" in the acts of making—and observing—love and art.

If *Lower-Class Heresy* is Hummer's agonistic volume, where he more fully depicts the battle between the ideal and the real, and if *The 18,000-Ton* Olympic Dream provides a view of the aftermath of that battle, its expense to the spirit, its field of destruction, then *Walt Whitman in Hell* shows all of Hummer's ghosts walking again. Published in 1996, Hummer's most recent book is a work of brilliant if bleak resurrection. Like *The 18,000-Ton* Olympic Dream this volume features a number of intense, meditative lyrics and a long, difficult central text, but for the first time there are no love poems. Instead, Hummer pushes further into politics, science, and religion and into wider dimensions of cultural history, with poems that seem to take place not only in the present day but variously in 1909, during the Civil War, and even at Walt Whitman's autopsy.

Whitman, the great Romantic optimist, is one of this book's two ironic, authorizing presences. "Zeitgeist Lightning" activates a central trope in *Walt Whitman in Hell:* the dismantling or compounding of the poetic self. Recall the powerful, singular "voice" that commanded our complex attention in *The 18,000-Ton* Olympic Dream. As though to deconstruct the last vestige of the Romantic ideal—what Keats, in reference to Wordsworth, calls the "egotistical sublime"—Hummer allows the fiction of self to shatter. At Whitman's autopsy the laboratory technician handling the poet's body dropped his brain, that "most god-like tumor of consciousness," and in the lightning strike of its dissolution, Hummer's doctor-speaker envisions the ensuing decay of Modernist history: "Conrad / Writes *Lord Jim,* / America elects / Coolidge, Hoover, / Karloff makes *Frankenstein. . . .*" This book proceeds as a dismantling of the self into fragments, as though the vessel of the text were dropped and restored, compounded, if monstrous.

It is as though the dead body of "the ideal" has decayed, yet from its dissolution new life forms evolve. "Now I begin again to refuse to say the things / I have refused to say all along," Hummer writes in "Mechanics." The third-person perspective widens his gesture:

> Something moves in the mirror's half-darkness.
> The shape she sees there could be anyone's,

> Living or dead. She thinks she does not care
>> what the dead are doing. She knows the dead
> Do nothing, exactly like the rest of us.
>> They are all on their way somewhere else.

The integrity of the self, the singular "person," is cast into doubt, where "poverty after poverty, each [grants] itself / The luxury of an *I*." In its place the journey "somewhere else" suggests the fluid transit of history and change, ghostly and anxious.

Once released from the self, the poem's point of view becomes plural, vast, and more capable. This may be the greatest development in Hummer's recent work. In a critique of the Romantic illusion of the self, perhaps he has also identified his true "lover," the aggregate other. In "Scrutiny," after a medical examination, a woman "desire[s] another life, a parallel dimension, / Translucent like our own, but in which the dial of consciousness / Is rotated one counterclockwise click, so every mind possesses / The body immediately to the left." As though stepping into another self, shape-shifting, her "reflection" is picked up in "Plate Glass," where another female character "tries to make out a tiny image of herself on the sidewalk / In front of the plate glass, staring in, trying to discover an even smaller self." The singular self may shrink in perspective, but a compound reflection emerges to enlarge the poems' visionary capacity. In subsequent poems, fascinating in their forms of wisdom and authenticating detail, Hummer is literally a ghost writer, stepping into and speaking out of the "self" of Hart Crane, John Keats, a farm wife struggling through the "drought years," a Civil War doctor haunted by the dismantling of bodies from amputation, and finally a tortured and abandoned "caucasian Male, 42" whose "forensic mystery" depicts the self-shattering loss within Hummer's project.

By exploding the limitations of the poetic self, Hummer has widened his field of history. Begun as a radical critique of the Romantic fiction, these poems often reach through invention toward sympathy and connection; they seem increasingly real, more vivid than illusory. After all, as Elisa New writes of Emerson's later work, "nothing is so original as an origin mislaid." That is the irony and aptitude of Romantic recursiveness. As much as Hummer has found discouraging and deceitful in history's circumstance, that judgment is a Romantic marker; it leads to rebellion, the mandate of reinvention. From the compound self, Hummer has learned to make a newly consequent art. In "Worldly Beauty," perhaps this book's clearest *ars poetica,* we see the combination of pain and beauty in the process of creation. *"Skin deep, you son-of-a-bitch,"* the poem's female speaker curses, as so many of Hummer's speakers have been driven to do. The body itself, the vessel of consciousness, is literally the artist's canvas, for the woman is being tattooed in a dingy parlor near San Francisco's port of entry, the Embarcadero: "The snake between the ribs, / Anchor, tiger, the daggered heart, *memento mori* of the skull." The images are drawn from a diversity of myths and historical scenes, painfully etched on the canvas of the receptive self: "I knew I could carry another flesh / On my flesh," she says proudly as she scans the room: "I stared at snapshots on the walls: images of the carriers of images, / Those who had come here before me, / done this thing and lived." As in the several other medical examinations and exhumations in the book, Hummer deploys a clinical precision in the process of crafting "the pierced and reborn body we call *the story / Of our lives.*" Physical pain is synonymous with the "beauty" of experience. The composite body becomes textualized in the subscendentalist's grammar of historical continuity.

No other poem measures Hummer's agon with the Romantic ideal more fully than the title poem, "Walt Whitman in Hell." Can we imagine a purer transcendentalist than Whitman, one unlikelier to be found in Hell? Hell for Whitman must be the inability to expand out of the individual into a wide, coherent spiritual self. Yet who more than Whitman is capable of embracing even these environs?

> The damned are ranged
>
> Before me, row on blighted row. I approach the first
> Prisoner or corpse or dead soul, a man dangled
> By the tissues of the soft palate for the felony
>
> Of his native tongue—he is effigied in the black rags
> Of an ancient uniform. . . .

Hell is here, of course, Manhattan. To Whitman the great city Manahatta, with its bustle and mixture, was the most appropriate metaphor for the wholeness, hence the holiness, of human experience. The urban was the natural, as the physical was the spiritual. But if Whitman is one of this poem's guiding presences, then Dante is the other. With its rich triplet stanzas Hummer's poem descends through dimensions of agony befitting *The Inferno's* rings of torture. The gothic is a malignant reproduction of the Romantic ideal:

> I enter from every gate
>
> At once, on every numbered street and avenue,
> Jackson Heights, Mt. Eden, Bleeker, Lorimer, 59th—
> And the enormity of my multitudinousness,
>
> This apocalyptic rush hour, eclipses even the brilliance
> Of the four quarters of the midnight city—
> Regions with designations, attributes, and enumerations:
>
> *North* the Quarter of the Vomiting Multitudes,
> *East* the Quarter of Suppurations, *West*
> The Quarter of the Pissing Millions, *South* the Quarter
>
> Of Investment Banking—but before I can say them,
> The great fluid weight of my entering
> Washes me forward, and the silent electric doors
>
> Of the silver cars open all together to take me in,
> Every human soul of me. . . .

In "Crossing Brooklyn Ferry," Whitman gazed through the evening rush hour at the multitudes "returning home" and urged the flood tide of time and humankind to "flow on!" Hummer's speaker is likewise swept into the flow, not rising but drawn down by the gravity of his circumstance, by the substantial "great fluid weight" of the human collective. Through the subway gate to the underworld Hummer's shadow-hero sinks into a world where nothing is forgotten. "This is my punishment," he realizes, "For forgetting to believe that blankness is the logical / Outcome of my passionate confusions." From the relatively innocent "tourist / From Michigan . . .

staring at the Empire State / When a cloud of noxious oblivion touched her," he falls further into history, where the landscape of "five hundred thousand blasted acres / Have been ripped apart by trenches and shells." He crosses the rivers of battlefields, "the Nile, the Rhone . . . The Mekong, the Tigris and Euphrates, / Where stealth bombers and F-111s vomit sulfur and acid on the Mesopotamian plain." Unlike the Lethe, these rivers provide no solace from memory's shame. He remembers the "vanished" poets of America—from Lindsay to Rolfe and Rukeyser—and driven further, to where the body has been blasted, where "the shattered ghosts come thick," he recalls with Dantesque clarity and zeal the unbearable shame of the politics of the day in a "seedy mercenary army":

> Dregs of ushers, gynecologists, thieves,
> And the fine ash of Iraqi cabdrivers,
> And the delicate grit of Marines,
>
> Dust of Bush, Baker, Schwarzkopf, Cheney,
> And beautiful Colin Powell: such a clay they made,
> Such a multitude molded, such drum-taps and battle hymns.

Hummer's art is drawn by an inability to forget or erase. Cultural memory is the opposite of the transcendental, as the utopian is outside history itself. Hummer's Hell, the Postmodern city, is dystopic instead, where nothing is forgotten and yet nothing means more than itself, "the body politic embracing / Self and nothing other." In *Lower-Class Heresy* Hummer depicted our reflections as ghosts "touched by fire, etched white / Against a pure black wall." But in "Walt Whitman in Hell" the "ghosts on the wall" do not reflect ourselves; they *are* ourselves. The great irony of Hummer's vision is that the ghostly, the hellish, has produced a remarkably clear image of the real. Even the spiritual torment of his Whitman in Hell is palpable as flesh:

> O I freely confess it now: America,
>
> I was wrong. I am only slightly larger than life.
> I contain mere conspiracies. What do I know?
> There is no identity at the basis of things, no one
>
> Name beneath all names. . . .

Hummer's poem provides neither for Whitman's transcendental resurrection nor for Dante's spiritual relief. After all, as he says, he is "the only one dead here." The world is just the world. His poem commands our memory of that world, with its compounded griefs and its difficult loves. "Maybe that is why I have to suffer / Everything I can. Maybe that is why," his afflicted Whitman muses, cursing, "I go on / Sounding my doomed eternal bodiless goddamned // *I, I, I, I, I*."

T. R. Hummer has become a powerfully innovative poet, a strong poet, to use Bloom's lexicon, whose ambitious vision intends to confront the very bases of Romantic idealism. He writes with high originality and an intellectual anxiety that are matched by very few other contemporary American poets. Throughout his work he contends that his evolving poetic is driven by "heresy," by his rebellion against the fundamental Romantic paradigms. His earlier work employs and his later work provides a severe critique of that ideal. But the central Romantic paradox remains. The ideal *contains* a heresy. Overseen, it continues to oversee. After all, the Romantic text maintains within itself, through the laws of its governing body, not only the means but the imperative for its own confrontation.

To Advantage Dressed:
Miller Williams among
the Naked Poets

To read the poems of Miller Williams is to brush against the dense, worn, muted fabrics of the world. It is to be asked to fit oneself inside a certain fashion—comfortable, casual, daily—as inside one's favorite work clothes. In fact, if as Alexander Pope asserts in "An Essay on Criticism" it is true that "Expression [or style] is the dress of thought," we might find especial value in examining Williams's poetry through its rhetorical methods, its styles, its fashions of expression. In his brilliant *The Motives of Eloquence* Richard Lanham also reinforces this type of project, "to look at words, not through them, to allow ourselves an extraordinary verbal pleasure." He continues:

> So with any detail of dress; it calls attention to, envaluates, an element of structure. It does not try to look natural, look unseen. If it really escaped notice . . . why bother? It wouldn't work. Like a verbal style, it must be seen as such in order to function as an analogue. . . . Thus the whole range of ornament . . . is equally rhetorical, equally deep or equally superficial.

And Pope, too, examining the "whole range" of poetic styles, returns to his tropes of ornament and dress to criticize poets he deems unable to portray or recreate simplicity:

> Poets, like painters, thus unskilled to trace
> The naked nature, and the living grace,
> With golds and jewels cover ev'ry part,
> And hide with ornaments their want of art . . .

as well as those who are unable to control or envalue their abundant, complicated styles:

> Others for language all their care express,
> And value books, as women men, for dress:
> Their praise is still—the style is excellent;
> The sense, they humbly take upon content.
> Words are like leaves, and where they most abound,
> Much fruit of sense beneath is rarely found.

Since the publication of his first book of poems, *A Circle of Stone,* in 1964, Miller Williams has worked to develop a distinctive "verbal style" primarily aimed at creating an environment of familiarity and acquaintance within the social or public arena. His is a world of surface commotion and texture; his overriding impulse is, persistently, to connect the chaotic, to stitch together the disjointed, to imitate habits of worldly behavior and patterns of public speech. His poetic seems fashioned to allow a rhetoric, a style, whereby he can move easily and comfortably in the world of the human— not to hide nor to transcend nor to boastfully strut, but to facilitate his movement among those he genuinely loves and wonders at: people.

In this regard, Williams's poetic style is often diametrically opposed to that of many of his famous contemporaries, poets whose projects have seemed intent on exposing, on defrocking, on stripping away layers of language to reach some primitive, alingual, and either pre- or post-conscious truth. I am referring, of course, to the related schools of poets known as the Deep Imagists, the Primitivists, and the Naked poets, that collective group (and its followers) most effectively identified in Stephen Berg and Robert Mezey's anthologies *Naked Poetry* and *The New Naked Poetry.* Especially during the late 1960s and through the 1970s—a period during which Williams published several volumes of his own poetry as well as anthologies, translations, and textbooks—this group attempted to define the limits of simple, stripped-bare style, pushing toward language's extinction as a way, ironically, to voice social discontent and as a way to mine the self's own anti-social or more mystical center. "It is a grammar of departure . . . without any of the comforting associations that had kept the world familiar," as Richard Howard, in *Alone with America,* says of W. S. Merwin's work. To reject language, to these poets, is to critique or reject society; to extinguish speech with silence is to commune with a ferocious, sublime, unhuman nature. One paradoxical result of such a poetic, of course, is its possible failure *as poetry*—that is, as a kind of language able to be shared—since a full transcendental experience may be impossible finally to express in language.* Point for point, Williams's project resists the doctrine of the Naked poets, as he counters their frequent despair with possibility, their privacy with public connection and concern, and their nakedness with well-fit wisdom. As Pope encourages: "True wit is nature to advantage dressed." Or as Williams states in "Ruby Tells All," to show the natural, hard-working goodness of the speaker as she laments her long-lost daughter:

> She's grown up now and gone though God knows where.
> She ought to write, for I do love her dearly
> who raised her carefully and dressed her well.

"Ruby Tells All" is surely one of Williams's central poems and should serve as an appropriate introduction to some of the signal tendencies of Williams's method. The poem's occasion, its plot, is simple enough. Now in old age, the character/speaker Ruby narrates some of the significant memories of her long life and finds herself wondering about the daughter she bore and raised but who has been gone for years. What Ruby projects into her relationship with her daughter—in fact, what she may be worried about in a larger sense than having lost touch with her daughter—is the inevitability of her own death, the growing awareness of her mortality:

---

* Harold Bloom sees more possibility in language's transcendental completion: "A transcendence that cannot somehow be expressed is an incoherence; authentic transcendence can be communicated by mastery of language, since metaphor is a transference, a carrying-across from one kind of experience to another." But I see a fuller problematic. The complete transcendental act must arrive at a condition where language ceases to exist (or where it has yet to come into being): language's absence. This would seem to involve significantly more than metaphor or trope transference, which is an exchange of language for language. I suggest instead the inherent frustration or grief of transcendence *as language,* since the transcending destination would be wholly irrelevant to words, apart from them. Transcendental poetry points to, but never arrives at, the transcendent: "Since then—'tis Centuries—and yet / Feels shorter than the Day / I first surmised the Horses' Heads / Were toward Eternity."

> Now, turning through newspapers, I pause
>
> to see if anyone who passed away
>
> was younger than I am.

She does not want to leave the world, its people, does not want to lose the thrilling contact—what Whitman calls the "necessary film"—between her body and "those early mornings, waking up . . . the moon full on the fields," when she felt so "important." Ruby is anything but a transcendentalist; she is entirely of this world with its "men who rolled in in Peterbilts," a world where "butterflies turn into caterpillars / and we grow up," and where the possibilities and mysteries of human love are vivifying, rejuvenative:

> There was a man, married and fond of whiskey. . . .
>
> I would get off work and find him waiting.
>
> We'd have a drink or two and kiss awhile.
>
> Then a bird-loud morning late one April
>
> we woke up naked. We had made a child.

Even nakedness here is a trope to express Ruby's desire to praise her attachment to the world rather than a means to transcend it. The child, of course, is the daughter for whom Ruby now laments and mourns. What she represents is Ruby's connection to, and her continued and continuing membership in, the world of the human. In addition to the narrative of the poem itself, Williams has charged this poem with other kinds of rhetorical choices which further reinforce Ruby's (and the poet's) connection to the world. He has chosen the method of the dramatic monologue as a vehicle for creating the rich fabric of such a knowing and fond voice as Ruby's, and he has juxtaposed Ruby's rural, uneducated, colloquial diction with the formalizing touch lent by the poem's blank-verse line. In other words, both the voice and the form of the poem—while initially rather contradictory partners—finally serve as effective companions to resist the possibility of Ruby's death. Ruby simply will not be quiet. Nor will the poem, its subject or form, vanish through the kinds of erasures favored by the Naked poets: "Every morning I forget how it is. . . . I belong to no one," Charles Simic writes. Ruby represents a kind of worldly persistence and presence, a generous faith typical of Williams's poems but quite unusual for Williams's contemporaries.

In the poem's final lines, as Ruby catalogues the small and grand gifts of knowledge she would pass on to her daughter, she returns us as well to the controlling trope of my argument:

> What could I tell her now, to bring her close . . . ?
> Maybe that I think about her father,
> maybe that my fingers hurt at night,
> maybe that against appearances
> there is love, constancy, and kindness,
> that I have dresses I have never worn.

The figure of clothing here might serve to establish two final aspects of Ruby's strength. She admits that her life has grown abundant and rich, though rich with pains as well as kindnesses; she feels still vibrant enough to want to put on a new dress rather than pass into feebleness or despair or anxiety. Moreover, her return to the metaphor of clothing again reaffirms her desire to belong to and in the world of human interaction; her final statement describes her sense of pride, of personal identity, to say nothing of her sexuality and her quiet confidence. She has sent her daughter off well-prepared, having "raised her carefully and dressed her well," and she concludes by maintaining her own intent now to send herself back into that world, participatory and wise.

It should be useful to slow down now and begin to trace more fully the kinds of rhetorical strategies which "Ruby Tells All" at least introduces, the strategies of a well-dressed (if rustic) poem, and to contrast these methods with the works of some of the Naked poets. A few lines from W. S. Merwin's "Snowfall" provide an adequate example to begin the comparision:

> Some time in the dark hours
> it seemed I was a spark climbing
> the black road
> with my death helping me up
> a white self helping me up
> like a brother
> growing
>   · · ·

I am beginning

again

but a bell rings in some village I do not know

and cannot hear

and in the sunlight snow drops from branches

leaving its name in the air

and a single footprint

brother

The power of Merwin's best work has always been its sense of the inex-pressible, its attempt to negotiate between our failing world and another kind of experience—impersonal, dream-like, symbolic. His work creates a mythic, other world perhaps preferable to this one with its Viet Nams and Watergates and pollution. Yet, though his work may initially have a social grounding, it generally operates by negation, by removing elements of this world from its canvas. As a result, his poems are frequently sparely populated and resound-ing with despair, with a deep longing to transcend and a sense of the failure to complete or articulate that transcendence. In *Mythologies of Nothing* Anthony Libby further defines such a poetic:

> It often reflects . . . the medieval *via negativa;* it tends to imagine fig-ural or literal death as the ground of revelation. . . . Often it comes from and leads to nothing. . . .

Here in "Snowfall," for instance, we find roads, villages, even brothers, yet these nouns seem to nominate no *recognizable* road, village, or brother. Even the speaker "[does] not know" them. These are instead more like archetypi-cal signs, and our inability to assign specific references to them indicates one aspect of Merwin's naked style—the impulse to erase references to the lit-eral world and to create in its place an alternative world which often seems populated only by a single speaker and his self-made mythology, a world of types and symbols. "To recur in its purest forms," Merwin has written in a commentary in *Naked Poetry,* "poetry seems to have to keep reverting to its naked condition." The obvious result of a language reverting to its naked condition must surely be silence, the death wish of language. In *The Still Performance,* describing Merwin's longing for such silence, James McCorkle identifies the obvious peril or paradox: "It [silence] is the only thing we cannot accumulate or lose. . . . Silence, however, can only be not-being and the lack of discourse between the self and others."

Miller Williams's poetry, if nothing else, is composed of references to the phenomena and minutiae of this world and to a life lived among a teeming, noisy population. It is the world of people:

> Out of Mobile I saw a 60 Ford
> fingers wrapped like pieces of rope
> around the steering wheel
> foxtail flapping the head of the hood
> of the first thing ever
> he has called his own.
>
> Between two Bardahls
> above the STP
> the flag flies backwards
> Go To Church This Sunday
> Support Your Local Police
> Post 83
> They say the same thing
> They say
> *I am not alone.*

Here, in "Plain," Williams has described a scene in some ways startlingly similar to Merwin's in "Snowfall"—a village with its attendant details and its inhabitants. But the particular differences of those details and inhabitants are telling. Williams's speaker travels not down a *via negativa* but down a more apparently literal road where people interact. Williams seems fascinated with the names of things specific to this world, and if the Merwin poem presents us with a semiology for his mythic landscape—giving us the signs of the psyche's longing for death and transcendence—then Williams's poem gives us a more literal signification in the images of the bumper and window stickers. They are clearly signs of life, signs of work, faith, and *be*longing. They do not accumulate into a mythology, or at least into *only* a mythology; they do not indicate a desire to be transformed or lifted or mortified, to be admitted into the brotherhood of the "white self" or the "snow drop." Yet they do resound with psychic import, albeit an import quite different from the Merwin poem. What they establish is a comfort in the human, a fascination with people, and the significant possibility that art can be made and comfort found entirely within the sphere of the this-worldly. Their tacit enemy is silence. Their apparent obligation is to capture or recreate the abundant richness of human and natural phenomena. They include rather than erase: Williams's art is torn from and restitched back into the fabric of the world.

One of Williams's most important poems, "A Poem for Emily," provides us with several more examples of the particulars of the poet's rhetorical methods, and each choice evident here seems again to affirm Williams's resistance of the naked condition and of death itself:

> Small fact and fingers and farthest one from me,
> a hand's width and two generations away,
> in this still present I am fifty-three.
> You are not yet a full day.
>
> When I am sixty-three, when you are ten,
> and you are neither closer nor as far,
> your arms will fill with what you know by then,
> the arithmetic and love we do and are.
>
> When I by blood and luck am eighty-six
> and you are someplace else and thirty-three
> believing in sex and god and politics
> with children who look not at all like me,
>
> sometime I know you will have read them this
> so they will know I love them and say so
> and love their mother. Child, whatever is
> is always or never was. Long ago,
>
> a day I watched awhile beside your bed,
> I wrote this down, a thing that might be kept
> awhile, to tell you what I would have said

when you were who knows what and I was dead
which is I stood and loved you while you slept.

Even as he considers the eventuality of his own death, the speaker here is much more intent on praising life, on *finding reasons* to praise life ("sex and god and politics"); in other words, he resists the elegaic impulse in behalf of the need to establish that "whatever is / is always or never was," to establish the on-goingness of things, as Ruby also articulated her abiding sense of continuity in "Ruby Tells All."

This is not a poem that wants to vanish from the page, that seeks its minimal condition. It suggests itself as a complete artifact rather than a naked archetype. Many of Williams's stylistic choices reiterate this impulse. The rhyme is quirky and memorable, rather like an adult's nursery rhyme; the playfulness of the syntax also serves to make apparent and delightful the rhythmic and alliterative qualities of the language; the five-stress, generally iambic pentameter lines and the even stanzas establish a formal regularity, a sense of the poem *as poem*—that is, willingly intact within the social traditions of poetry. Williams uses these conventional devices and lends them a rather unconventional voice. Here, as often in his poetry, Williams's speaker finds the language of poetry within the colloquial voice, locates the written within the oral; the lines of the poem are "poetic" lines, yet the syntax is that of speech. The remarkable sentence which makes up stanzas three and four is a good example of Williams's marriage of the written and the spoken, the formal and the idiomatic, as the misplaced phrases and entangled zeugmas characteristic of speech wed themselves to the strict lineation. Even this charming and personal voice, I contend, helps to ground the poem's experience in *this* world, as Williams persists in exploiting the peculiarities of language rather than filtering them out.

Again, a poem by W. S. Merwin will serve as an effective counterpart to Williams's poetic in "A Poem for Emily." The whole text of Merwin's severe, collapsed "Elegy" is:

Who would I show it to

Where Williams revels in the possibilities of continuity, Merwin laments. His elegy, of course, cannot be an elegy for the death of a person—the way Williams's poem served as a celebration of the birth of a granddaughter—

for indeed there is no person in the poem. Merwin seems to suggest that the form and/or the impulse of the elegy is itself hopeless or impossible, since the human subject of any elegy will naturally never read that elegy. Rather, Merwin's poem elegizes the elegy, sings a dirge for the possibilities of language itself, turning its failure back on itself. Merwin's implicit desire to speak to, even to save, the departed must remain unfulfilled, since his language cannot be capable of completing the journey to the other world, to death. So it must vanish in its attempt, reverting more and more to the conditions of transparence, of absence, of nakedness.

"Poetry is the wasted breath," Galway Kinnell's note in *Naked Poetry* reads. "The subject of the poem is the thing which dies." Merwin's typical erasure of punctuation, the taut brevity of his utterance, the apparent absenting of personality and contact, the sense that the poem itself is an inadequate translation from another, better condition, all serve to reiterate the poet's desire to transcend experience as the poem vanishes necessarily into silence, into Kinnell's "wasted breath." Conversely, as in "Ruby Tells All," as if to counter the Naked poets' condition of privacy and despair, Williams fills his poems with voices—of aging starlets, associate professors, men on buses, even grandfathers—to find in such populous occasions an encouragement, a means to go on in the world. In the final stanza of another poem, "The Aging Actress Sees Herself a Starlet on the Late Show," the speaker seems not only to answer her own question but also to provide a good example of Williams's continued leaps of faith out of despair into connection and persistence:

> How would you like never being able
> to stop moving, always to be somewhere
> walking, crying, kissing, slamming a door?
> You can feel it, millions of images moving;
> no matter how small or disguised, you get tired.
> How would you like never being able
> completely, really, to die? I love that.

To examine more fully the function of imagery in the work of the Naked poets and of Miller Williams demonstrates further the telling differences in their respective poetics and positions. Anthony Libby has rightly identified the "deep image" as one of the most important characteristics of the Naked poets:

> The successful deep image strikes with the force of a newly discovered archetype, minor or major, coming from the depths of the poet's subjectivity with a paradoxically universal force, his private revelation made ours.

Libby supposes that the poet must "describe his psychic state in images which despite their novelty seem more discovered than made," and may do so by employing "concrete surrealist imagery as the result of 'leaping' from conscious to unconscious mind and back again." Robert Bly's "After Long Busyness" may serve as a suitable example:

> I start out for a walk at last after weeks at the desk.
> Moon gone, plowing underfoot, no stars; not a trace of light!
> Suppose a horse were galloping toward me in this open field?
> Every day I did not spend in solitude was wasted.

Typical of the Naked poets, here Bly recites a list of images which seem elemental, natural, stripped to basics. It is not unimportant that the speaker has been working hard—his writing at the desk, in fact, wants to be seen as parallel to the physical labor of plowing a field—and now has turned to the blank natural world for healing. The wild flight of the horse is his release, his obliteration, and so the totemic images attempt to express his delivery from the tiresome, workaday world into the solitary world where language itself, again, seems inadequate to express "this open field." The images, in fact, suggest a sort of stock formula; they become a set of symbols which leads the speaker from his human self at home into the dark expanse of nature and finally, necessarily, into the erasure of "solitude."

Jung must certainly be one of the immediate parents of this poetic. His following passage defines the Naked poets' own impulse to discover deep, natural, elemental imagery as a way to locate the absenting spirit or the soul, using the tropes of clothing and bareness to articulate an essentially mystic, transcendental project:

> And if we hide our nakedness . . . by putting on gorgeous robes and trappings . . . we are essentially lying about our own history. It would

be far better simply to admit our spiritual poverty. . . . The spirit has
come down from its fiery high places . . . but when spirit becomes
heavy, it turns to water. . . . Therefore the way of the soul leads to the
water, to the dark mirror that lies at the bottom. Whoever has decided
to move toward the state of spiritual poverty . . . goes the way of the
soul that leads to the water.

Every impulse in Miller Williams's poems resists or contradicts this atti-
tude. If Merwin, Bly, and other Naked poets wish to discover deep images,
Miller Williams is thrilled at presenting social images, images raked from
the surface of the populous world. It is not inappropriate that he has titled
his selected poems *Living on the Surface*. One of his most frequent methods
is to assemble disparate images, abundant, even chaotic images, which hardly
ever seem to reveal a formula or a means by which to transcend the phe-
nomenal world, "to move toward the state of spiritual poverty," as Jung says
above. In other words, his poems are composed of images of the outer world,
the tangible, the particular, where inner meaning is relinquished in favor of
sheer *being*, where individual identity is not erased but clarified and savored.
As if in praise of this very impulse, his "A Toast to Floyd Collins" is a joy-
ous, strange catalogue of people, events, and ideas. After toasting the likes
of Trotsky and Nicanor Parra, the speaker continues:

> To whoever dies tonight in New Orleans
> To Operator 7 in Kansas City
>
> To the sound of a car crossing a wooden bridge
> To the Unified Field Theory
> To the Key of F
>
> And while I'm at it
> A toast to Jim Beam
> To all the ice cubes thereunto appertaining
> To Jordan knitting
>
> A silver cat asleep in her lap
> And the sun going down
>
> Which is the explanation for everything

This is, it seems to me, a decidedly untranscendental poem, a totally anti-Jungian compilation of images that leads not to the "white spark" of the self but to the social self who loves bodily pleasures such as music, who loves the contact of voices, even the small delights of family, and the *making* of these things into poetry. He has not stripped away the idiomatic or the impure, as the Naked poets tend to do, but has relished the exotic and the familiar alike, clothing his imagination with the simple material which surrounds him in his daily habitat. Even when those phenomena are not explicable—as, of course, there is in physics no particular formula yet devised for the Unified Field Theory, only the supposition that such a formula may exist—he raises his Jim Beam in praise. The effects here, then, come from the mind's responses to the body's sensations, its delights in the sensory pleasures replete in the world and in the poem. Even the combined images of "Jordan knitting / A silver cat asleep in her lap / And the sun going down" do not, though he says they do, explain anything. The sun's going down cannot be an explanation, only a cause or simply an event. But the speaker knows that; he delights in the irrational, not seeking to transcend a difficult or hard-to-explain existence, happy to feel implicit in the busy, chaotic, surface world.

The impulse of the Naked poets is finally an anti-intellectual one. When Charles Simic states in *New Naked Poetry* that "poetry is the orphan of silence," he sides with Merwin and Kinnell in his suggestion that poetry is in some essential way a negating art, that it is unable finally to "save" itself from eventual obliteration back into silence, or at least that, in trying to resist the merely-worldly, poetry must inevitably deny or reject the intellectual processes of the merely-human. He continues: "There is a need here, an obsession with purity. . . . In the end, I am always at the beginning. Poverty—an endless condition." The poverty he mentions is surely both Jung's "spiritual poverty" and a poverty of imagination, of language. It is the poverty of mortification that Merwin implies in "Plane," where "my will [is] like a withered body muffled / in qualifications until it has no shape." In this poem Merwin desires a "vision of the essential nakedness of the gods" and defines nakedness as "the seamless garment of heaven," again making use of the trope of clothing and nudity to express the issue of humility and selflessness, of the otherworldly.

Williams's poems do not trust the anti-intellectual. Williams is, more thoroughly, devoted to the thoughtful processes available within the traditions of poetry and of language. His treatment of images should prove his faith in the capacities of the human mind, even the deliberate capacity or decision to resist logic. Where the Naked poets finally distrust the intellectual, choosing instead to obliterate the self and the self's language (language being, of course, an intellectual enterprise), Williams resides entirely in the particular, the individual, and the intellectual—even when he cannot explain a particular phenomenon. Instead of being anti-intellectual, frequently his poems and his schemes of imagery are irrational, finding intellectual delight in their own irrationality. The world is, after all, sufficient for Williams's speakers; they sense that it is far larger than they are able to comprehend.

In a marvelous example of the world's abundance and a speaker's sense of awe and joy in the irrational, Williams's "Love Poem" is at once a catalogue of apparently unconnected events from around the world and from within the speaker's own neighborhood:

Six o'clock and
the sun rises across the river.
The traffic cop wakes up and
crawls over his wife.
The naked professor will sleep another hour.
The dentist wakes up and reaches for a smoke.
The doctor reaches for the phone
and prescribes
his voice full of rust. . . .
It is midnight now in Samoa.

As he imagines the unconnected activities of his neighbors, the speaker still creates a connection by the sequences he chooses and by the repetition of words (such as the double "reaches"), the repetition of syntax, and the repetition of events (suggested by the several sleepers as they progressively waken, act, and speak). As the day passes in the poem, the speaker allows his imagination to range into schoolhouses, hospitals, and stores. He follows, or invents, the random activities of his neighbors and juxtaposes these with the passing of time in Berlin, Djakarta, Osaka, and elsewhere, creating a relativist's connection to things. He never wants anything more, never wishes to reject or deny the inexplicable complications and sadnesses of daily human life; instead, as we have seen earlier, he witnesses and names and so ultimately praises. The poem's final lines complete the cycle of the imagined day, returning from their world journey back to the speaker's own home, having travelled but not transcended. The speaker has confronted a chaotic world where "in Mercy Hospital a man is dying" but has as well found a renewed need for love or connection, even if love is irrational, even if life and imagination are limited by time and place:

> Eleven o'clock:
> The children are gone to bed and we are here
> sitting across the room from one another
> accustomed to this house
> that is not ours to keep
> to this world that is not ours
> and to each other.
>
> Sands run through the children in their sleep.

The final possible insufficiency of the deep image is its implication that the phenomena of the world contain a meaning within themselves that is greater than themselves. In writing about James Wright's short-lived but famous phase as a Naked poet, Williams himself identifies the difficulty of such a poetic:

> Leaping . . . requires a symbolic approach to a poem, and so does the deep image, which is simply the sensory end of a leap; both assume that a thing has an aura of significance beyond its physical fact, or no less important than the fact. . . . And I suspect that [James Wright] left the leaping alone, on the whole, after *Saint Judas,* because it so easily begins to parody itself.

Williams finds delight and significance in things themselves, in the imaging of things, and seldom strains to invent their psychic or archetypal meaning.

His comment about the availability of the deep image to self-parody is also important, for certainly one of the dangers of the deep image (here interestingly akin to the Puritans' sober and severe *plaine stile*) is the temptation of self-imposed exile and therefore of narcissism. Recall again Jung's description of the soul, seeking spiritual poverty, as it leans to "the dark mirror" at the bottom of its watery essence. The style of the Naked poets is designed to create simplicity, humility, honesty, sobriety, and probably even to suggest guilt (implied in Jung's "spiritual poverty"). Importantly, this desire to strip away, to unclothe the language, can also turn into a kind of auto-eroticism, a love of the self's ability to appear simple, stripped, nude of contrivance, even morally superior. This is precisely the point where the Naked poets finally run into trouble, as Williams predicted above and as Paul Breslin outlines in his article "How to Read the New Contemporary Poem"—when their plainness becomes a sort of fetish evident in self-plagiarism or unearned drama, when the deep image myth becomes its own subject. This weakness is to be found in recent work by some of the poets I have used here to represent the Naked poets. In the mid-1970s and 1980s their work too often turned into a kind of rhetorical narcissism, as if they fell in love with their own naked, mortified selves. The unfortunate result is that their personal agonies and transformations ring untrue and do not, as Libby says they must, turn their "private revelation[s]" into ours.

Williams seems to identify explicitly the danger of transcendence, the failure of the private revelation to connect, in "One Day a Woman":

> One day a woman picking peaches in Georgia
> lost her hold on the earth and began to rise.
> She grabbed limbs but leaves stripped off in her hands.
> Some children saw her before she disappeared
> into the white cloud, her limbs thrashing.
> The children were disbelieved. The disappearance
> was filed away with those of other women
> who fell into bad hands and were soon forgotten.
> Six months later a half-naked man in Kansas
> working on the roof of the Methodist Church
> was seen by half a dozen well-known

and highly respected citizens to move

directly upward, his tarbrush waving,

until he shrank away to a point and vanished.

Nobody who knew about the first event

knew of the second, so no connection was made.

The tarbrush fell to earth somewhere in Missouri

unnoticed among a herd of Guernsey cows.

While I do not want to go so far as to claim that Williams wrote this poem *about* the Naked poets, still the details of the poem certainly give us plenty of invitation to read it as such. The woman's disappearing in a "white cloud" while working in her perhaps Edenic garden, the "half-naked man" who moved "directly upward" while tarring his church with a brush (like an artist's tool), the absurdity of the pious, pure situations, all point to Williams's tacit attitudes toward art-as-transcendence. Such privacy fails to become valid as a possibility for art, since "no connection was made." Over and over, Miller Williams's poems desire connection over transcendence, delight over despair, the pleasures of verbal texture and formal fabric over nakedness and simplicity.

The conflict described here between the styles of Miller Williams and the Naked poets is not new to the contemporary realm. Nor is it limited in the contemporary scene to these poets only—for certainly we could usefully see the works of Howard Nemerov or Richard Wilbur as sympathetic to Williams's aesthetic and many of the works of Peter Everwine or James Dickey (a Southerner, like Williams, but worlds apart from Williams's poetic) as essentially transcendental in the manner of Merwin, Bly, or Kinnell. Still, it might be useful in conclusion to outline some of the traditions within which Williams's worldly vision operates, as well as those which underlie the Naked poets' impulses.

The conflict, as I see it, is most probably the conflict between Philip Rahv's "palefaces and redskins." Or, to avoid Rahv's unfortunate racism, it is the conflict in America between Eliot and Robinson, or earlier between Emerson and Twain, or even between Edwards and Franklin. It is probably traceable to the very deep, essential tension between Platonic and Aristotelian inclinations—that is, to the most basic rift in Western thought.

To the Puritan in Edwards, the transcendentalist in Emerson, and the Modernist-turned-mystic in Eliot, the function of language is ultimately otherworldly, Romantic, Platonic. Its impulse is to resist and deny or despise the public, to develop the private and the self-reliant, in order to allow the individual a means to transport himself away from this world. Its components include a transparent or naked language, high seriousness or morality, associative leaping, and objects loaded with spiritual, symbolic significance. This literary philosophy, like most religions, is markedly sublime, and as Thomas Weiskel observes in his *The Romantic Sublime,* "the essential claim of the sublime is that man can, in feeling and in speech, transcend the human." Harold Bloom identifies, in his *Ruin the Sacred Truths,* two of the greatest difficulties of such an aesthetic:

> Transcendence of the human in speech, particularly in the utterance within a tradition of utterance that is poetry, necessarily relies upon the trope of hyperbole, an over-throwing . . . that is closer to simplification through intensity than it is to exaggeration. Transcendence of the human in feeling is a universal experience (or illusion) and itself transcends most modes of utterance.

We have identified the dangers of "naked" simplification and have also explored the paradox that a transcendental experience itself transcends our capability to express it. Nakedness is simply not enough, as Richard Lanham complains: "Naked into the world [we] came, *but not without resource.*"

In the other camp, to the Deist in Franklin, the social humorist in Twain, and the formal realist in Robinson, the function of language is this-worldly and thereby classical, Aristotelian. For such writers the impulse is to participate in the public discourse, to revel in and learn from the things of this world, to admit the irrational and the particular, even the peculiar, and to remain at last "well-dressed" in the public's presence by making use of ornament and the personalizing intricacies of style. Their work will not erase but employ and relish the peculiarities of human experience and behavior. Again Lanham defends this aesthetic with clarity and precision:

> Ornament, in a way then, seems more honest than plainness. It does not affect a naturalness in the nature of things unattainable. . . . The way to naturalness lies through artifice, not around it.

The correlary ingredients of this aesthetic and style may include colloquial and idiomatic language, humor, practical or worldly knowledge, images which resist merely symbolic significance, experience which resists the otherworldly or the merely private, and the willing inheritance of traditional formal and/or narrative structure. This literary philosophy is decidedly untranscendental, and it is Williams's home.

As if directly to confront the temptation to vanish into a Naked poet's typical landscape, Williams's poem "Waiting for the Paper to be Delivered" gives us a final, ample example of this poet's vision and faith:

> Late January.
> Snow is on everything.
> No matter how far I listen there is only silence.
>
> Two yellow machines have worked for a week
> cutting away the hill in front of the house
> I have come to live in for the rest of my life.
>
> On the highest part of the hill
> one oak is standing.
>
> Nothing else is vertical on the horizon.
> It locks the white sky to the white earth.

Though he hears only silence, he is, importantly, waiting for the news of the world to be delivered. The silence of line three is immediately subsumed by the human commotion implicit in the second stanza. Time and again, Williams resists Merwin's erasure, his "white self." We find here instead remarkable assurance in the one oak standing "on the highest part of the hill." Though he says the oak "locks the white sky to the white earth," it must also surely be true that—like a pencil propping open a window, or like the poet's own desire—the oak also keeps the two clearly apart. It keeps the speaker safe to live in his house "for the rest of [his] life." Like a good winter coat, buttoned and well-fit, this poem takes its speaker out into the spare landscape and lets him come back, alive.

PART TWO

Culture, Inclusion, Craft

Culture, Inclusion, Craft

We live in extremely public times. The narcissism of the media, the omnipresence of advertising and gossip, an almost Victorian titillation at things overseen—we just can't take our eyes off of everybody else. Our quickening publicness is frightening especially as its surface images come popping relentlessly, joylessly, out of the popular media; the reductive nature of the media is greatly to blame for the fear and suspicion with which we typically respond to change or to any perceived foreign or "other" cultural phenomena. Confronted, for example, with an increasingly empowered women's movement, with a homosexual community demanding acknowledgment and fairness (even survival), with a growing minority population, and so on, our "majority" citizenry often responds with impatient judgment, blame, exclusion, or dismissal—allowing only the surface image projected by a hasty medium to register, hence allowing that image and its human foundation little credibility, little chance to connect.

What disturbs us in one realm may nurture us in another. The impulse to include, document, and monitor our changing cultural phenomena is one of the saving graces in our current poetry. It offers understanding and sympathy, an alternative to the judgments encouraged or inflicted by the popular media; within the ranges of poetry this impulse may lead us out of the narcissistic self-confessions of previous decades, out of the exclusive attitude that the private is the only legitimate locus for art. Compared to the media's typically reductive nature and the public's learned response to pass quick judgment, a poem's desire is more likely to be to name, to include, to praise, to sympathize with—to make room, in this case, for the other.

On Popular Culture by Albert Goldbarth, Ohio State, 1990; *Let Evening Come* by Jane Kenyon, *Graywolf*, 1990; *The City in Which I Love You* by Li-Young Lee, BOA, 1990; *Ode to Anna Moffo* by Wayne Koestenbaum, Persea, 1990; *Mystery Train* by David Wojahn, Pittsburgh, 1990; *Powers of Congress* by Alice Fulton, Godine, 1990.

Albert Goldbarth is a poet with a voice and vista large enough to seem like multitudes. He is, in fact, a sort of cultural phenomenon himself, writing and publishing with fervor for the last two decades; he has been one of poetry's most enthusiastic makers, articulating some of the widest of public goings-on. Goldbarth's culture, his abiding project and frequently his subject, as the title of his splendid book declares, is "popular" culture— that is, both the culture of the masses as well as, more ironically, the immense popularity of that culture. His is a vast, inclusive, electric, rambunctious, even downright messy poetic vision, but it is capable of articulating wisely and sympathetically the chaos and clutter of the popular imagination. In short, he is poetry's answer to the superheroes of childhood —comic and eminently capable at once—who "come back sometimes . . . with their lightningbolts sewn / the size of dinner utensils across their chests, with their capes / rayed out, with their blue lamé boots," and whose tools include "pharaonic rings, / atomic lariats, stun guns, mystic arrows, tridents, with / such amulets as hinge the Earth and Heavens into symbiotic grace," as he writes in "Powers."

Goldbarth struggles in his poetry to develop a stance whereby he might see from this perspective, where Earth and the Heavens "hinge." He wants nothing less than to see, say, and bear it all. In the opening poem of *Popular Culture,* "By One," he begins to negotiate an appropriate locus and "law" to enable his poetry: "That's all it requires. The law of even / miracles is economy, and one / resourceful angel is all it requires." But if an angel might prefer the "symbiotic grace" of economy and evenness, Goldbarth places his own faith in the inclusive and the impure. His grace is decidedly not the grace of angels; after all, "the night sky [is] full / of too much to be familiar." He dismantles the miracle of the heavenly with a single flourish of his popular method: "There's a theory / UFO's are the 20th century's angels." By the end of the first poem the economical and angelic have been transformed into the abundant and the human-all-too-human, as Harold Bloom might say—folklore, machine parts, and sugar cubes of Salk vaccine having replaced the pure and sublime. For Goldbarth the miracle is what follows. Appropriately, the poem succeeding the one about angels is his raucous, wacky "Donald Duck in Danish," so earthy and off-the-wall, so alternately funny and desperate, that the vast human sphere with its Disneyworlds, Danish silks, and DNA is undoubtedly sufficient for all of his poetry's needs.

Goldbarth's is a universe in expansion, or rather a "multiverse," as he prefers to call it, where mass and matter are extending with blinding speed, held together only by the human will to contain. Though his poems are jampacked with so much stuff, Goldbarth is consistently willing and able to grapple with abundance:

> A single 'paragraph' might draw
> the picture of two grass-appraising oxen, a parrot their
> same size, fish, a huge central tree with a husband and wife
> enjoying a supper under its reach, each leaf a word, each feather,
> scale, flex of flesh . . .
> The whole of Creation, literally
> from language. . . .
>
> *("Qebehseneuf")*

Goldbarth could be describing his own poetry in this passage, since a single stanza of his may appear to include "the whole of Creation, literally / from language." He rides the black-and-white range with the Cheyenne; he visits the intestines of Tutankhamun "folded in linen, then / set in a miniature mummiform coffin"; he even turns the capitalist enterprises of the World Trade Center into a frenzied beauty pageant: "Miss Pet Food. Miss Circus Equipment . . . Miss-Pickle-handing-out-gherkin-slices." Language and imagination are the tools of the maker. If Goldbarth lets his lines spill awkwardly and forces his stanzas to break into occasionally bizarre enjambment, it is to mirror the pressures resulting from the increased mass and movement of an evolving existence. He wants his poems to look like they are barely able, but *able,* to contain whatever odd-shaped thing he flings their way. But he's sneaky; for instance, there are, in *Popular Culture,* two quite formally subtle but splendid sonnet sequences, "The Quest for the Source of the Nile" and "Of the Doubleness," and several other poems in regular stanzaic patterns. In fact, the collection itself, composed of fourteen poems, is something of a humongous sonnet, marking its most radical shift at the ninth poem, "Pop. Cult. Crash Course." His poems shine with the high gloss of a low style intelligently made.

Goldbarth makes his home among doubleness, plurality, relativity. He fuses the loss of a father or the longing for love with subjects normally forbidden in "high art"—physics, folklore, comic book magic, for example. His voice is as capable of joy and awe as of hyperbole and screech, and his rhetorical models are as likely to be discursive as lyrical. He reports in "Quebeheneuf":

> An Indian medical text of the 15th century
>
> discusses closing intestinal wounds by lining
>
> black Bengali ants along the rupture. Really.
>
> They clamp it together. Their bodies are snapped off
>
> and the jaws remain, as ample sutures
>
> that dissolve by the time the wound heals.

Quebeheneuf is, it turns out, "the hawk-headed god and spirit-of-the-intestines." But even given the fascinating fact of the technique described, indeed given Goldbarth's compulsive, interesting head for information and tidbit, it's the lilt of "Really" that marks Goldbarth's poetry. He wants so badly to convince, to be believed—to charm and cajole us into finding value in what we might otherwise dismiss as weird, unusual, marginal, or mundane. Instead of altering or ignoring the unevenness of experience to fit poetry, he adjusts his poetry to fit the strangeness of the world, in a stance approaching pure energy, sheer will. It's an original, highly entertaining conglomeration, locating legitimate and lasting value in the imagination of the popular culture.

If Goldbarth's multiverse is rapidly expanding, blasting outward, then the universe of Jane Kenyon's *Let Evening Come* is undergoing a severe contraction, a collapse, a falling inward toward density and gravity. It's a poetry common to the minimal, primitivist impulses of the past three decades. Even while I acclaim the noises of cultural inclusion in contemporary poetry, I want to continue also to find solace and beauty in plainness, in solitude. Unfortunately, Kenyon here seldom raises her private, spare utterances to the conditions that, I believe, the plain style aspires to—prayer, song, grace.

In her best poems Kenyon documents the culture of the solitary—an impulse which, I admit, conflicts with the qualities I am generally praising here. But it is of course possible and surely desirable, in a poetry as abundant and various as ours, to have it both ways. Here is Jane Kenyon having it her way quite well:

August. My neighbor started cutting wood
on cool Sabbath afternoons, the blue
plume of the saw's exhaust wavering over
his head. At first I didn't mind the noise
but it came to seem like a species of pain.

From time to time he let the saw idle,
stepping back from the logs and aromatic
dust, while his son kicked the billets
down the sloping drive toward the shed.
In the lull they sometimes talked.

His back arched unrelentingly, he assumed
from all the stooping. Sundays that fall
they bent over the pile of beech and maple,
intent on getting wood for winter, the last,
as it happened, of their life together.

Restraint, melancholy, a watcher's whisper—these qualities mark "Father
and Son" as they do most of Kenyon's poems. In poems of the plain style
the stance of simplicity, of natural observation, is a predominant rhetori-
cal gesture. But the humility of this poem becomes more interesting, even
ironic, when one notices how much more than mere reportage Kenyon
employs. The narrator is in clear control, for it is she who turns the saw's
sound into a "species of pain" and she who knows what the father
"assumed" about his stooping and she who suggests a deep, final awareness
in the piercing touch of "as it happened." Each image bears both storyline
and a deeper, suggestive resonance; even the "blue plume of the saw's
exhaust wavering over" the father's head clarifies his action and prefigures
his death with hovering ominousness. This poem's structure is simple, effec-
tively unassuming. Each stanza is a closed chronology, a life shutting down.

Kenyon seldom strays from a style of observation, image, plain speech.
Unfortunately, too many of the other poems fail to suggest the quiet magic
of "Father and Son." Too few of her details have the suggestive pitch nec-
essary to resonate as emblems or archetypes. Simple details and plain speech
remain merely, well, simple and plain. The point of the plain style—as I

think of the work of James Wright, Mary Oliver, William Heyen—is to leap from the personal to the universal by a connection through archetype; that finally is a deeply cultural connection. But Kenyon seems too seldom interested in such a leap or contact, and too many of her poems read more like merely private or mundane journals. Sometimes she is a downright grouch:

> At dinner I laughed with the rest,
> but in truth I prefer the sound
> of pages turning, and coals shifting
> abruptly in the stove. I left before ten
> pleading a long drive home. . . .
>
> Why do people give dinner parties? Why did I
> say I'd come?

Lord knows, I want to say to "Dinner Party." The company she keeps in *Let Evening Come* is of five types: mostly herself, but also her husband, their fairly distant few neighbors, the things in her garden, and some famous figures from the art world. With this last category, for instance, I grow impatient with such presumption. In one poem she concludes, "Like Beethoven's head [her geranium's] head had grown too large," and in another she begins, "Like Varya in *The Cherry Orchard* I keep the keys . . ." and in others we follow Keats and Severn yet again bravely straining over the Spanish Steps in Rome.

Days begin and end, the seasons change, nature follows its cycles. *Let Evening Come* monitors the pulse of a rural life, but it often feels as if the presiding spirit is inherently suburban or nonagrarian, the spirit of a passer-through. Not much happens, not much work gets done, and so the difficult life of the rural seems pastoral, even occasionally melodramatic:

> The first snow fell—or should I say
> it flew slantwise, so it seemed
> to be the house
> that moved so heedlessly through space.
>
> Tears splashed and beaded on your sweater.
> Then for long moments you did not speak.

No pleasure in the cups of tea I made
distractedly at four.

The sky grew dark. I heard the paper come
and went out. The moon looked down
between disintegrating clouds. I said
aloud: "You see, we have done harm."

"While We Were Arguing" is crisp, its pacing reserved and apt, but its whole presumption is grandiose, finally arrogant. This argument was so shattering and important that all of nature seemed to respond? I find no leap here, no connection with mystery or magic, nothing to turn the private into communal or cultural music—only ego and sentiment.

There are genuine pleasures here in "The Letter," "After an Illness, Walking the Dog," and the especially fine "At the Public Market Museum: Charleston, South Carolina," among others, and yet there are many more instances of mere happenstance and the mundane. I think of this as a slender book, so I was surprised to count its fifty-seven poems; many of them just haven't stayed with me. Only eleven are longer than a page; none is longer than two. They are often interchangeable—short, stylistically repetitive, rhetorically flat. Given Kenyon's earlier work, I had hoped for a book sharing the mysteries of solitude and an essential involvement with the land. But too often the brevity of these songs also marks the duration of their pleasures.

Li-Young Lee's second collection, *The City in Which I Love You,* is the 1990 Lamont Poetry Selection and follows his award-winning *Rose.* Like Jane Kenyon, Lee is a poet of the plain style, but where Kenyon holds her poems with a tight, spare rein, Lee writes with a loose, relaxed, open plainness. His work depends very greatly on the charms of character, as does the work of his presiding influence, Gerald Stern. But where Stern is our most powerfully ecstatic poet, whose skill seems to reside in sheer will and exuberant directness ("Today I am letting two old roses stand for everything I believe in"), Lee is more of an ironist, a poet of doubleness and wariness ("After all, it was only our / life, our life and its forgetting"). Even in lines that directly pay homage to or borrow from Stern, Lee shows his occasional tendency toward flatness or dissipation:

> I am letting this room
> and everything in it
> stand for my ideas about love
> and its difficulties.
>
> *("This Room and Everything in It")*

I have to admit that I admire the desires this book expresses more often than I am able to admire the writing.

The City in Which I Love You is predominantly concerned with two impulses: to document the collisions and possible resolutions of Asian and American culture as enacted by an immigrant population and to trace that cultural evolution personally through Lee's changing relationship with paternity. The repeated mournings of the loss of the father, I think, also bespeak the grief and dissociation resulting from a loss of Asia:

> I wander
> a house I thought I knew;
> I walk the halls as if the halls
> of that other
> mansion, my father's heart. . . .
> While a rose
> rattles at my ear, *Where*
> *is your father?*
> And the silent house
> booms, *Gone. Long gone.*

Here, in "Furious Versions," the speaker mourns that "memory revises me," but he will learn to carry his loss into the future—as story and as the desire to become himself a father. In the first half of the book this loss of the father is a loss of homeland and a loss or probing of faith—faith both familial and Christian. In the second half his making of a new home through marriage and fatherhood and his growing enculturation as an Asian American provide the speaker with the means to renew his faith and to restore his past. By "The Cleaving," the book's best and final poem, he has learned to embrace severing and doubling as the paradox of his existence:

I thought the soul an airy thing.
I did not know the soul is cleaved
so that the soul might be restored. . . .

No easy thing, violence.
One of its names? Change. Change
resides in the embrace
of the effaced and the effacer. . . .

Lee's finest achievement as a poet, in fact, is his persistent blending of cultural politics and personal desire, a doubled subject that seems to me essential to American poetry, given America's admirable but troubled character as a culture comprised largely of immigrants:

. . . this dark
dancer, this Jew, this Asian, this one
with the Cambodian face, Vietnamese face, this Chinese
I daily face,
this immigrant.

Where Albert Goldbarth can make an art form of the lumpy and inclusive, Lee hasn't yet mastered his craft sufficiently to fully support his large embrace. The importance of his double theme notwithstanding, his poems are too loose and tend to dissipate. Even in his longest poems, Lee typically eschews a narrative stance in behalf of a lyric or meditative one and therefore seldom provides a sufficient chronological or dramatic intensity to drive what tends to become reverie. For instance, again in "Furious Versions," a poem of seven sections, the very powerful opening sections decay into redundancy and hesitation in the poem's sixth:

It goes on and it goes on,
the ceaseless invention, incessant
constructions and deconstructions
of shadows over black grass,
while, overhead, poplars
rock and nod,

> wrestle Yes and No,
> contend moon, no moon. . . .

The problem is that Lee doesn't always muster a powerful enough rhetorical voice to convey his imagery. Further, he prefers a very loose, usually irregular stanza and ragged line, suggesting that material presides over structure. At its best here, this technique is effectively humble, a rhetoric of prose-like informality, a democratic or popular site-of-oration. But Lee allows the open-endedness of his technique to seem like unendedness or helplessness; he gives himself few reasons to close or control a line (or stanza or poem) besides his energy, his breathiness. Too often in *The City in Which I Love You* my energy and interest to finish simply deplete before his do.

Ode to Anna Moffo is Wayne Koestenbaum's first book of poetry, but he writes with such finesse, power, and intelligent joy that to identify it as such seems almost misleading. Of all the poets considered here, he is by far the most willing to exert the pressures of traditional formality, yet he is also likely to let the voice and experience of a poem grate against his own formal gestures, launching by turns into raw confession, roughhouse, and rage as well as into aria and art-speak. His sense of sound is sophisticated and capable, for his rhymes, his complex, subtle rhythms, and his precise syllabic or accentual lineations invariably seem natural—or so unnaturally evident as to be uncannily right:

> My sister made up kennings for what she hated: "Socks Fall Down"
> > Meant rolled-down socks with robin's-egg-blue patent leather
> Mary Janes. I secretly loved fancy dress, but drowned
> > My plumage in the closet where I hid my zither,
> Xylophone and bells. I locked them in a box because I'd joined Cub Scouts
> > And wished to kill the songbird, the prissy bluethroat
>
> That I had been before I donned the regulation neckerchief.
> > Fish gut veins and scouting knife were the same Prussian blue.
> My merit badge for knots stood out from my navy shirt in bas-relief.
> > Had they awarded a merit badge for fancy hairdos
> I'd have won it, I took such pains to fix my Beatles bangs.
> > But my attempt to be an outcast boomeranged. . . .

"Fugitive Blue" also identifies the predominant dilemma in Koestenbaum's poetry and his recurrent subject: the wish to destroy the "prissy blue-throat" bird above is more deeply an expression of the confusion, loneliness, and self-loathing of a young gay person in a loudly heterosexual society. Koestenbaum turns circumstance into power. Where the young boy of "Fugitive Blue" sought to hide, the adult narrator of these poems makes self-conscious use even of the clichés of male homosexuality, delighted, if you will, to try on racksful of "peacock" clothes and "pants of lapis lazuli" as a way to flirt with or examine his own indignation at prejudice and intolerance: "The widow / Calls 'Vain' to me, meaning 'Wayne,' and I answer." He can be bawdy, showy as a diva, even purposefully decadent, but will always modify his delights with indignation, pride, anger, or grief.

"Doctor Type" demonstrates the conflicting joy and sadness that complicate nearly every poem in this book. Its opening stanzas introduce the young neighborhood doctor, who "wears jeans / faded so white his butt 'reads' (is discernible) across / the street before I recognize / his face," and establish the playful, even aroused interest of the speaker who shouts, "'There's Doctor Type!' / in private / jubilation meant for no ear." The poem's first half nearly doubles over with wit and wordplay, with self-conscious delight in language as metaphor for the physical, since language is the nearest, most affectionate contact the speaker can afford. Each line is loaded with desire; virtually every line break lingers over an especially wishful notion. But the imagined relationship turns quickly to matters more lethal, as the speaker rehearses the Doctor's inevitable warnings and prognoses. Even his own requisite case history would "blind me to look back that far— / to the embrace that will have been / the deadly / blow." And so the omnipresence of AIDS shadows not only the speaker's imagined tryst but also his past. As the poem modulates, the doctor becomes less a figure of desire and more a figure of distance, conventionality, and impossible peace, and the speaker's initial wit and passion resolve by degrees into damage and regret:

My body,

pale, attracts mosquitoes. The bite by my left
nipple will be worse tonight: I predict

by dawn it will eclipse the swelling on my knee. Wounds shift
powers, degrees, intensities.

Elsewhere, indeed throughout *Ode to Anna Moffo,* Koestenbaum per-
sists in this most serious paradox. "Ecstasy is viral"—as he succinctly for-
mulates in "Erotic and Sepulchral Epigrams from the Cinquecento"
—could rightly stand as the book's clear curse, for throughout these daz-
zling poems the erotic and the deadly, the witty and the grief-stricken, the
bawdy and the enraged, the impassioned and the poisoned do their duets
which "[sew] the body to its sorrow." If there is redemption or hope for
peace or chance of survival, such a hope lies in the figure who sings through-
out. The diva Anna Moffo, from the book's beautifully complex title poem,
the genie-soprano of "Scheherazade," and the poet himself spinning his
educative or doom-deferring charms all conspire to enchant and perhaps
defeat contagion—the diseases of the body or the sicknesses of intolerance.
Koestenbaum's voice and talent insist on inclusion; his passion is buoyant,
his culture only human.

The centerpiece of David Wojahn's third book, *Mystery Train,* is a rowdy,
enjoyable, but often dark concert of sonnets and sonnet-approximations
whose subject is mainly rock-and-roll. In the thirty-five poems comprising
the sequence "Mystery Train," he proves himself to be a new formalist in
the best sense (unlike many who go by that label) by doggedly reworking
and reapplying older formal notions to new arrangements, in much the same
way that the blues is replayed and recast by rock. One of the most signifi-
cant projects throughout *Mystery Train* is Wojahn's struggle to amend con-
ventional form, voice, and gesture in his search for the relevant, pliable, and
memorable.

"Mystery Train" is a veritable jam session of sonnets, and in addition
to the sonnets also includes a poem in nonce stanzas and a remarkable
villanelle-variant, the title piece. Wojahn employs half-rhyme, stanza frac-
turing, William Carlos Williams's triadic line, John Berryman's near-
sonnet—whatever he can get his hands on—to "dismember" as well as
reconstruct. Likewise, the multiple narrative of "Mystery Train" blends the
histories of rock-and-roll and blues music, the damaged and often suicidal
lives of Confessional poets, the equally wrecked lives of several musicians,

and the now iconic events of the period since the Korean War, including the Kennedy and King assassinations, the Vietnam War, and Nixon's sly entanglements. The timeline traces the birth and development not only of Confessional poetry and rock-and-roll but also of Wojahn himself, who was born in the early fifties. It's cacophony as harmony, cultural history as autobiography.

As in any good jam session, the players in "Mystery Train" are from disparate schools, but each is a distinctive stylist. In the third poem, "W.C.W. Watching Presley's Second Appearance on 'The Ed Sullivan Show': Mercy Hospital, Newark 1956," Wojahn uses Williams's terse voice and triadic line as counterpoint to the future King's flirtatious style:

> The tube,
>> like the sonnet,
>>> is a fascist form.
> I read they refused
>> to show this kid's
>>> wriggling bum.
> "The pure products
>> of America. . . ."
>>> etc.
> From Mississippi!
>> *Tupelo,*
>>> a name like a flower
> you wouldn't want
>> beside you . . .
>>> a goddamn
> hostage to yourself.

The ailing Williams bemoans and curses the passing of one age into another—sonnet to television, poet to rock star—and lends perspective on things to come as only the outgoing can:

>> This pomped-up kid,
>>> who preens

and tells us

    "Don't Be Cruel."

            Kid, forget it.

You don't know

    a fucking thing

        about cruelty yet.

Indeed the story of "Mystery Train" is a story of cruelty—of noise inflicted, lives shattered, destruction wreaked, form threatened. For Wojahn these are the true impulses of the era, articulated best by rock-and-roll. He improvises and maneuvers within the sonnet form like a longtime member of the band.

    Bookended around the center of *Mystery Train* are sixteen longer, more meditative poems. They don't have the cumulative density or the linear distinction of the sonnet sequence, but they provide a more reflective, spacious counterpoint to the sonnets' wail and rubble. They are also reminiscent of Wojahn's earlier work—his melancholy, his looser narratives of meditation, his typically spoken voice, his technique of second-person address. To lend drama to these poems and to enlarge their voice, Wojahn uses form and syntax more often than modulation or variety:

It goes up, engulfed in flames in seconds, until everyone
    is silent, having put,
on instruction, their cameras down, mothers boosting children
    to their shoulders,
straining for a better view. A minute or two, and the canopy
    festooning the pyre

also ignites, shrinking to ash but not falling, tumbling
    upward in the breeze,
over the crowd, and gone.

                  ("No Gesture: Ceremony")

Like the sonnets these poems are thickly populated; their audience, their immediate "you," ranges from John Berryman to Private Gabriel Calvin Wojahn. Wojahn approaches his general audience by first corralling and addressing a specific one: "Say that your days and nights have grown somnambulant," he supposes or commands in "Double Exposures," as if directly to identify this technique's recent master, Richard Hugo ("Say your life broke down").

Whether in his fine medley of sonnets or in his longer, meditative poems, Wojahn is haunted by the forms and formulas of catastrophe. His poems record the decadent noises of the past four decades, making a kind of music out of popular culture and taking care to preserve even the sounds of destruction so we will never forget the consequences of silence. In a scene of literal instruction, from the sonnet "Francis Ford Coppola and Anthropologist Interpreter Teaching Gartewienna Tribesmen to Sing 'Light My Fire,' Philippine Jungle, 1978," this paradox is meticulously clear:

> CAW-MAWN   BAY-BE   LIGHT
> MY FOY-OR they chant.
> > "What mean Apocalypse Now?" asks Leader.
> Dr. Singh: "Mean: *everybody-die-together-here.*"

Most of these poets are crafting an art of inclusion and complication, a poetry where one and the "other" may dance without fear of unfair judgment, a poetry of cultural tolerance and connection. This strength is formulated by the title of Alice Fulton's new book, *Powers of Congress.* The power of congress—that is, the phenomenon produced at the meeting or colliding point of any entities—is energy. When two forces come together, they make heat, sparks; each affects the resultant course and condition of the other. That is a fundamental precept of physics and congressional government alike, and that is the especial project of these poets. "Let my glance be passional / toward the universe and you," Fulton offers in "Cascade Experiment." Her merest glance is catalytic, a vehicle for connection.

Alice Fulton writes with great flash and jazz, yet the confident ease of her song belies the complexity of her method. She rivals Goldbarth in her ability to include facts and information from nearly anywhere, and no one matches her ability to perform a marginal sneak attack, a slipping-in of subject, substance, sound—to insinuate the unknown into the known, to fracture, fuse, repair. Her strategy of layering results in a poetic equivalent of the fractal theories of physical science, where apparently arbitrary or chaotic structures are often proven, on closer examination, to be self-similar, where part may serve as emblem or representation of larger part. Here is the whole of her splendid title poem:

> How the lightstruck trees change sun
> to flamepaths: veins, sap, stem, all
> on brief loan, set to give all
> their spooled, coded heat to stoves called
> *Resolute:* wet steel die-cast
> by heat themselves. Tree, beast, bug—
> the world-class bit parts in this
> world—flit and skid through it; the
> powers of congress tax, spend, law
> what lives to pure crisp form
> then break forms' lock, stock, and hold
> on flesh. All night couples pledge
> to stay flux, the hit-run stuff
> of cracked homes. Men trim their quick
> lawns each weekend, trailing power
> mowers. Heartslaves, you've seen them: wives
> with flexed hair, hitched to bored kids,
> twiddling in good living rooms,
> their twin beds slept in, changed, made.

This is a poem about, and enabled by, the resolute force of fusing, of combining. This "law" is replicated in Fulton's overall structure. (Practice makes pattern, she writes in "The Fractal Lanes": "Repeat a thing till the again / sculpts presence.") Using a rhetoric similar to fractal repetition or self-similarity, she fuses parts of stories and images into a single, evolving scenario or culture linking "tree, beast, bug" to the suburban couples. Within Fulton's cosmology each of these is essentially alike, a diminished or enlarged image of the other, since each life form responds to the politics of biology, where the "powers of congress tax, spend, law / what lives to pure crisp form / then break forms' lock. . . ." As fusing is a result of applied heat, Fulton's method is realized through the heat of juxtaposition; her blunt omission of conjunctions and articles results in a dense, slow syntax whose elements seem linked, welded.

Again like Goldbarth, Fulton is embarked on a project to redefine or recreate poetry according to the multiforms of experience and intellect rather than to shape experience by modelling it on a received poetic vision. With her "passional glance"—the mediating presence of the poet—she keeps one eye focussed on the smallest of phenomena:

> In the window, frost forms cradles
> more fail-safe than the beams
> of string kids knit
> between their fingers.
>
> Listening deeply, we might fancy
> infinitesimal clicks
> as each tailored wafer builds
> its strict array . . .

and, as this single, remarkable sentence demonstrates, she keeps the other eye peeled toward the hugest of connections:

> though the tiny silence
> of the crystal's
> like the giant quiet
> of the heavens in full swing.

It's as if she's searching for a poetic equivalent of the unified field theory, the governing "law" which would unite the minute and the massive. The already wonderful leap from the window's ice crystals to the swirl of galactic matter in "Disorder Is a Measure of Warmth" is still incomplete for Fulton; she insists on making another more human and happily absurd link:

> No wonder hundreds
> named their daughters Krystal
> after the goblet
> of blond starlet

> on TV. Madonna Paradox, she
> > forges a perfection
> > older than enzyme or ferment
> > > within the human melo-
>
> drama of protoplasm and cell.

This is an altogether delightful act—to correlate science and wonder, protoplasm and the popular mind. This strategy continually invigorates Fulton's poetry. She works to find within the apparent randomness of the universe an essential pattern or system of repetition. Whether snowflakes or goblets or "ignorant things / that succeed in being / gorgeous without needing to be / alive," Fulton writes:

> How deeply we,
>
> the products of chance collisions
> > between wrinkled linens
> full of eccentricity and mission,
> > want to be like them.

To find or invent likeness is, of course, to suppose a kind of order on which we can rely. That is the "reasonable ecstasy" of Fulton's poetry, to "love what we're given" so much that we find its substance reproduced by the form of our own imaginations. Indeed, the strength of an inclusive, sympathetic imagination may be the one force capable of keeping things— things cultural, things humane—from falling apart.

The Push of Reading

After disparaging the predominance of the confessional lyric mode over the past several decades, a number of poets and critics have lately turned to the long narrative poem as a popular antidote to the supposed self-absorption of the contemporary lyric. Would that it were so. While the impulse of this loose coterie—I refer mainly to the New Narrative poets, but to others as well—may be laudable, in their attempts to broaden the scope, subject, and stance of contemporary poetry, too often I find their means to be unimaginative. It is quite true that there are a few fine poets working in this mode, as there are in nearly every poetry school, but in general the work of the New Narrative poets is graceless, formally stiff, rhetorically unremarkable. Too often the formula of their strategies is merely chronological, a sort of proselike clockwork, plodding through plot, arguing that sequence *is* event. But surely we must know that there are many ways to measure experience and idea. It seems obvious that after Bors and Jung, after Riceour and Cage, after virtually every theoretical physicist and mathematician, storytelling must reconsider and refigure the notions of time, progression, sequence, narrative, and ultimately idea.

Perhaps what these poets do sense is the need to "push" the lyric poem, to extend its capacities both formally and thematically. That does seem to be the project of many poets currently—from the New Narrative poets to Language poets to the myriad of others exploring ways to make the contemporary lyric less pure. Few poets have embarked on a more serious, more substantial reconfiguration of the lyric episode than has Jorie Graham. She is, to my mind, one of the few contemporary poets who ought to deserve a label like "new narrative"—or "new formalist" for that matter—since her

---

On *Materialism* by Jorie Graham, Ecco, 1993; *Red Trousseau* by Carol Muske, Viking, 1993; *The City of Women* by Sherod Santos, Norton, 1993; *Garbage,* by A. R. Ammons, Norton, 1993.

project is nothing less than to reformulate the elements of story, structure, drama, and idea within an expanded and highly speculative lyric frame.

Since her 1987 *The End of Beauty* Graham has written in an extended, proselike line, dotted with parentheses, ellipses, and open spaces; much of the work in her distinguished *Materialism* follows that method, though other, shorter poems here recall the more compressive lineation of her earlier *Erosion* and *Hybrid of Plants and of Ghosts.* In *Materialism* she desires to take us deep into a lengthening lyric matrix itself, inside its fragments and its apparatus and inside the creative, shifting imagination as it weighs, values, and makes aesthetic decisions:

> What do you
>
> want, *you,* listening here with me now? Inside the
>
> > monologue,
>
> what would you insert? What word?
>
> What mark upon the pleating blacknesses of hotel air?
>
> *What,* to open it? To make it hear you. To make it hear
>
> me.
>
> How heavy can the singleness become?
>
> Who will hear us? What shall we do?
>
> > *("In the Hotel")*

Her attempt is to situate a voice, a "self," and a readerly partnership with the presence of other (both competing and aiding) voices and factions. She wants to make an expanding poetic field that includes, and withstands, the pressing facts of politics, economics, and science. In the manner of Czeslaw Milosz, in his *Unattainable Earth,* Graham has interspersed among the twenty-two poems of this book actual texts by Jonathan Edwards, Emerson, Wittgenstein, and Dante; an extremely germane passage from Bacon's *Novum Organum;* and other passages from the patriarchy of high Western thought. Even in her own poems the polyphonous voices of others rise and fall inside her own; in the passage above I can clearly hear Whitman's passionate attempt to situate himself and his readers within the fluid yet constant tide of time in "Crossing Brooklyn Ferry." Whitman's own phrase "the push of reading" especially suggests Graham's resolute, dramatic method.

In many ways *Materialism* reads like a single, sustained poetic effort, a long poem whose methods strive toward a coherent stability, but Graham brings to bear so many forces against each other that we must see her ultimate stance as dynamic, fluid. *Materialism* enacts this constant push throughout, a persistent negotiation among competitive energies. Hence her predominant tropes are those of expansion and growth, on one hand, and compressive tension or power on the other. Bacon describes these impulses, among others, as "motions": "When bodies, for instance, being placed not altogether according to their natures, constantly tremble, and are restless, not contented with their position." Even the "materialism" of Graham's title negotiates between matter-as-mere-substance and matter-as-consequence. As she warns us in "Who Watches from the Dark Porch," from her previous book, *Region of Unlikeness,* these are the two basic forces of history, of being: "mother Matter—the opposite of In- / terpretation." From her earlier *The End of Beauty,* in "Pieta," she identifies this same conflict: "the spirit of matter, there, where the words end." Her poetry skirts the edges where these forces collide, as if in search of a sort of unified field where meaning and being—or where history and the transcendent—can be conceived of as complementary parts of a single, phenomenal law: "like a vast silver page burning: the black hole / expanding: / like a meaning coming up quick from inside that page."

Over and again Graham probes the relationship between the still, lyric instant and the inevitable push of history or matter. In "Event Horizon" a domestic scene initiates the poem, as the speaker washes a red dress in a basin where "sunlight hovered . . . in the chasm of the millisecond" and where she sees "two still jays in the swelling instant." For Graham every instant "swells" into *chronos.* Within the initial stillness of this scene, the necessary continuities of nature instigate the speaker's meditation on history: "Strutting of sun over fencepoles, river. // Strutting of wind over tops of pines. // There is history—the story of the man carrying his father / on his back. . . ." This distinctive leap is decidedly non-narrative, barely associative; it depends on the mere motions of phenomena and therefore of time. The "strutting" of matter and the consequential passage of time conspire to threaten the simplicity, even the possibility, of a transcendental instant. Instead,

> Inside, the anchorman's back, the minutes tick by.
> The government in Beijing *has cut off all satellite*
>
> *transmission*
> and all we get is the anchor's face
>   and sometimes voice-over onto the freeze-frame
> where coverage
>   was interrupted.

From its serene, lyric beginnings the poem has become a speculation on light, radio signals, news reports, the revolution in China, warfare, and imperial domination; even "the face of the most beautiful woman in the world" ends in the fires of collision, "a smile on her face as the hair starts to burn." The momentum of history quickens until all of experience is flung together due to hastening proximities. Graham fruitfully employs the language and imagery of physics to enact this view of history. The definition of an astrophysical "event horizon," in fact, holds that as matter nears a black hole, it quickens until it becomes invisible, flung into the area around a black hole too dense for light to escape—and the speaker's TV screen fades to black.

Every poem in *Materialism* bears a similar gravity and high seriousness. The language and imagery of astrophysics animate her rhetoric, but so does the discourse of economics ("it is plain / that commodities / cannot go to market / and make exchange / of their own accord . . . that commodities are without / power of resistance against man,") and of politics ("What is it, the spot inside Mary, the punched-out spot of / blood which is *not her?* / to whom does it belong?—immaculate / garden—red idea; truth held *self- / evident /* through which the crowd can cross // and *take possession / of the earth*") as well as theology, aesthetics, cultural history, and philosophy. In "Manifest Destiny," a title she also used in *Region of Unlikeness,* even a simple trip to a museum results in Graham's reimagining the history of America, from James Town to Shiloh to the present. In this poem, as throughout *Materialism,* she superimposes an entire field of colliding, worldly impulses over the purest, isolated lyric sensibility. America is her perfect laboratory, with its history of growth and attendant guilt, with its Romantic politics and its eminently more practical methods. She makes use of McGuffey's Reader,

Audubon's journals, and Whitman's encouragements in order to frame the fullest expression of the American dilemma: that the insatiable taming and ownership of open spaces has depended on cruelty, repression, and loss.

Materialism is a book about America, its Old World heritage and its perilous New World freedom and responsibility. In a sustained apostrophe to a cluster of trees, as well as to her companion Reader, Graham identifies in "Young Maples in Wind" this driving impulse in her work:

> And you, green face—mournful, tormented, self-swallowing, graven,
>
> navel-and-theory face, what is it you turn towards, green history-face,
>
> where is your migration from?

This book is a weighty, often brilliant achievement, characterized by long, speculative poems and difficult readerly tasks, an intermixture of songs and stories, of meditation, experiment, and assertion, of Graham's voice amidst the polyphonic chorus of others. Graham's wish is to make a complete examination of the empirical evidence in her search for a coherent and compassionate self. (Five of her twenty-two poems are entitled "Notes on the Reality of the Self.") This is a very ambitious task, and in a few places the poems with their overextended lines and absolute tones seem ponderous, heavy-handed; sometimes all the visible apparatus and mechanism can overwhelm the poems' other effects. Further, since Graham's tactic is to provide this book with its own critical context—employing many quotations, allusions, and references—readers might feel occasionally beset rather than invited. But at more generous durations *Materialism* is moving, often chilling, and surprisingly passionate. Jorie Graham is a challenging and important poet, and *Materialism* shows her working at the top of her form. I can think of no other current American poet who has employed and exposed the actual mechanics of narrative, of form, of strategic inquiry more fully than she has—at least no other readable poet—and no other poet able to deploy so fruitfully and invitingly the diverse systems of philosophy, science, and history. If anyone can unify the disjointed fields of contemporary discourse, I think it might be Jorie Graham.

Carol Muske is by far the most lyrically pure of the four poets under consideration here, the one whose governing impulses have always been more compressive, enclosed. That has been her method and her strength;

yet even here in *Red Trousseau,* her strong fifth book of poetry, Muske pushes her own lyric inclinations toward inclusive and expanding destinations. While this is a more miscellaneous collection than the other three discussed here, still it is similarly driven by several longer poems. Rather than, like Graham, stretching her poems by infusing them with colliding tropes and complex speculations, Muske makes longer poems out of a sequence of shorter sections. It's as if she wants to stitch together a poem's peaks of dramatic action and forego the duller narrative valleys. As a result, her poems have the clarity of narrative poetry without much of the discursive framework.

Muske's intimate and familiar poetry is charged by two primary proclivities: it is driven by highly visual imagery, and it is animated by a performative impulse. Her poems are self-conscious but rarely self-centered, intelligent but not pedantic. And throughout *Red Trousseau* they are sparked by the title's color—the red heat of passion, the flamboyance of action, and the fires of the decadent or decaying. In "In-Flight Flick" a motion-sick traveler is beset by a drunken fellow passenger, who recounts to her the story of his estranged family. His story quickly takes on the drama of a performance:

> His mouth opens
> above the red slash of his silk tie.
> He imitates, hands flat, a plane
> taking off—*zoom*—so split
>
> the wife and child. Then to show how
> they broke him, he slumps in his seat . . .

and this whole narrative is superimposed on the cabin's lowering movie screen:

> Together, they watch his made-up plane
> bank before the dropping movie screen. . . .

Finally, when the movie begins, the whole scene becomes a densely textured palimpsest, text-over-text, one history transcribed onto others:

> Now it's dark. His drink flashes in the blue-
> and-flesh beams shot from the credits.

His hands work in the air before Pompeii:
a long shot of ancient courtyard and whole

families frozen in domestic poses. One fall,
he says, flashing a wound, a torn screen scarred
him. He was only putting on storms.
Before us, the time-traveler turns an Uzi

on the plane, the robot girl cracks a smile.

His anger is reflected in the terrorist's weapon; the cinema screen seems torn, three-dimensional, like the drunk's ripped window screen back home; and the history of one brutality reflects all brutalities. Muske's dense, exacting final line captures the essential sameness of each narrative's inevitable conclusion: "Every motion a betrayal, every gesture a fall into fire."

The world in *Red Trousseau* is comprised of images and appearances—an intimate's account of friendship, marriage, and parenthood, on one hand, and a resident's account of the fabrications and dailinesses of contemporary Hollywood, on the other. Where Graham's voice is speculative, probing, Muske's is more descriptive and tightly interpretive. Graham pushes through the static image toward the more dynamic motivations of history and interpretation; Muske doesn't so much push her poetry outward but rather opens it from the inside, looks for the play within the play, admires the highly artificial center because it depicts not detail but abstract desire. Few poets have made more of the fascinating collision of surface imagery and real, knowing intimacy. There are actors, performances, glitter-and-gilt everywhere, but Muske's stance toward them is engaged, not awed or culpable. Hers is the perspective of the resident and the critic, not the tourist or the naive viewer, and she writes with a gorgeous lyric voice and a fine-tuned ear for phrasing and modulation. Here is "Lucifer," printed entirely, a good example of her drive toward insight and her talent for song:

Two A.M. and we're on Lucifer, arguing, drinking,
one of us a Believer. I say if that beautiful
light-named angel, once most loved of God,
fell, he must have kept falling into insight—
scattering his illumination, plummeting, coming apart

into a broken new deity, one that divides
as the woman's face in darkness,
the man's face in quick rip-slashes of light.
Starry dark: down and down She falls into her empty glass,
the night sky lights up with all He refuses to let go.

Muske's several longer poems are characterized by this same tight phrasing, these leaps of association and analysis; they are extended dramatizations composed of compressed parts, like still photos arranged into a film. In "My Sister Not Painting, 1990" Muske brings together her strongest talents to produce a terrific nine-page poem. It is a study of repression and of memory's powerful insistence, a portrait of the speaker's sister: "She lives in a little town. She's afraid. / She imagines herself facing some ignorant, powerful / tribunal: giving advice on how not to paint." A broom, a story, a brush "skin-painting / over her belly, over the unborn body within," each of these provides the sister with a tool for "painting not painting," for a kind of metafictional representation of creation and erasure. At the poem's center is a long narrative about the sisters' uncle, who was the lone survivor of a war massacre in the Alps, whose eventual savior was "a young man in a military uniform, standing/ before him in a bright light. Then the youth's clothes / melted away and the boy became a woman." In his dementia, he sees this figure as, simultaneously, a "man-woman," a lover, a Christ figure whom "he longed to fuck." Later, after subjection to electrotherapy, he is driven to alcoholism and random obscenity by his experiences and finally is "walled up in the family business, a man / in a glass elevator."

Through the framed absences of the sister's not-paintings, Muske's speaker sees the origins of her sister's fear. These pantomimes of the act of creation serve as compelling figures of memory, of the family's nightmare. The unrelenting *presence* of the sisters' shared horrors—their virtual co-authorship of the story—is depicted by the sister's rush of negations:

Terrific, she says, how *not* to paint this story:
Not paint *here:* the snow riddled with holes,
shrapnel pocks, little yellow lacework of piss
or *here,* not paint Uncle bearded, raving,
on his knees? Not paint *here,* his friend, the corpse,

boots and helmet, mouth open in song—half of
a silent aria, the cement duet of *pain, sky, pain,*
sky? Here. Not paint the soldier-Christ-woman
with her removable heart atorch, her black brassiere,
sheer black stockings?

                Not paint *here,* the center,
bruisecolored, tumescent, his bloody hand on himself?

Reenacting her own "skin-painting over her belly," the sister portrays this final figure as half-erotic, half-tortured—created and destroyed. Muske's own striking visual imagery, her subtle conversion of one narrative into layers of others, her flair for performance and for metafictional representation, all unite in this frightening, brilliant poem, which becomes an extended excursion into the regions of repression, memory, and artistic creation. As here, throughout *Red Trousseau* Muske's poems are driven not by the structures of chronological sequence or narrative formality but rather by the "plots" of non-temporal memories and by leaps of imagery and association.

Muske's constant reminder in *Red Trousseau* is just this: the most self-conscious representation of artistic expression, the most artificial of surfaces, yields the most effective and acute emotional trigger for an audience. As she writes in "Unsent Letter": "Presented with the mirror of our sentiments, it seems / possible to believe that we love the world, ourselves." In a few poems I feel Muske's drive toward meaning or metapoetic drama to be forced, an insistence on self-explanation that can seem arbitrarily connected to the poem's local or narrative situation. Abruptly shifting from a description of her daughter's backyard play, the speaker of "Stage and Screen, 1989" informs us:

Misunderstanding passion (the old poet told me),
a poem goes wrong in two ways: first,
like an amateur tragedian milking
the best lines for emphasis,
pushing quite innocent everyday dialogue
to enormity. Then what remains to be seen
can't be.

Though she turns this sudden, theatric advice knowingly against the feigned innocence of her own poem, still I feel that the speaker has insisted on, rather than discovered, this intellectual exercise. But in this book, one of whose primary strategies is to interpret, such moments are few. Carol Muske's collection is best characterized by its more wholly realized achievements: its lyric grace; its fiery desires; its startling and effective connections; and its original mixture of dramatic pizazz and serious, brooding love:

> Like Art featuring Life, the real
> sky behind the starry backdrop fills with stars. The lovers kiss.
> I want to cry out How much? How much do you love each
> other? But the director in his cherry-picker signals another take:
> The sky grows light. It's late.

Sherod Santos's third book of poems, *The City of Women,* permits us to see the effects and fine successes of another method by which to "push" the lyric poem. Where Graham is speculative, compelled by rhetorical exercise, and where Muske is connective and interpretive, Santos is extendedly meditative, the most deliberate, inner, and anxious of the poets under consideration here. His book-length work *The City of Women* is a foray into the erotics of memory and memory's access—and its invention—through language. Comprised of blank-verse lyrics, prose poems and fragments, journal-like entries, and a variety of other formal tactics and arrangements, Santos's poem sustains itself by its diverse, contrapuntal method as well as by its compelling depth. Like Roland Barthes's *A Lover's Discourse,* Santos's book is a sort of plotless novel, an intense, personal discursion into complex webs of erotic encounters and relationships as well as into the intellectual and emotional provinces of love, language, and representation. It is a love poem to a wife—and to women—but moreso to the imagination, its fancy, its hunger, its obsessions.

In his book's first poem Santos seems to be following Barthes's description of a "lover's discourse," which is to Barthes "no more than a dust of figures stirring according to an unpredictable order." Still, Barthes says we can "assign to love, at least retrospectively . . . a settled course: it is by means of this *historical* hallucination that I sometimes make love into a romance, an adventure." Santos's book begins with a similar paradox, with an image thirty years past, at once inexact and meticulous:

> She is seated somewhere—I can't recall where
> Exactly now, the young Algerian shopclerk
> From a bookstore Mother frequented those days—
> And she is seated alone, in a café, let's say,
> Looking out onto a crowded square in Châteauroux,
> On a market day in the early fall, a shifting
> Fretwork of pushcarts, string bags, makeshift stalls,
> The gutters a rubble of spoiled fruit, rinds,
> Bread crusts, dung, stray dogs snuffling at
> The entrails too bruised to lay out in the pans,
> An acrid smell off the *pissoirs*. . . .

In a passage that must refer to one of the speaker's first enamored encounters—here his youthful enchantment with a bookstore clerk—Santos depicts the doubleness of Barthes's description: an indistinct, purposefully fictionalized scene which, nonetheless, begins to take on the remarkable clarity and sensual detail of actual memory. The clerk provides this book with an initial muse-figure, whose memory Santos evokes and creates: "Across that time which in some ways / Does not exist, will never exist, the story of my life / In love, the buried life I know little about, / Perhaps know nothing at all."

Here, and throughout the rest of the book, such figures of and abbreviated encounters with women function in two ways. They establish a kind of linked, non-narrative history of the speaker's various experiences with love towards women—erotic, matrimonial, fantastic, mundane; the loves of a child, a son, and a man. But further, they are the primary mirror in which the speaker identifies his own personality, his own being, as if only in proximity to others does he exist at all. This "self" is the fundamental fiction of Santos's book, a figure created by story and desire. Barthes concurs: "I cannot *write myself*. What, after all, is this 'I' who would write himself?" While *The City of Women* seems to assume characteristics of an autobiography through its detail, its confessional richness, its vigorous exploration of memory, it is more accurately a moving, impersonal representation of eros in general, where every figure is an erasure of the actual or particular, where each scene is an unfolding seduction between the duplicate fictions of writer and reader, "as though you and I were somehow united in the fundamental joy of *creating* a self." Santos's "as though" reinforces the playfully serious artifice of language itself which Barthes, again, identifies: "To try to write love is to confront the *muck* of language: that region of hysteria where language is both *too much* and *too little,* excessive . . . and impoverished."

Though this work's project is to inspect the role of women in his life, the speaker of *The City of Women* does not fall into the trap of voyeurism or exhibitionism, nor does he allow his speculation to become a pleasure dome for male heterosexuality. He exhibits sympathy and patience toward the women figures; he more willingly allows them to wield power over him than the reverse:

> Following a late-night dinner and a bottle of wine . . . Zoë asked if I would do something to her.
>
> I said yes, anything. Anything she wanted. This is what I wanted too. Whatever excited her. Whatever she most desired.
>
> But what if it repelled you? What if, secretly, it filled you with disgust?
>
> I told her again I wanted what she wanted. However dark it was. There was nothing she couldn't ask of me.

Santos's speaker avoids tropes of adoration or wish-fulfillment, and his tones and stances—of peril, humiliation, and grief, as well as of intimacy and discovery—are more expressive of his own exposure than of the women's. When they reveal themselves to him, it is through their stories. In one prose episode, the wife-character L. narrates an event from her childhood but reveals—or invents—herself with the name Marianne; then, before finishing her story and "faraway now . . . [s]he said nothing more about it, but from then on I believed she carried a name she'd chosen, in time, for the shy, lost boy she'd missed the chance to love." The personal stories for which the speaker is audience are, in the end, often enigmatic or concealing, parables of mystery or suspended drama; yet their purpose is intimately connective: "The loss in her voice awakens, simultaneously, a loss in me."

I mention this rhetorical strategy because it is one of the many risks which Santos seems purposefully to suggest and fruitfully to employ. He wants to expose the speaker, the rawness and confusion of *his* identity as it is created through the histories of others:

> My mother's family was Southern, affluent, aristocratic; my father's,
> working-class, immigrant, resettled near the hops fields in northern
> California. When they met in 1942, at the height of the War, they were
> both, so to speak, in disguise: my mother in the somber, pin-striped
> outfit of the volunteers at the USO; my father in the full military
> splendor of an Air Corps pilot on R & R.

Elsewhere we follow these parents' divorce as well as the speaker's many other involvements with family members and lovers. Santos seems acutely aware of his own rhetorical designs and qualities. Through a number of devices he instructs us to see not only his but our own pasts as useful fictions and further encourages us to share the representative burden of the book's speaker. Referring to another episode of apparent "memory," he speaks now in plural:

> Already, in advance, our lives owe something to those moments [out
> of the past]. An induction. A knowledge. An unlikeness between our-
> selves (before) and ourselves (thereafter). And a barely perceptible
> disharmony with all of our surroundings, as though the world had
> just contracted around a newly engendered set of senses. As though
> the world, in vast but incalculable ways, had put a DIFFERENT
> FACE ON THINGS.

The "different face" is a profoundly important difference. He refers, I think, not only to the changing faces of loved ones—like Yeats, "who loved the sorrows of [his love's] changing face"—and not only to the self's changing face, but to the essential conversion of both memory and imagination into "the world" of a work of art whose "newly engendered set of senses" arouses and tutors us. He urges us to see the introspective details of autobiography—with its confessional foundation, its inquiry, its sometimes unbecoming honesty— as a means by which to understand *each other's* desires and fears in what Barthes calls "the lover's anxiety: it is the fear of a mourning which has already occurred, at the very origin of love." *The City of Women* is an obsessive scrutiny into this phenomenon, into the emotions of language and art, and into the self-sacrificing relationships of lovers and of poets and their readers.

Not only is Santos masterful at weaving the rhetoric of lovers, their intimacies and fears, but he also demonstrates the lovers' myriad moods and inquiries through his formal tactics. Form functions to establish and enhance rhetoric, as if Santos deploys each form's conventional strength to turn those strengths against themselves. The many blank-verse sections of *The City of Women* demonstrate Santos's most finished, highly glossed articulations:

> Early morning, a woman sits up in bed
> With a cup of coffee and an ashtray in her lap,
> Though she isn't smoking and the coffee
> Has long since cooled. For the last two months
> She and her husband have slept in separate
> Rooms, and now, by habit, it's decided this room
> Is "hers." Outside, the sky is overcast,
> As it usually is in the mornings in the fall,
> And there's a stillness on the world, which
> For once she doesn't find threatening.

The restraint of the woman's posture is captured, formalized, by the gravity of the writing and by the ode-like form itself. It's a way of dignifying the scene and, at the same time, of estranging it, like the woman who "manages once more / To turn a loss into the semblance of a loss." Santos uses his prose sections for other purposes: to be more instructive or theatric, full of stage directions or self-conscious inquiry; to suggest the note-like intimacy of a private journal; or, as here, to invoke the reader's complicit curiosity:

> Imagine, for a moment, that in matters of love everything we're told is a lie. . . . Then imagine—if only for argument's sake—how BEING IN LOVE might well depend not on each of us *coming to know each other,* but on each of us actually struggling to guard that which knowing would give away. And imagine, moreover, how love may not be a "union" at all, but the willed preservation of that *otherness.* . . .

It's as if, in Santos's hands, the forms themselves take on the aspects of dynamic, distinct personalities, like characters in this fascinating drama.

Sherod Santos's *The City of Women* is a passionate and powerful study of love and desire, as whole, as intimate, and as knowing as Barthes's *A Lover's Discourse*. For its rhetorical range, its formal variety, its remarkable insight and sympathy, and its intensely focussed concentration, I can think of nothing to compare it with in contemporary American poetry; yet it feels as disturbingly familiar, and as thrilling, as the subject it explores.

A. R. Ammons's *Garbage* is a brilliant book. It may very well be a great one, as fine as, or perhaps even superior to, his previous long masterwork, *Tape for the Turn of the Year,* with its massive, connective inquiries, or *Sphere,* that most dense and eloquent longer poem. To be honest, this book caught me off-guard, following, as it does, fairly closely on the heels of Ammons's *The Really Short Poems of A. R. Ammons. Garbage* is a 121-page poem in eighteen sections, composed in couplets, and nearly composed of a single, winding, astonishing sentence. Ammons is famously capable within the short lyric mode—distinctive, intelligent, quirky—but the long poem extrapolated from a lyric base is his genius. Sherod Santos's book-length sequence is an intense concentration on a single motif; *Garbage* is about, well, everything—especially since, as Ammons insists, garbage is the primary building block of the universe. In the wonderful cosmos of this poem, there is nothing that is not "garbage":

> garbage has to be the poem of our time because
> garbage is spiritual, believable enough
>
> to get our attention, getting in the way, piling
> up, stinking, turning brooks brownish and
>
> creamy white: what else deflects us from the
> errors of our illusionary ways. . . .

Beginning with a description of a trash dump alongside a Florida highway, *Garbage* soon finds itself evolving into a series of connected meditations, each about a different order of refuse, of the wasted, whatever is unused, overgrown, or cast aside. Ammons's speaker discovers that nature everywhere is composed of the decadent and entropic, the aged, the tired—"toxic waste, poison air, beach goo, eroded roads"—and sees in nature, then, enough models to be able to state that "this is a scientific poem, //

asserting that nature models values." The speaker himself, nearing retire-
ment from his professorship as a writing teacher, feels discarded, decaying,
worried about social security and disease:

> a pain in the knee or hipjoint or warps and
> knots in the leg muscles, even strange, binding
>
> twinges in the feet ought to cause you to include
> in the list of possibilities that the high
>
> arch in one of your feet has slipped, shortening
> you shortlegged, your weight misdistributed. . . .

But Ammons knows his science well; he knows that no amount of material
substance ever vanishes, only converts into other matter or energy. And this
is the magic of *Garbage*. We become witnesses to something of a genera-
tive and evolutionary process—the turning of garbage into utility, decay
into new life, an idea into further ideas. A sort of latter-day, practical opti-
mist, the speaker transfers his initial observation into aesthetic and peda-
gogical usage—"I say to my writing students—prize your flaws, / defects,
behold your accidents, engage your // negative criticisms—these are the
materials of your ongoing"—and then takes his own advice, instructing
our readerly expectations as well:

> this is just a poem with a job to do: and that
>
> is to declare, however roundabout, sideways,
> or meanderingly (or in those ways) the perfect
>
> scientific and materialistic notion of the
> spindle of energy . . .
>
>   in value systems,
> physical systems, artistic systems, always this
>
> same disposition from the heavy to the light,
> and then the returns from the light downward
>
> to the staid gross: stone to wind, wind to
> stone: there is no need for "outside," hegemonic

> derivations of value: nothing need be invented
> or imposed: the aesthetic, scientific, moral
>
> are organized like a muff along this spindle,
> might as well relax: thus, the job done. . . .

As simply as "thus," a story about aging, about worldly disgust, sharply converts into an encouragement to see that the world is necessarily composed of such leavings. An early morning's "senseless" vision of the future with its "strokes, hip replacements, // insulin shots, sphygmomanometers" brings with it "a tiny / wriggle of light in the mind that says, 'go on': // that's what it says: that's all it says." And death's own inevitability becomes an invitation to see, in essence, the entirety of time within the space of a moment:

> [if] death is so persuasive, can't life be: it is
> fashionable now to mean nothing, not to exist,
>
> because meaning doesn't hold, and we do not exist
> forever; this *is* forever, we are now in it; our
>
> eyes see through the round time of nearly all
> of being, our minds reach out and in ten billion
>
> years: we are in so much forever. . . .

By the poem's end the speaker has so thoroughly embraced the connectedness of things, the cyclic give-and-take of matter, that he sees his own body now, even in old age, as a kind of garden, a place where life is not lost but nourished:

> if you've derived from life
> a going thing called life, life has a right to
>
> derive life from you: ticks, parasites, lice,
> fleas, mites, flukes, crabs, mosquitoes. . . .

Many of the values of *Garbage* seem to be grounded in the practical, encouraging Romanticism of Emerson. Emerson's insistence on the values of utility and frugality precedes Ammons's own compulsion to see that every iota of material substance is used and appreciated, every bit of waste turned to order and meaning. Emerson spoke of this notion in "The Young American," a lecture in 1844 to the Mercantile Library Association of Boston: "Nature is the noblest engineer, yet uses a grinding economy, working up all that is wasted today into tomorrow's creation—not a superfluous grain of sand. . . ." There is coherence in such a universe, where a natural order of "work" performs the tasks of converting matter and energy into more of the same and where, for both Emerson and Ammons, these physical transformations signal similar transformations in understanding, improvements in the spirit. Even in its more skeptical moments, and even in the ironized language of Postmodern wit and banter, Ammons's *Garbage* enacts an Emersonian cosmology, where the wastes of the contemporary soul are converted into consolation, connection, even hope: "I have a low view of us: but that is why / I love us or try to move to love us."

Still, this does not begin to characterize the brilliance of the poem itself, its tremendous variety of tones, its astonishing range of subject matter, its sheer readability. The voice in *Garbage* is almost disarmingly direct, neither the mundane voice of an "average" person, as in so much contemporary lyric verse, nor the hyper-dogmatic expression within a scholar's *texte,* nor the epic-like inflations of a character like Paterson. I almost want to characterize this voice, again in Emerson's terms, as Man Thinking. He is brilliant, interested in the political and personal, in hard critique as well as praise, fascinated by science and philosophy but also by the day's weather and market fluctuations. He can be very funny but, even so, uses his hilarity for multiple means:

> I just want you to know I'm perfectly
> serious much of the time: when I kid around
>
> I'm trying to get in position to be serious:
> my daffydillies are efforts to excuse the
>
> presumption of assumption, direct address, my
> self-presentation: I'm trying to mean what I
>
> mean to mean something: best for that is a kind
> of matter-of-fact explicitness about the facts. . . .

He can wink at us with his self-aware presence; "(check that rhyme)" he nudges at one point. He can let rip the most inventive, spirited catalogues of "stuff":

> The heap of knickknacks (knickknackatery),
> whatnots (whatnotery), doodads, jews-harps,
>
> belt buckles, do-funnies, files, disks, pads,
> pesticide residues, nonprosodic high-tension
>
> lines, whimpering-wimp dolls, epichlorohydrin
> elastomotors, sulfur dioxide emissions, perfume
>
> sprays, radioactive williwaws . . .

and then minister to our most practical necessities. Here he employs (and mimics) the instructional pragmatism of Franklin's *Autobiography* and of *Walden* in his enumerated "elaboration to prize the essential":

> (1) don't complain—ills are sufficiently
>
> clear without reiterated description: (2) count
> your blessings, spelling them over and over into
>
> sharp contemplation: (3) do what you can—
> take action: (4) move on. . . .

Ideal and useful, punning and pensive, this voice is a dazzling dance of purposes and speculations, made of whatever material it finds at hand, a patchwork of the cast-off, the trashy, the high-brow, the stern, the inventive, and the true.

This poem's technical style is as sinuous and connective as its subject. Speaking about the cyclic patterns in nature, which "likes a broad spectrum approaching disorder so / as to maintain the potential of change," Ammons also reminds us that such is the method of his writing: "things that go around sometimes go / around so far they come back around: if you // like my form, experience my function." In this way, subjects transmute into others, often recurring and winding back around to themselves. Where *Sphere* was composed in triplets, *Garbage* is made of couplets—

open-ended, highly enjambed, cracked open, making for dramatic momen-
tum. The connection of phrases here illustrates a sort of formal curiosity
and encouragement, a push of aesthetic energy. This is not blank verse or
syllabic construction (lines here range from seven to twenty-four syllables,
most often running between ten and thirteen) nor a reintegration of
William Carlos Williams's triadic line, though I have heard each of these
explanations supposed. Nor is Ammons's lineation accentual, though a five-
stress line predominates. In fact, I find the most consistent and remarkable
formalization in *Garbage* to be the sentence rather than the line. Indeed,
in a poem whose length is nearly twenty-five hundred lines, there are only
a handful of sentences. Ammons much prefers the colon to the period, as
if to suggest the evolving pattern of his vision. Ammons's colon serves two
important purposes: it is connective, extending the imperative relationship
of one idea or image to another, and it is explanatory, indicating that each
new discourse or narrative is the *result* or solution of the last and that each
new clause will serve as the forebear of the next. The result is a tumbling,
dynamic, resourceful rhetoric and form, able to contain and employ what-
ever comes its way:

> the rabbit's
> leaps and halts, listenings, are prosody of
>
> a poem floating through the mind's brush: I
> mix my motions in with the mix of motions, all
>
> motions cousins, conveyors, purveyors, surveyors,
> rising from the land, eddying coils of a wash,
>
> bristling with fine-backed black clarity as with
> brookripples over stone, spreading out. . . .

Garbage may be one of the central poetic accomplishments of our time.
With Galway Kinnell's *The Book of Nightmares,* with Adrienne Rich's
achievements, with W. S. Merwin's dark lyrics, this poem can tell readers
of poetry far into the future what our lives were like at millennium's close,
what we thought, what we feared, where we looked for hope. When their
archaeologists assess our rubble, they will find this simple dignity there: "to
pay attention is to behold the / wonder, and the rights, of things. . . ."

Framed in Words

The first sentence of G. S. Fraser's introduction to D. B. Moore's *The Poetry of Louis MacNeice,* published in England in 1972, promptly bespeaks the ongoing problematic of MacNeice's career and reputation: "If asked who were the most exciting new English poets of the 1930s, many readers would have said then, and would say now, 'Auden, Dylan Thomas, Louis MacNeice. . . . '" Even MacNeice would have agreed with everything in this assertion except, perhaps, the ordering of the list. Of course, the nomination of his membership (and Thomas's, for that matter) to the ranks of English poetry is the other sticky point. MacNeice was born in 1907, in Belfast, and spent most of his childhood in the coastal village of Carrickfergus. Though his father was a staunch advocate of Irish Home Rule, MacNeice was sent to preparatory school in England at the age of ten, eventually forsaking Dublin's Trinity University to begin study in 1926 at Merton College, Oxford. For the rest of his life he would remain a virtual exile from Ireland, if never quite an expatriate. Still, after Yeats, MacNeice is undoubtedly the most influential and accomplished poet of the Modernist period to have emerged from embattled Ireland.

It is not hard to see why the British designation has stuck throughout MacNeice's career as a poet. Even aside from England's habit of claiming the achievements of its small neighbors as its own, and aside from the certain uneasiness attendant on the MacNeice family's devout Protestantship in Catholic Gaelic Ireland ("My father made the walls resound, / He wore his collar the wrong way round," the poet confirms in "Autobiography"),

---

On *Selected Poems* by Louis MacNeice, Wake Forest, 1990; *Selected Poems 1966–1987* by Seamus Heaney, Farrar, Straus and Giroux, 1990; *Outside History: Selected Poems 1980–1990* by Eavan Boland, Norton, 1990.

MacNeice himself persisted in his desire to be a spectator of Irish affairs from outside its borders. Not only his British schooling but also his life-long connections with W. H. Auden and Stephen Spender, his sustained involvement with the BBC's literary productions, and his eventual direc-torship at the British Institute in Athens contributed to his detachment from Ireland and from the Ulster literary circles in particular. His life would never comply with his Irish past. But Irish poet and critic Michael Longley has compiled a new selection of MacNeice's poetry which should seriously urge us to renew our acquaintance with his work and perhaps even to con-sider more carefully his Irish heritage.

If MacNeice rarely walked the Irish soil after his youth, he insisted on maintaining an Irish habitation in his poetry. An early poem, "Carrickfergus," bears a striking resemblance to Yeats's own early "The Lake Isle of Innisfree," where a still romantic Yeats idealizes his imagined, pastoral residence, his "small cabin . . . of clay and wattles made." Composed in 1937, "Carrickfergis" seems initially to echo Yeats's great poem with its long, lyric lines and rhymed quatrains, its precise imagery and detail, its locus-as-subject, its compression. But where Yeats looks dreamily forward toward a perfected and private resi-dence, MacNeice turns a more realistic and typically skeptical eye to the past, to the commotion and grim fact of his Irish background:

> I was born in Belfast between the mountain and the gantries
> To the hooting of lost sirens and the clang of trams:
> Hence to Smoky Carrick in County Antrim
> Where the bottle-neck harbour collects the mud which jams
>
> The little boats beneath the Norman castle,
> The pier shining with lumps of crystal salt;
> The Scotch Quarter was a line of residential houses
> But the Irish Quarter was a slum for the blind and halt.

Yeats's poem finds its speaker spurning "the pavements gray," but MacNeice typically rejects the pastoral ideal, even in imagination, and attends to the sobering imagery of the urban and, by extension, the real. He locates here again some of the causes of his dissociation: "I was the rector's son, born to the anglican order, / Banned for ever from the candles of the Irish poor."

When "the war came and a huge camp of soldiers / Grew from the ground in sight of our house," the young speaker leaves his home, though "the steamer was camouflaged that took [him] to England." As if articulating the difference between late Romanticism and early Modernism, MacNeice answers Yeats's wish to "live alone in the bee-loud glade":

> I went to school in Dorset, the world of parents
>> Contracted into a puppet world of sons
> Far from the mill girls, the smell of porter, the salt-mines
>> And the soldiers with their guns.

Certainly we can hear in these measured, factual tones his clear disapproval, but perhaps we might detect also a touch of the starkest nostalgia, a complex regret at having been displaced from an admittedly painful past. Many years later, in "Carrick Revisited," published in the mid-1940s, MacNeice found himself pulled back by the same impulse to try to probe the reasons why he was "Torn before birth from where my fathers dwelt, / Schooled from the age of ten to a foreign voice." Here his dislocation speaks mournfully, as his memories of "Fog-horn, mill-horn, corncrake and church bell" transcend the circumstances of his residence; he presents himself "dumbfounded to find myself / In a topographical frame—here, not there." The trope in this poem, of Ireland as bedrock and castle, of his circumstance as being somehow lost at sea, accompanies MacNeice through much of his poetry. And the figure of a "topographical frame" identifies one of MacNeice's most significant representations:

> Whatever then my inherited or acquired
> Affinities, such remains my childhood's frame
> Like a belated rock in the red Antrim clay
> That cannot at this era change its pitch or name. . . .

If MacNeice found himself outside the margins, the legal borders of Ireland, at the same time he insisted on framing his imagination and his art often within its premises. The metaphor of the frame recurs frequently in his poems; it serves, I believe, as a way for MacNeice to continue to situate himself within the borders of Ireland, his "childhood frame," and it also places MacNeice's imagination squarely in the Modernist mode. That is to say, like Stevens, Pound, and Joyce, MacNeice creates a persona whose preferred residence is framed by, is *within,* the work of art itself.

"To Posterity," written in the mid-1950s, completes what may be seen as the three stages of MacNeice's attitudes toward habitation and art. If "Carrickfergus" begins to restore Ireland to MacNeice's imagination, and if "Carrick Revisited" more exclusively frames that restoration within the regions of art, then "To Posterity" places its entire faith in the power of poetry to salvage and to claim:

> When books have all seized up like the books in graveyards
>
> And reading and even speaking have been replaced
>
> By other, less difficult, media, we wonder if you
>
> Will find in flowers and fruit the same colour and taste
>
> They held for us for whom they were framed in words,
>
> And will your grass be green, your sky be blue,
>
> Or will your birds be always wingless birds?

Here poetry has evolved for MacNeice into the necessary mediation between existence and appreciation; in short, real life is appreciably less real without the very artifice and sensual difficulty of language. Without language the world is literally not itself—lesser, duller, incomplete, scarred. Language may even be a *more* real experience than the experience of "real life," or it may perhaps be a prior experience. In addition to being importantly Modernist, this notion prepares the groundwork for the most engaging fields of current poetic and critical theory.

Longley's prudent selection of MacNeice's poems encourages such tracings of thought. But at just over 150 pages, it is also a fairly severe representation of a writer whose corpus is quite large. Not represented at all, for instance, are any of his popular verse plays written and produced for the BBC, though two of his dramatic eclogues, "An Eclogue for Christmas" and "Eclogue from Iceland," are included. His central long poem, "Autumn Journal," is only partly reprinted here, and its flawed but fascinating partner, "Autumn Sequel," is represented only by parts of two of its twenty-six terza-rima cantos. "Autumn Journal" is an especially notable poem, a complex, extended interweaving of several narrative impulses. On one hand it is the story of an exuberant, if doomed, love affair:

Shelley and jazz and lieder and love and hymn-tunes
  And day returns too soon;
We'll get drunk among the roses
  In the valley of the moon.
Give me an aphrodisiac, give me lotus,
  Give me the same again;
Make all the erotic poets of Rome and Ionia
  And Florence and Provence and Spain
Pay a tithe of their sugar to my potion
  And ferment my days. . . .

But among these amorous reveries, MacNeice weaves a sterner picture of his always-present, "jumbled" Irish heritage:

Nightmare leaves fatigue:
  We envy men of action
Who sleep and wake, murder and intrigue
  Without being doubtful, without being haunted.
And I envy the intransigence of my own
  Countrymen who shoot to kill and never
See the victim's face become their own
  Or find his motive sabotage their motives.
So reading the memoirs of Maud Gonne,
  Daughter of an English mother and a soldier father,
I note how a single purpose can be founded on
  A jumble of opposites.

And an even more haunting circumstance provides the framework inside which his erotic and inherited obsessions intertwine, for the poem (written during the Munich crisis) is also an account of anxiety and grief at the imminence of World War II, the probability of its effect on Europe and on MacNeice's adoptive London. The successful blending of personal and political anxieties, and of dramatic and philosophical modes of discourse, makes "Autumn Journal" one of MacNeice's finest, most inclusive accomplishments.

Longley has generally opted to show MacNeice in his more lyric and compressed mode. That does mean his famous and often-anthologized poems show up—the brilliant "Sunday Morning"; "Bagpipe Music," with its rollicking, long-winded measures; the sensually haunting "Snow"— along with a number of other formally exacting, finely crafted poems. Indeed, during an age of stylistic experimentation, MacNeice chose, like Frost or Spender, to locate his doubt and discovery within the contexts of content; addressing Auden here in "Postscript to Iceland," he could have been describing his own attitude toward style and form:

> For the litany of doubt
> From these walls comes breathing out
> Till the room becomes a pit
> Humming with the fear of it. . . .
>
> So I write these lines for you
> Who have felt the death-wish too,
> But your lust for life prevails—
> Drinking coffee, telling tales.
>
> Our prerogatives as men
> Will be cancelled who knows when;
> Still I drink your health before
> The gun-butt raps upon the door.

Longley has been careful also to include a generous supply of MacNeice's lesser-known poems, many of which will be new to all but his most faithful readers. The resulting selection, while compacted, shows MacNeice to be impressively various—probing, wry, playful, and gifted with a lyrical realism in both his narrative and meditative mode.

MacNeice was a lovely, important, devoted poet; even his early death in 1963 revealed his commitment to his art. He was, as Longley describes, taken with fatal pneumonia at the age of fifty-six after "descending into Yorkshire pot-holes with BBC sound engineers . . . recording effects for his last radio play." Nor was he alone in his life of exile. It is a familiar irony that so many Modern writers found themselves bodily or psychically removed from their origins and, therefore, found themselves members of the community of exiles.

For MacNeice this resulted in a complex mixture of impulses—a grim, realistic, unsettling vision of the modern world; a formal, even bardic sense of poetic style; and an increasing faith in the redemptive or retrieving powers of art, within whose frame he finally claimed his birthright.

There is no doubting Seamus Heaney's preferred and established precinct. He is Irish through and through, already (at the age of fifty-two) a cultural or at least a literary icon in the history of twentieth-century Ireland. Not since Yeats has Ireland embraced a poet so wholly. His distinct voice and beautifully made lines seem to trill with a refined brogue, and his large project—to document the culture of Ireland at once personal, historical, and mythical—is indeed matched by his large talent. He rigorously maintains his Irish identity despite his international habitat; born in County Derry, Northern Ireland, now a resident of Dublin, he holds teaching posts at Trinity, Harvard, and Oxford.

This is not to say that Heaney has willingly embraced all the conventions of Irish poetic history. Despite an inheritance of the formal texture of Irish poetry and an unmistakably Irish idiom and vista, and even despite his deep involvement in Irish lore and myth, Heaney has persisted in his attempt to situate himself at least partly outside the frame of the traditional Irish pastoral, outside the Romantic and naturalist impulses generally characteristic of earlier Irish poetry. From his first book with its telling title, *Death of a Naturalist,* Heaney has maintained a difficult, partial distance from the fact (or stereotype) of his inherited past.

Surely that is why he has chosen to begin *Selected Poems 1966–1987* with "Digging," an announcement of his intentional withdrawal or at least his self-conscious, apparent distancing from the Naturalist tradition. Most of this well-known poem is a narrative memory of the speaker's father working in his flowerbeds. The father's physical and rustic labor connects him not only to the earth but also to the lineage of fathers and earth-workers before him:

> By God, the old man could handle a spade.
> Just like his old man.
>
> My grandfather cut more turf in a day
> Than any other man on Toner's bog . . .

> Nicking and slicing neatly, heaving sods
> Over his shoulder, going down and down
> For the good turf. Digging.

The fertile, even sensual earth with its "cold smell of potato mould, the squelch and slap / Of soggy peat, the curt cuts of an edge" provides the speaker (and this book) with a sense of origin and birth, a paternal and erotic order of work. And clearly, the speaker seems proud of his masculine lineage, unabashed about boasting of his grandfather's toil and victory. But in the poem's most significant passage, the speaker also asserts:

> But I've no spade to follow men like them.
>
> Between my finger and my thumb
> The squat pen rests.
> I'll dig with it.

These concluding lines echo a description of the poet's tool earlier in the poem: "Between my finger and my thumb / The squat pen rests; snug as a gun." The pen as pistol, the pen as spade—that which shoots and plows—certainly encourages us to examine its figuration. The speaker removes himself from the hardy earth-workers of his past, his Irish fathers, by means of his studious, inner occupation, but he also assigns to the pen the qualities with which to continue their work—to control and to cultivate. Less obviously but still clearly, the speaker also experiences an erotic, if isolated pleasure, a masturbatory self-interest, which connects him further to the father figures, all of them "loving [the] cool hardness in our hands." If he is detached from the fathers, he is like them too.

Throughout his career Heaney has situated himself in precisely such a stance. He maintains a location outside the frame of the pastoral and natural, at least outside the more naive versions of such, by his continual suspicions that the artist's vocation removes the artist from physical participation. But to do so, to parlay this notion into practice, Heaney continues to refer to, and to make use of, the very conventions which he claims to suspect. The irony obvious in such a strategy is, I think, a mark of Heaney's more rewarding and authentic position—not that he has removed himself from the natural past, but rather that he regards it and his relationship to it with a mixture of detachment, loss, and anxiety.

This is precisely what makes Heaney such an intelligent and acute correspondent. His doubled belief—in the integrity of the past and the anguish of the present—provides his most abiding and important strategy. He documents the past, its artifacts, history, and austere beauty, in order to demonstrate its relationship to a changed and changing present. To retrieve the past Heaney very often goes literally into the earth, digging and sifting and sorting, as in "Bog Queen":

> I lay waiting
>
> between turf-face and demesne wall,
>
> between heathery levels
>
> and glass-toothed stone.
>
> My body was braille
>
> for the creeping influences. . . .
>
> I lay waiting
>
> on the gravel bottom,
>
> my brain darkening,
>
> a jar of spawn
>
> fermenting underground. . . .

The bog queen is one of Heaney's central figures, one of his most characteristic and telling metaphors. Having sunk and "fermented" long ago in the ancient bog, she is also, significantly, fully preserved, able to speak in rich, thoughtful, even (again) erotic terms: "I knew winter cold / like the nuzzle of fjord / at my thighs." Part human, part earthen, at last she may be on the way to ruin, but it is the wholly human present which ruins her, the meddling diggers who "robbed" her:

> I was barbered
> and stripped
> by a turfcutter's spade

who veiled me again
and packed coomb softly
between the stone jambs
at my head and my feet.

So her ascension to the world of the human, her rebirth, is more accurately and paradoxically her death, for only in the fresh air will her decay commence and her fertile correlation with the bog cease:

The plait of my hair,
a slimy birth-cord
of bog, had been cut

and I rose from the dark,
hacked bone, skull-ware,
frayed stitches, tufts,
small gleams on the bank.

Heaney's sympathy with the past—the wounded primitive—is indisputable. In many poems in this selection, as in "The Gutteral Muse," it is downright personal: "I breathed the muddied night airs off the lake / And watched a young crowd leave the discotheque. . . . // I felt like some old pike all badged with sores." This feeling drives Heaney's most powerful poems, from his early "Gifts of Rain" and "The Tollund Man" through the brilliant, long sequence "Station Island" to the best of his most recent work.

Selected Poems 1966–1987 is Heaney's second go-round at such a gathering, following by a little over a decade his *Poems 1965–75.* Between then and now he has published three significant collections of poems, *Field Work* (1979), *Station Island* (1984), and *The Haw Lantern* (1987), as well as *Sweeney Astray* (1983), a splendid and generous retelling-as-translation (he calls it a "version") of the medieval Irish narrative *Buile Suibhne.* This selection includes much from these recent books and severely cuts back on his early work, generously shown in his previous selection. Specifically, his first five books receive one hundred pages here while his last two obtain the same. That's an especially conspicuous fact, given that he even reprints quite a number of his Sweeney versions from "Sweeney Redivivus" in *Station*

Island (and deletes a number of wonderful, original poems from that volume, like "The Loaning" or "The Sandpit"). I wonder whether this is all a little off balance—especially if the later books are more likely to be available than the earlier ones. Heaney may be making an assumption that his more recent work is his best. But many of the tight, splendid lyrics from his first five books are among his most important poems; indeed, while *Field Work* and *Station Island* are brilliant books, especially energized by Heaney's growing concern with the long sequential poem and the more overtly political poem, *The Haw Lantern* is something of a letdown.

A letdown for him, that is. Even in his modest poems, Seamus Heaney is gifted with impeccable control and a clear, intelligent, enchanting voice. In his best poems, throughout the remarkable achievement of *Selected Poems 1966–1987,* he packs his tightly traditional lines with rich, fertile detail and endows his poems with cultural and often political acuity, severe grace, and an abiding regard for the past—a past at once enthralling and remnant.

Eavan Boland is only five years younger than Seamus Heaney, and she is author of six previous books of poetry, but *Outside History: Selected Poems 1980–1990* is her first collection to be widely distributed in this country. Ontario Review Press did publish its *Introduction to Eavan Boland* in 1981, and Carcanet distributed here, modestly, her 1987 *The Journey.* Still, while she clearly has not sprung overnight fully formed and brilliant, this collection may suggest so to an American audience. She is a splendid, graceful, demanding poet who has been evolving for some time, having published her first book, *New Territory,* in 1967.

I have been interested in showing how MacNeice positioned himself outside the literal framework of Ireland and how Heaney situates himself at least partially outside, or apart from, the tradition of the Irish pastoral. Boland derives much of her considerable power from a similar strategy, locating herself outside of history, as her title stipulates. More specifically, she pursues an important, feminist revision of the history-making so often praised or inherited by MacNeice and Heaney. Not so much outside of history as counter to it, or in the process of amending it through addition, Boland has developed in her poetry what Harold Bloom might call an agonistic relationship with the paternal, natural, and often silencing history of traditional Irish poetry.

Recall, in reading the whole of Boland's "Bright-Cut Irish Silver," the lineage specified in Heaney's "Digging":

I take it down
from time to time, to feel
the smooth path of silver meet the cicatrix of skill.

These scars, I tell myself, are learned.

This gift for wounding an artery of rock
was passed on from father to son, to the father
of the next son;

is an aptitude for injuring
earth while inferring it in curves and surfaces;

is this cold potency which has come,
by time and chance,

into my hands.

The scars earned in "Digging" by the passing down of male power and responsibility are learned in Boland's poem—that is, gleaned as well as learnèd. In other words, what she inherits is a reminder or artifact of the male imagination dominant in the making of history and poetry. The male "gift" is a wounding one, a turning of the earth into scars, as well as a subtly misogynistic impulse to injure the female figure "inferred" onto the earth; recall, for instance, the fertile, if impossible bog queen and the violent act performed on her by the turfcutters and by history itself. Heaney's men loved the "cool hardness" in their hands as they performed their desires on the earth or on the page, but Boland finds such manipulation to be "cold," an oxymoronic potency at best—and an inheritance that she "takes down" only occasionally as a reminder of her own difference and obligation.

The image of a cicatrix—a healed scar, specifically of a tree—provides Boland with a complex figure for the revising of poetic history. In "Mise Eire," as she swears not to "go back to . . . my nation displaced / into old dactyls," she realizes again that her "roots are brutal." The brevity of her lineation suggests a clear-minded, resolute intent to confront

the scalded memory,
the songs
that bandage up the history,
the words
that make a rhythm
of the crime.

Here the speaker performs an act of sympathy and synthesis, imagining herself into the voice of a previously silenced persona:

I am the woman
in the gansy-coat
on board the *Mary Belle*
in the huddling cold,

holding her half-dead baby to her.

Having identified and called into question the patriarchal character of history, Boland now seeks to replace that "criminal" paradigm with another model, maternal, uprooted, immigrant. It is most important that the female figure also possesses the skill of language—not the "old dactyls" of her antique nation, but rather

a new language
[which] is a kind of scar
and heals after a while
into a passable imitation
of what went before.

Language frames or marks the location of the wound and, as well, provides the element which authorizes the wound to begin to heal.

To identify and name a problem is to make such a beginning. Boland's overall poetic involves an even more thorough transumption, and many of her strongest poems take up the challenge of containing the past while revising it into relevance. To amend the traditional estate of women in poetry, Boland locates her women in their more probable situations—not as unreal nymphs or muses, but as working, dignified, if domestically bound women.

It's not that Boland wishes an exclusively domestic occupation for women, but such an occupation (instead of membership in a male myth-wish) is their more likely, accurate history. "The Women" presents a landscape and a vocation more like Dickinson's than Heaney's:

> This is the hour I love: the in-between
> neither here nor there hour of evening.
> The air is tea-colored in the garden.
> The briar rose is spilled crepe de Chine.
>
> This is the time I do my work best,
> going up the stairs in two minds,
> in two worlds, carrying cloth or glass,
> leaving something behind, bringing
> something with me I should have left behind.

The poet at work deals with a reluctantly inherited past and with the homely materials at hand, stitching them together. At the doubled crossroad—of night and day, and of the past and present—she witnesses in her lines a remarkable metamorphosis:

> in the words I choose, the lines I write,
> they rise like visions and appear to me:
>
> women of work, of leisure, of the night,
> in stove-colored silks, in lace, in nothing,
> with crewel needles, with books, with wide-open legs
>
> who fled the hot breath of the god pursuing,
> who ran from the split hoof and the thick lips
> and fell and grieved and healed into myth,
>
> into me in the evening at my desk. . . .

This is a "vision" of the history of women heretofore "outside" poetic history. So that "my sister will be wiser," as she writes in another poem, "Daphne with Her Thighs in Bark," she exposes a past vulnerability toward the myth-maker, the "god pursuing":

Look at me.
I can be cooking,
making coffee,
scrubbing wood, perhaps,
and back it comes:
the crystalline, the otherwhere,
the wood

where I was
when he began the chase.
And how I ran from him!

Pan-thighed,
satyr-faced he was.

Boland repudiates the role of victim-shepherdess within the mythol-
ogy of male history-making. Or rather, she recognizes the role her gender
has played in that mythology and refuses to frame herself there any longer.
In "The New Pastoral," Boland explores the possible hazards of cutting
loose from such a pervasive system:

I am a lost, last inhabitant—
displaced person in a pastoral chaos.

All day I listen to the loud distress, the switch
and tick of new herds.

But her speaker reasserts that she's "no shepherdess" and turns instead
toward the actual circumstances of women's lives. Even within the con-
temporary domestic scenery, Boland senses a possible, familiar (and famil-
ial) entrapment:

am I
at these altars,
warm shrines—
washing machines, dryers

with their incense
of men and infants—
priestess
or sacrifice?

The answer, here in "Domestic Interior," depends on her ability to trans-
form her circumstances past and present into art, into a schema of imagery
appropriate to her own sense of self, and finally into an identity *she chooses*
within and beyond the poetic tradition:

The woman is as round
as the new ring
ambering her finger.
The mirror weds her. . . .

But there's a way of life
that is its own witness:
put the kettle on, shut the blind.
Home is a sleeping child,
an open mind

and our effects,
shrugged and settled
in the sort of light
jugs and kettles
grow important by.

Boland seeks to describe a poetic location, an "effect"—that is, a property
as well as a force—which includes an indicted past and a possibly ensnar-
ing present. What prevents the continuation of oppression is the voice of
the woman as she elects the substance of her own history and the manner
of her own presentation. Even from within her daily surroundings, or per-
haps especially within such, she finds an alternative to the unreal myth of
her fathers:

There is
about it all

a quiet search for attention,
like the unexpected shine
of a despised utensil.

Eavan Boland is an attentive, powerful, encouraging poet. Part of her power derives from her ability to confront a past which might otherwise force her into complicity or silence. That dubious inheritance includes, in part, Louis MacNeice and Seamus Heaney. But there may be a remarkable kinship between her work and theirs: the consistent antagonism of modern Irish poets with their past. These poets all very carefully and purposefully situate themselves outside a large and traditional notion. Most significantly, the stance of a chosen exclusion allows each poet to maneuver more freely *within* the conventions held in question. For MacNeice, exile provided him the freedom to retrieve his Irish birthright within the frame of his memory and art. Heaney questions the pastoral ideal to reinvigorate it, modernize it, even politicize it. Boland subverts the male ideal of history even while she instigates a parallel history, feminist and alternate, to witness the "unexpected shine" of otherwise mundane, mythologized, or suppressed lives. Due in part to their skeptical, doubled stances toward their respective subjects, these poets express a deep and intelligent love for something related to, but clearly not the same as, what they hold in doubt.

PART THREE

Kinds of Knowing

Smarts

Poets these days want us to think they are smart. This strikes me as I read much of the poetry written in the last few years. If the decade of the 1970s favored the shorter lyric, and the 1980s became a decade of narrative extension, then the 1990s are shaping up as an age of discourse, of poetry infused and sometimes laden with obvious smartness: the Poem Thinking. That's certainly a preferred rhetorical method, one of the most common stances, among poets currently. I think, therefore I instruct.

This should not be an altogether surprising development, given the circumstance of a dramatic number of poets these days. They teach. But perhaps the current instructive and discursive modes may be explained by considering other matters, too. Perhaps poets are articulating a desire to engage their audience and educate it toward a further enjoyment. Perhaps poets feel overshadowed by the critical superstars of the day and so wish to appear *au courant* with the more hip talk of theory. Perhaps they feel critically abandoned and therefore charged with the task of explicating their own work. Perhaps, in widening the scope of poetry from the personal to the historical, political, scientific, or more broadly cultural, poets are struggling to find appropriate voices and forms to bear such heavy weight. Indeed, it's finally not a bad development. Poetry had better be able to think hard. But our best poets are careful also not to destroy the passions, humilities, and mysteries that make poetry—not merely to talk so smart that only a few other poets (or critics) will care or pretend to understand them.

Susan Howe is an obviously speculative poet. She is by far the most didactic or patently "smart" of the five poets here considered. She is also a

On *Singularities* by Susan Howe, Wesleyan/New England, 1990; *The Never-Ending* by Andrew Hudgins, Houghton Mifflin, 1991; *Bethlehem in Broad Daylight* by Mark Doty, Godine, 1991; *Star Ledger* by Lynda Hull, Iowa, 1991; *Questions about Angels* by Billy Collins, Morrow, 1991.

Language poet. That is to say, her poems quite readily abide by the primary tenets of Poststructural poetics: they partake of visual experimentation; they are only loosely syntactic; they appear to want to question the structures of power and authority often tacitly or openly accepted by traditional poetics; they depend to a surprising degree (given their claims of social justice and political equity) on a thorough and privileged awareness of scholarly discourse and exercise, treating language as such; they are not pretty.

Singularities is comprised of three long poems and describes a fairly conventional view of American history. Its project is to participate in and concurrently to revise the ongoing American experiment: the rugged individual who traipses or is forced to flee into the wilderness to construct a new Eden. The structure is chronological, from "Articulation of Sound Forms in Time," with its partial grounding in seventeenth-century Puritan America, to Howe's alternately sympathetic and parodic rendering in "Thorow" of a writer's exile in the wilderness, to "Scattering as Behavior Toward Risk," the shortest and perhaps most overtly theoretical of these texts. The wilderness into which Howe travels is not really a setting but rather a circumstance, an occasion for the enacting and revising of language and history. Howe's hero/sojourner takes along a hefty literary armament— the letters of the Rev. Hope Atherton, Thoreau's *Walden*, the critical theory of Deleuze and Guattari, and more:

> Fence blown down in a winter storm
>
> darkened by outstripped possession
> Field stretching out of the world
>
> this book is as old as the people
>
> There are traces of blood in a fairy tale

The figure of the trace serves throughout these poems as a clarifying mark, a "track of Desire" as Howe calls it in "Thorow": a footstep out of the erasures of history, by whose remnant presence we are connected to the past and by whose heading we are directed to the future. The trace is as well a recurring literary device: a deconstructionist's trace, a lingual clue or currency by which we may, as Jonathan Culler translates Derrida, "think the present starting from/in relation to time as difference, differing, and deferral." Howe seeks to tell the history of the individual by tracing the history of language, reiterated, renewed, and revised in its reuse. In astrophysics, as in Howe's theory of language, a "singularity" is an event which can happen or be proved to happen once and only once. History is to Howe a field of singularities rather than a unified, linear construct with constant integrity. The Postmodern American wilderness is language itself, and its meaning is ever-shifting in an ongoing, explosive dynamic of destruction and renewal.

The Rev. Hope Atherton, the first minister of Hatfield, Massachusetts, provides Howe with a forgotten hero in "Articulation of Sound Forms in Time." In May, 1676, forced into the woods where he hid for days after witnessing a battle between English soldiers and members of a Mahican tribe, Atherton, upon capture, was forced to watch the torture by fire of several soldiers. He later emerged to find his story disbelieved and his reputation ruined. His "literal attributes" as hero are clarified by Howe:

> Effaced background dissolves remotest foreground. Putative author, premodern condition, presently present what future clamors for release?
>> Hope's epicene name drawn its predetermined poem in.
>> I assume Hope Atherton's excursion for an emblem foreshadowing a Poet's abolished limitations in our demythologized fantasy of Manifest Destiny.

A mere letter away from Howe, Atherton's female forename is an obvious misnomer, suggesting peace and optimism, hope for salvation. It ironizes his eventual "baptism by fire," his estrangement from his community, and his ignominious death. He is Howe's personification of American experience, where a journey into the wilderness is more likely to result in tribulation and default than in spiritual vision or material creation. Howe absorbs Hope's voice and proceeds by word gaming—by puns, sound-alikes, phonetic spellings, and revisionist remeaning. Her poetic method derives most often from the palimpsest, the text overwritten by subsequent texts, as a means to suggest a "Visible surface of Discourse // Runes or allusion to runes." She integrates Atherton's language and experience, his "Cries hurled through the Woods," with more contemporary discursions into theory, history, and politics, to create a many-layered, plural, difficult, sometimes exasperating text:

We turn suddenly

Lords of the Lay

Letters sent out in crystalline purity

Muddled and ravelled

Sigh by see

Smoke faces separate

Lore and the like

Sucked into sleeping

—Hegelian becoming

—Hugolian memory

Patriarchal prophesy at the heels of hope

Futurity. . . .

When this technique works, it is a startling and generative achievement. It surprises, and it smartly resists the doldrums of typical poetic stances and modes. Poetry in Howe's hands becomes a sort of battleground for sense-making, a constantly altering field of matter and language whose self-aware purpose is to resist being permanently fixed—that is, permanently situated as well as reliably repaired. When it fails, and indeed I believe it often does, its failure stems from a few primary causes. What can be joyful or inventive can turn mightily severe, off-putting, superior, or intellectually indulgent, as in this section of "Scattering as Behavior toward Risk":

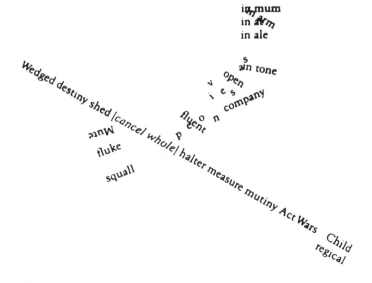

The difficulties of Howe's poetry derive from her commitment to one of the oldest theories of art: mimesis. She insists on replicating, in form and syntax, the unstable or unfinished conditions of language, story, and meaning. Her aesthetic so depends on this notion that she often willingly foresakes sense in favor of sensation, signification in favor of sound and sight, our patience in favor of our tolerance. Perhaps this is the largest risk of Language poetry. It too completely depends on the kinds of knowing-ness and receptivity gained through very special scholarly preparation, sym-pathy, and privilege. Not that it is ultimately hard or even strikingly new, but this poetry *requires* a prior, exhaustive, and specialized theoretical edu-cation. And there's the rub: if poetry abides by or merely proves a critical agenda, if indeed the theory is more engaging than the poem, what good is the poem? Though Howe's poetry is about people and their language, not very many people can read it.

Andrew Hudgins writes the kind of poetry with which Susan Howe's poems strenuously argue. If Howe is experimental, speculative, then Hudgins is apparently mainstream. His primary methods in *The Never-Ending* include linear narrative and anecdotal drama, a static speaker, traditional lineation with formalized line breaks. He has a fondness for blank verse, clarity, pub-lic expression, and shared experience. He writes what in most hands is the tidy, safe, party-line poetry favored by many literary magazines. But Hudgins can be brilliant. Sometimes the most valuable and difficult articulations are those originating from deep within the confines of traditional method, those that reinvigorate otherwise conventional gestures. If Howe's theory is based on the variability or unreliability of the text and its meaning, Hudgins's response might be, indeed, that poetry must acknowledge chaos but then resist it rather than abide by its demands.

There are many admittedly orthodox properties in Hudgins's new book. Even his primary subjects are familiar, hackneyed in most hands. Hudgins writes about childhood, a conventional Christian and Southern background, and the rather placid pastime of gardening. In other words, he reiterates the primary and common topics of the Romantic lyric—the innocent, the sublime, and the pastoral:

> Though wild, each flower has its name:
> sweet william, dogtooth violet,

> wild iris, wild geranium.
> Some of the headstones, too, bear names:
> Rucks, Murphry, Bookout. Mostly, though,
> it's *Unknown Soldier CSA.*
>
> It's late. At dusk, cool slanted light
> glows opalescent on white stones,
> and at the end of a long row
> we stand and talk about—what else?—
> mortality. . . .

If it weren't for the wink of "what else?", the opening lines of "New Headstones at the Shelby Spring Confederate Cemetery" might suggest a competent mere repetition of convention. But Hudgins is too knowing, too insistently self-subverting to allow us to believe the obvious. In "The Adoration of the Magi" again he hurries to expose an otherwise objective narrative strategy: "A boy—okay, it's me—wears a fringed / blue tablecloth and fidgets as Joseph / in his church Christmas play."

Hudgins has the skill and will to have it both ways—innocent and knowing, formal and unruly. He's a faithful skeptic. In "The Ugly Flowers" he abides by the strictures of iambic trimeter *as if* to say that poetry ought to replicate the deep formal structure of the natural world: "Because there's little else / to love in March, I love / the ugly flowers." The closer he looks, however, the more his eye discerns a nature described by entropy and randomness rather than by order and form. Hudgins's poetic is therefore a reversal of Howe's mimesis. Both poets suggest that the universe is in some basic way logically unpredictable or impenetrable, but rather than disorganizing language and syntax in imitation of variability, Hudgins imposes a formalizing pressure onto chaos. This is his poetic as well as his cosmology. His style's organic paradigm may be the tidy garden, but his vision's as turbulent as the compost heap:

> The beauty of the compost heap is not
> the eye's delight.
>   Eyes see too much.

> They see
>
> blood-colored worms
>
> and bugs so white they seem
>
> to feed off ghosts. Eyes
>
> do not see the heat
>
> that simmers in
>
> the moist heart of decay. . . .

As here, in "Compost: An Ode," it's out of decay and friction that things grow in Hudgins's poems, out of the pressure applied by oppositions:

> The compost heap is both—life and death—a slow
> simmer,
>
> a leisurely collapsing of
>
> the thing
>
> into its possibilities . . .
>
> the opulence
>
> of everything that rots.

Hudgins treats spiritual matters with the same determining eye with which he treats the organic. A number of these poems consider Christian mythology and artwork, but Hudgins looks so clearly and deeply that again he's more likely to find rot than faith or form. In "Lamentation over the Dead Christ," Hudgins examines Botticelli's details, locating distortion, not salvation:

> . . . and Mary, fainted virgin, her body huge,
>
> distended, bulging, because she suffers more
>
> than anyone can grieve until she loosens
>
> her human shape, becomes impossible.

If grace is possible at all in these poems, it is through the beneficence of the artist, not God. Mary Magdalene, "hunchbacked, wrenched . . . by sorrow," pleads *"Erase my eyes!"* so she won't see Christ's brutalized form: "She begged, / and Botticelli, unlike God, said *yes.*" Hudgins's prayers are so close to curses in *The Never-Ending* that it's impossible to tell them apart. And his humor veers so close to sorrow or loss (or meanness) that his tone inflicts even as it entertains. That's apparent in the opening lines of "Drunk":

> Our Father who are in heaven, I am drunk.
> Again. Red wine. For which I offer thanks.
> I ought to start with praise, but praise
> comes hard to me. I stutter. Did I tell you
> about the woman whom I taught, in bed,
> this prayer? It starts with praise; the simple form
> keeps things in order. I hear from her sometimes.
> Do you? And after love, when I was hungry,
> I said, *Make me something to eat.* She yelled,
> *Poof! You're a casserole!*—and laughed so hard
> she fell out of bed. Take care of her.

Communion is debauchery; a joke is a curse; a plea for care is, under the breath, a clear condemnation. What begins in gratitude for "birds and trees, / that nature stuff," ends in ironic acceptance of human failure:

> What makes me think of me
> is the poor jerk who wanders out on air
> and then looks down. Below his feet, he sees
> eternity, and suddenly his shoes
> no longer work on nothingness, and down
> he goes. As I fall past, remember me.

The measure of Hudgins's ability is the tremendous leap his poems take, from conventional beginnings to original, fatal, ironic ends. He writes accessible, public poetry, with wonderful faith in his readership and in his language, and yet his vision is unsettling, even horrific. His demanding intelligence finds articulation not in fragments and theory but deep within the structures of story, image, tone, and formalized prosody. For Hudgins the human imagination strives for order in a universe that clearly does not.

Like Hudgins, Mark Doty writes well-ordered poetry whose primary method is anecdotal, whose speaker is singular and personal, and whose vision is skeptical. But where Hudgins takes each of these current conventions into startling, sometimes brilliant directions, Doty seems satisfied with humdrum competence. His narrative drive turns frequently into lineated prose; his speaker often prefers detachment and judgment over involvement and sympathy; his view of things seems rather self-contained or meager.

Doty's *Bethlehem in Broad Daylight* shares Hudgins's interests in the experiences of adolescence and art. In "A Box of Lilies" a professor/poet is "driving to work, late, / *Tannhauser* on the tape player— // the skittering violins spiraling down / in their mortal pull. . . ." Juxtaposed with the "grand theme" of Wagnerian opera is the speaker's appointment with a young student who "tells me he's fallen / in love, an old girlfriend / still lingering somewhere." To the speaker the student's dilemma is overblown, even compared to the conflation of Wagner's grandiose style:

> There's something bravura,
> something nineteen in even saying it,
>
> and I can't decide whether
> to love or blame him. . . .

From here Doty's speaker shifts to consider a friend who has embarked "on a kind of going / we don't know the least thing about." The journey seems to imply a terminal illness, but again the speaker reorients his description, this time to the misdirected gift of a box of lilies and his neighbor's subsequent desire to see the flowers blossom:

> it's the beautiful event
> in the garden she waits for,
>
> and their fragrance goes hurrying
> up; she's an interruption
>
> en route to heaven.

Doty's desire to connect narrative threads is admirable. The blooming lilies suggest operatic trumpets, his student's dilemma parodies Wagnerian tragedy, and the whole scheme attempts to make sense of the friend's terrible loss. But Doty's treatment is just too easy. His drive to understand is dramatically undercut by facile philosophizing:

> Maybe dying's like being given
> a box of what will be trumpets,
>
> maybe it feels like a mistake,
> and you plant them with all
>
> the requisite attention
> and wait for something. . . .

Matters are too either/or in Doty's work, too quickly explained, vaguely confronted. How indeed is dying like a box of "trumpets"? Why were his speaker's only two possible reactions to his student's story either "to love or blame him"? He reduces, forcing things into tidy polarities: "I don't know which I love better— // knowing the bulbs are there, this March . . . or the brief July spangle // smudging our faces / with that golden lipstick."

Doty's preferred method is to connect and juxtapose anecdotal episodes. He often demonstrates good instincts for such correlations; he doesn't want to be pure. But he also doesn't manage enough stylistic rigor to convert anecdote into poetry. Often I feel as if I'm reading lined prose:

> The school bus rattled around more turns
> in the desert roads than I'd ever
> be able to trace again, the summer I worked
> in Head Start and the lead teacher
> arranged a field trip from the barrio
> to the Valley of the Moon.

The opening stanza of "The Garden of the Moon" is cleanly lined but typifies Doty's limited voice. I find little resonance, little figurative intensity, little dramatic significance; instead the tone is flat-spirited, the voice of reportage and self-satisfaction.

My other hesitation with Doty's style concerns a related easiness. Doty possesses the admirable desire to turn instance into meaning; he wants to philosophize and thereby instruct. His method here is often to conclude a long narrative passage with a short general observation. In "The Death of Antinoüs" the opening thirteen-line sentence describes in moving, concrete language the agonies of the drowning hero and his eventual immortality as statuary, but Doty follows up his precise description with nearly meaningless generality: "What do we want in any body / but the world?" I have some strong opinions about that question, if he really wants to know, but he doesn't seem to. Rather, in the poem's final sentence he again confuses abstract emptiness with epiphany: "Longing, of course, / becomes its own object, the way / that desire can make anything a god." Doty's impulse is often good—to make serious meaning out of detail and episode—but he smudges and reduces so much that his arrived-at theses seem sentimental, artificial, wrong, or at least seriously debatable.

The overall problem in Doty's work—and I feel the same about much contemporary poetry in this fashionable mode—is its detachment from its own story. Doty doesn't seem possessed by his content as much as he seems a distant and privileged observer and commentator on it. "All we have of our neighbors' lives / is noise, and the stories we can make of it," he asserts in "Against Paradise," though in the same poem he claims that he "couldn't love any world but this." It's not sympathy but disconnection, not "love" but a final, subtle unconcern, that he describes. Within the realm of art Doty's speaker is hopeful, faithful; otherwise he's an uninvolved skeptic: "That's the lesson," he theorizes; "art is remembering, and turning away." If that's the lesson, it may also be the obvious damning problem.

Lynda Hull makes her poetry out of displacement and trouble, too, deeply seen and intelligently wrought, but she never settles for the sentiments of abstract theory. Nor does she allow her language to devolve into prosaic discourse or her ideas into pedantry. She is both smart and accessible, a poet for whom passionate engagement becomes her most vivid means of thinking. She makes noise—funky, concrete, difficult, demanding noise—and she sounds like nobody else writing these days. She's not always easy to listen to. Her view of things can be mightily severe, her style measured equally by sobriety and relentless tension, but she is starkly original and possesses a stern, bodily manner of cognition. If Howe's involvements are critical and Hudgins's are conventional, then Lynda Hull's are primarily social. She scours cultural history, urban immigrant neighborhoods, and the troubled imaginations of artists and addicts alike to find impulse for her poems, and her formal tactic derives from her hunger to make a line, stanza, and poem spacious enough to contain her multiplicity of subjects.

"Lost Fugue for Chet" may serve as Hull's most clear statement of design. An elegy for jazz trumpeter Chet Baker, who dove to his death from an Amsterdam hotel in 1988, the poem maneuvers among points of view as among dingy streets, changing the rules, like a jazz improvization:

> . . . the horn's improvisations purl & murmur
>
> the narrow *strasses* of *Rosse Buurt,* the district rife
>
> with purse-snatchers, women alluring, desolate, poised
>
> in blue windows, Michelangelo boys, hair spilling
>
> fluent running chords, mares' tails in the sky green
>
> and violet. So easy to get lost. . . .

Hull's fugue refers not only to the formal apex of neoclassical music, whose strategy is multi-voiced, contrapuntal, but also suggests the fugue states of psychology (the pathological inability to focus on or to control action) and of physical science (the state of variability or chaotic plurality). It is an impressive element of her style to mesh such tropes into a singular narrative. Just so, the brilliance of the musician's talent depends on nearness to disaster, on a willingness to "get lost," to taunt the limit:

> After surviving, what arrives? So what's the point
>
> when there are so many women, creamy callas with single
>
> furled petals turning in & in upon themselves
>
> like variations, nights when the horn's coming
>
> genius riffs, metal & spit, that rich consuming rush
>
> of good dope, a brief languor burnishing
>
> the groin, better than any sex. Fuck death.

Carefully wrought sound is an aspect of thought. It bears a grammar, a logic, and strives for a distinct effect. Here each phrase and image pattern—the music, the women's sexuality, the smoke furling, blood blooming—winds and curls into the next. Hull takes her sympathetic, troubled characterization into another register, too, moving unannounced from third person to second, pushing Baker closer to the literal edge: "What do you do / at the brink?" The obvious answer is that you jump:

> this is the tied-off vein, this is 3 a.m. terror
> thrumming, this is the carnation of blood clouding
>   the syringe. . . .
>
>   Cold chestnuts flowering April
>   & you're falling from heaven in a shower of eighth notes
> to the cobbled street below & foaming dappled horses
>   plunge beneath the still green waters of the Grand Canal.

Hull's formal strategies replicate her interest in variation, inclusion, and complication. The sheer bulk of her very wide lineation suggests the accumulative capabilities of prose, though unlike Doty she rarely allows the tonal pressure of her lines to exhale into depletion. More likely, Hull's voice can become so intense or severe it may border on fright. Typically, the long line invites quicker or more steady reading than the short line, yet Hull's abbreviated phrasings, her slow syntax, mid-phrase enjambments, heavy accentuation, and abundant punctuation all conspire to increase a reader's anxiety. Hull wants us constantly to be aware of the difficult going in her poems. Her purposeful stylistic impediments are appropriate to the hazards and disjunctions of her stories.

The opening sentence of "Love Poem during Riot with Many Voices" demonstrates the two forces which propel her poems—difficulty of style and a complicating of convention and theme:

> The bridge's iron mesh chases pockets of shadow
> and pale through blinds shuttering the corner window
>
> to mark this man, this woman, the young eclipse
> their naked bodies make—black, white, white,
> black, the dying fall of light rendering bare walls
>
> incarnadine, color of flesh and blood occluded
>
> in voices rippling from the radio: Saigon besieged,
> Hanoi, snipers and the riot news helicoptered
> from blocks away.

The lovers' landscape is anything but conventional—darkly urban, its privacy compromised by cruelty. The complex syntax of this single sentence is further enhanced by the plural possibilities of the words themselves. In just the first two lines, several words (mesh, chases, show, pale, blinds) could be several different parts of speech. Parsing the syntax is part of the rigor of discovery here and part of the danger of discordance, the fugue of "getting lost." Hull's wisdom and difficult sympathy find their expression in her considerable ability to suggest "the riot within" her characters by means of the many riots and crises outside. Occasionally the result can be clotted, her insistent figuration almost relentless, but more often her poems hold up remarkably even in the most severe conditions.

The overall movement of *Star Ledger* follows the same strategy that informs Hull's best poems, for the book's three sections become increasingly complicated by the grime and grit of earthly concerns. By the third and strongest section of the book, Hull's "star ledger" has fully evolved, not into a charting of distant celestial bodies but into a monitoring of earthly turmoil; after all, the *Star Ledger* is also Newark's morning newspaper. Here Hull is most at home, ranging through the rough neighborhoods of Amsterdam or Barcelona, smelling the odors of Chinatown, finding "strange good fortune" in a Newark hospice. Throughout, Hull's unflinching attention, her "silent complicity," is with the outsider—the poor, the misunderstood, the excluded. Her voice is as likely to bear a slap in the face as a drugged caress. Her speakers want a poetry able to contain the whole "shuddering world," even if embracing the world means losing themselves. That's the exacting wisdom of this book:

> Whatever I meant
>
> to say loses itself in the bend of winter
> toward extinction, this passion of shadows falling
>
> like black orchids through the air. I never meant
> to leave you there by the pane, that
>
> terminal hotel, the world shuddering with trains.

What else but brilliant crafting could result is such a "terminal" closure in the poem "Black Mare"? Even the word "terminal" resounds with awful, harmonic resonance, and its double usage reinforces our hearing other types of doubleness or rhyme. The final hard syllable of "train" reaches back to "pane" (itself a dark, homonym pun), while the double "meant" echoes with "winter" and the interior music of "there" and "air" also reiterate "winter." Hull deploys so many closings-down, a kind of fateful or inevitable series of endings, that, finally, the poem locks itself with the force of a sonnet's couplet. Lynda Hull is a powerful, intelligent poet. The measure of her wisdom is the measure of her song and her passion—flamboyant, full, connective, flirting with the dangerous edge.

Billy Collins's new book finds its title in a celestial or quasi-religious image. He shares that with the other four poets here, though little else in his poetry is like theirs. Howe, Doty, and Hull write in a primarily serious tone, verging at times on the severe. Hudgins is also generally serious, since even his jokes are meant to pierce. Billy Collins can be downright funny; he's a parodist, a feigning trickster, an ironic, entertaining magician-as-hero. Indeed it is a heroic (or mock-epic) journey which we undertake in *Questions about Angels*. Collins shares with Susan Howe a dubious regard for many of the conventions of contemporary poetry, and the progress of this fine book describes a killing-off of these usual customs, a requisite descent into the underworld of cliché and sentiment and a gradual rebirth or restoration of imaginative vigor. He exposes many of the tired assumptions of current poetry which Howe, too, seems to disrespect, yet his effect is much more open and inviting.

The book's first section requires a number of deaths—the death of naive mimesis, of allegory ("I am wondering what became of all those tall abstractions / that used to pose, robed and statuesque, in paintings / and parade about on the pages of the Renaissance . . ."), even of the traditional reader ("we were forgetting how to look," he warns in "First Reader"). He dismantles the sonnet in his twenty-one line "American Sonnet," ripping its insides open to expose the conventional gestures:

> We write on the back of a waterfall or lake,
>
> adding to the view a caption as conventional
>
> as an Elizabethan woman's heliocentric eyes.
>
> We locate an adjective for the weather.

> We announce that we are having a wonderful time.
>
> We express the wish that you were here. . . .

And in "Forgetfulness" he kills off the author himself, "as if, one by one, the memories you used to harbor / decided to retire to the southern hemisphere of the brain. . . . " Like a kind of dying, forgetting leads to freedom and a possible rebirth of imagining. So when the poem's hero "rise[s] in the middle of the night," he begins to discover anew the possibilities of the world: "No wonder the moon in the window seems to have drifted / out of a love poem that you used to know by heart." Much of Collins's capability here derives from his double stance; he can engage as he criticizes, educate as he entertains. He will not be pinned down to a single or singular pronoun nor to any one historic period, as if he is blasting these minimizing tendencies. He wants to make his readers hyper-aware of his strategies and thereby of their own assumptions. He's a meta-poet with charm and compassion.

The two middle sections of his book find Collins, having killed off his hero, descending into a sort of poetry underworld, seeking reeducation before reentry. Here, in a poetry "afterlife," Collins's speaker must face his mortal sins: "My life is an open book," he admits in "Cliché." He lays bare his imagination's conventional leanings in "Purity":

> In this condition I write extraordinary love poems,
> most of them exploiting the connection between sex and death.
>
> I am concentration itself: I exist in a universe
> where there is nothing but sex, death, and typewriting.
>
> After a spell of this I remove my penis too.
> Then I am all skull and bones typing into the afternoon.

His tone is self-aware and parodic. His quest steers him toward the self-regard and mortification of the omniscient dead. "Memento Mori" follows up:

> There is no need for me to keep a skull on my desk. . . .
>
> It is enough to realize that every common object
> in this sunny little room will outlive me. . . .

In these two sections Collins strips down the experiences of daily life and of poetry, exposing the "skull and bones" of convention and readerly expectation. His landscapes become increasingly desert-like or deserted, terminating at last with "Invective," a subtle mockery of Yeats's "Lake Isle of Innesfree." Here Collins's speaker suggests his readiness to reenter the world, to "stare" with "cold, unblinking eyes" skeptical of the usual poetic vision.

And indeed the book's final section is a catalog of transformations and discoveries—from retellings of fairy tales and Kafkaesque metamorphoses ("I would feel the pages of books turning inside me like butterflies") to a parody of Wallace Stevens in "Saturday Morning." History is rewritten ("the Stone Age became the Gravel Age, / named after the long driveways of time"), jazz is rediscovered ("something / that sounded like / bop ah dooolyah bop"), and the world is revitalized into the strange and provocative place it should have been in the first place. That's the dazzling, disorienting strategy of "On Reading in the Morning Paper that Dreams May Be Only Nonsense":

> We might have guessed as much, given the nightly
> absurdities, the extravagant circus of the dark.
> You hit the pillow and moments later your mother
> appears as a llama, shouting at you in another language. . . .
>
> Or the nonsense is just a scrambling of the day before,
> everyone walking around the office stark naked,
> the elevator doors opening on to deep space,
> the clamshells from lunch floating by in slow motion.

The poems in Collins's final section swirl in a mixture of familiarity and strangeness, where family life and a dance step from 1340 may coexist, where the promise of discovery with its "secret patterns" invigorates the mundane. This is the gift of Collins's work—to make new, to redescribe poetry's creative capability. To do so, he battles the usual gestures and our own anticipations, making them obviously suspect before he gives us back the world.

Questions about Angels is a considerable achievement, though I might mention one or two slight misgivings. Collins's method depends heavily on the vitality and pliability of his voice; occasionally his charisma becomes merely cute, his smartness too close to smart-alecky. Also, while Collins calls into question many current poetic stances and assumptions, he doesn't veer far from the formal properties (and possible slacknesses) of a fairly tidy free verse—though this is not so much a problem as a small curiosity. To be sure, these are minor notes about a big accomplishment. Without question, Collins writes with verve, gumption, and deep intelligence. Not many poets can infuse humor with such serious knowledge; not many can range so far through history and look so freshly into the future. Not many can please so thoroughly and still manage to chide, prod, urge, criticize, and teach.

Kinds of Knowing

Philosophy is, in its first definition, a love of wisdom. Philosophical poetry must be particularly fashioned not only to bear wisdom but also to sustain a rhetoric by which wisdom becomes lovely, bodily, metaphoric, passionate—that is, poetic. But it's hard to be philosophical in poetry, the difficulty stemming in part from the lyric poem's conventional resistance of direct discursion, overt methodology, or sophistry. The Modernist credo "No ideas but in things" lingers with an old half-true resonance. Contemporary poets usually do better with the particularity of experience than with the inductions of wisdom; they prefer to suggest that sensation and incident are types of initiatory intelligence. Or, when they undertake a sustained and overtly philosophical project—for example, the Language poets' rigorous Poststructural engagement—their work likely evinces as many failures as successes. The poets at hand try to strike a balance, to infuse poetry with lucidity as well as with more conspicuous, sustained, and sometimes notably *un*lyrical thinking. To be sure, their work is not philosophical in the sense that *De Rerum Natura* or Blake's more didactic tracts or most Language texts are. These poets are not particularly interested in epistemology or rational analysis. But to some significant if varying degree, they undertake schemes of intellectualization which are sustained, abstract, as well as lyrical.

Eric Pankey is outstanding among the members of an emerging generation of talented and accomplished poets. Indeed, given the excellence of his previous two books and given the particular maturity, confidence, and graceful intelligence of this new one, his age—he was born in 1957—seems all the more remarkable. *Apocrypha* is one of the most carefully

On *Apocrypha* by Eric Pankey, Knopf, 1991; *The Wild Iris* by Louise Glück, Ecco, 1992; *Heart and Perimeter* by Linda Bierds, Holt, 1991.

composed, subtly constructed books of poems I have read in years, and one
of the most moving. It is also Pankey's most cohesive collection, virtually
a sequence, comprised of short lyric and meditative poems arranged to sug-
gest a subtle narrative design, a story of one man's faith and doubt. Its faith
is both religious—specifically Christian—and poetic, and its doubts derive
from the speaker's probing of his own convictions in these spiritual and
aesthetic matters.

Pankey writes compressed, meditative poems in the manner of Wallace
Stevens's and Czeslaw Milosz's short lyrics. His work is sharpened by an
exactness of imagery, but it is driven by its speculative method. For Pankey
an image may serve as representation of an idea—as in the artful, Stevens-
like "The Plum on the Sill." More often, however, image is an idea's foil. In
fact, these poems typically portray a sort of imaginative battle between detail
and Pankey's impulse to synthesize. The opening sections of *Apocrypha* are
marked by this technique as well as by Pankey's conditional wonderment.
"Between a laugh and rare luck," he begins in "Provision," "A man makes
provision for clarity." His speaker, "the beholder who holds little," grapples
with a central dilemma: his compulsion to understand the world versus his
desire to see past its mere details. Not satisfied by particularity, he hungers
for a method of knowing which comes from abstraction and distillation,
from an absenting of detail in behalf of something like faith:

> As in the cold world, the sheltered world,
>
> The air of earth and foundation,
> The example overshadows the argument
> And is illumination: a cast, a casting.
> Clarity is not precision, the particular
> Intersection, the crude *X*.
> It is what the tools cannot measure:
> The gap, the lack, the verge of arrival.

Revising Stevens's "arrogant, fatal, dominant X," Pankey marks his method
by seeking the "clarity" of negation or humility. The point of "arrival" is
the point of using but then relinquishing precision in favor of synthesis
and (as he comes to call it) belief.

Apocrypha is rich with such complex poems. The book itself is comprised of six sections, each with nine poems; its organization creates its own narrative of the speaker's faith and doubt. In the first sections he dramatizes small crises of understanding and perception—from a lover's receding relationship to an "apocryphal" argument between two translators who can't agree on the meaning of words to the parable of a neighbor who nourishes himself with whiskey made from stolen corn: "It tasted of ash, as did the snow, / Which he melted for water and drank / When he woke at night with a terrible thirst" ("Neighbor"). A quiet "chaos," as he calls it, runs through the book's first two sections, reaching its crisis in the third section, in poems which directly or obscurely reenact a sacrifice or crucifixion: "Underfoot / This land is a wreck of wheel ruts and gravel, / Crazed with aftermarks, a hill that levels / Here where the killing's done," he writes in "Tenebrae."

Sections four and five become both more nostalgic and more knowingly confessional:

> I was not the type to call forth angels,
> But if I said there's a swallow rising as it banks
> Over the white flat of the rail yards,
> Tracing the long ellipse of its hunt,
> You could believe me. I talked like that.

Here, in "Fool's Gold," the speaker's demeanor is restrained but critical, his speculation shaped through direct Biblical allusion. He sees that his previous innocence lent him "precision," the direct (if now naive) correspondence between verity and language, but it also prevented his awareness of or his need of "angels"—that is, of a spiritual life. As both the poem and the book develop, the speaker finds that his maturity and skepticism are clouding his ability to see (or speak) precisely: "I'm not talking / About miracles," he says, as if trying to appease his sense of bewilderment at this new incapacity. Nature possesses the characteristics of language, a kind of metaphysical intelligence, but the speaker does not have the ability to read it. What he locates instead is

> Nothing but rills and deltas, intricate
> Markings I thought I might decipher.

Each stone in the rift was placed
As if a clue. If the water
Sifted a fistful of pyrite
Glimmering beneath the surface
That too was evidence of a language
I was just beginning to learn.

If this poem both yields and depends on paradox, so does Pankey's poetic. *Apocrypha* is studied but deeply felt. Probing both individual faith and the conditionality of language, it is remarkably intimate but never personal —confessional in a spiritual rather than Plathian sense. Each poem is highly elliptical, contemplative. Yet the whole sequence describes a clear narrative movement from innocence to knowingness, from the willing crucifixion of naivete through punishment and loss, pointing finally toward humility and acceptance. Pankey is unusual, and admirable, in the way his intelligence demonstrates an abiding modesty rather than either pride or scholarly performance. The individual poems are wonderfully well-composed —often accentual, compressed, in stanzas so even and balanced they seem chiseled. Their power may be especially cumulative. I suspect some of them, separately, may be more cryptic. Also, while Pankey's use of Christian allegory is both subtle and central, and while his speaker's doubts are disconcertingly honest, Pankey accepts the myth itself as universally viable and meaningful. This last comment is less a complaint than a descriptive hesitation.

Pankey's Christian paradigm not only informs but enables his demanding speculations about language, poetry, selfhood, and good and evil. The book's final two sections release its speaker into a world inevitably fallen ("Cumbersome grief, grief, / By its form fragmentary, is now our history," he says in "The History of the World") and yet also newly promising. He senses the coming of "a belief that joy will come, / That joy is relief" ("Eschatology"). The speaker's involvements range from the practical and familial to the spiritual in these final poems; the predominant tropes are of measuring, rebuilding, and curing. For "each brute act" in *Apocrypha* Pankey answers with an intelligent, faithful reply. His responsive "echo" is wonderfully enacted in the final lines of "The History of the World," where Pankey's speaker constructs a figurative cathedral "To every dodge and contrivance." As if replicating the lovely method of Pankey's poems, the belltower sounds its complicated, clear song: "The toll—a three-note scale, / A song that calls us to celebrate and mourn // That each day is not the day of judgment."

Pankey speaks about God and faith in *Apocrypha;* God talks back in Louise Glück's *The Wild Iris.* Her brilliant new book is audacious and daring, even though its rhetoric may seem initially unassuming. The voices in these fifty-four compressed lyrics become at different times a dialogue, a chorus, and an argument; the individual poems are "spoken" not only by Glück's human character and by God but also, as if to complete her Romantic trinity, by the garden itself, where Glück's speaker works and through which God makes himself (he *is* a he in these poems) manifest. There is actually very little to distinguish these speakers from one another, poem by poem, other than a few details and our own readerly, mediating inferences. Throughout, Glück's style is consistently introspective and abstractive. Nor is her flower garden especially Edenic, for little original innocence resides among the trillium, lilies, and iris. Rather, the book is a spiritual conference in the aftermath of the fall, closer to the *fin de siècle* than to any first cause.

Like Pankey, Glück has organized *The Wild Iris* to suggest a clear narrative progression, even though the poems separately are never driven by plot, chronology, or overt dramatic action. Each is highly meditative. Still, the book seems finally like a long poem, organized by three narrative paradigms: the passing of a single day (seven of the poems are entitled "Matins," nine are "Vespers"); the beginning and fading of a single growing season, from early spring through September; and the modulation of the speaker's own faith and understanding as she observes patterns suggested by the Biblical Garden and other fertility myths. The early poems take place in the morning, describe spring flowers (snowdrops, trilliums), and introduce the human character's circumstances: "This is how you live when you have a cold heart. / As I do: in shadows, trailing over cool rock, / under the great maple trees." Here, in "Lamium," the speaker's chilliness —her inability to love fully—is suggested through the small flower's traits. Like the trillium, which "woke up ignorant in a forest," the speaker finds herself remote but alive in a world as natural as she can make it. Her curiosity and desire to know God directly are intense, as in "Matins":

> I see it is with you as with the birches:
> I am not to speak to you
> in the personal way. Much
> has passed between us. Or
> was it always only
> on the one side? I am
> at fault, at fault, I asked you
> to be human. . . .

God's own early stance, in "Clear Morning," is both annoyed and parental:

> I've watched you long enough,
> I can speak to you any way I like—
>
> I've submitted to your preferences, observing patiently
> the things you love, speaking
>
> through vehicles only, in
> details of earth, as you prefer. . . .

But now, because he chooses not to "go on / restricting myself to images," God decides to "force clarity" on Glück's speaker. God's original gift of images—that is, nature, with its educative and representational powers— is finally insufficient to carry meaning to his disappointing subjects.

The clarity which Glück's God compels is remarkably similar to the clarity to which Pankey aspires—that is, the clarity of abstraction and distillation rather than of detail or "precision." The speaker in *The Wild Iris* wants to see, through the phenomena in her garden, into the heart of desire, faith, and love. Perhaps even more than Pankey, Glück avoids concrete images in favor of abstract nouns: grief, wisdom, anguish, illusion, glory— these are the nominal elements of her hieratic garden, growing next to the iris and lilies. When heaven and earth do meet in *The Wild Iris,* precisely at the book's center in "The Doorway," the present tense shifts to the past, and Glück looks back to see a most important paradox, already recognizing failure: "I wanted to stay as I was / still as the world is never still," her speaker intones. Though it is only late spring, "the grass not yet / high at the edge of the garden," she senses that her previous condition was as close to peace or "stillness" as she will ever be. As "the epoch of mastery" approaches, the time of most abundant flowering, she realizes that her creation bears certain ruin. That is the central knowledge of *The Wild Iris*. Whether centered in sex, family, God, or the self, the paradox of love is that its possession inevitably results in its loss.

The Wild Iris is a stunning book. Glück has never been more explicit or more severe in her radical confrontation of the Romantic ideal. This book is all the more remarkable given that Glück wrote it during a ten-week period in the summer of 1991. The pace is both exceptional and, in a few ways, evident. The poems are marked by a sameness of style and method, which effectively reinforces Glück's obsession, her tireless intellectual probing. But sometimes redundancy can blur the wonderful and the sufficient. Glück also tends to dramatize her rhetoric: "Hear me out: that which you call death / I remember," she writes in the title poem, following a few lines later with "Then it was over: that which you fear, being / a soul and unable / to speak, ending abruptly, the stiff earth / bending a little." The clauses are forceful but also a touch forced, and Glück's technique of introducing assertions with colons, in a deliberate rhetorical announcement, is one of the book's customary gestures. There are also one or two grammatical weeds among the flowers: "I can only extend myself / for so long to a living thing," she writes in "September Twilight," perhaps misplacing the adverb. To be sure, this may be more descriptive of the eccentricities of Glück's method than of its flaws. I am amazed throughout this book at how something so cool, so remote, can be so intimate and exacting.

A garden is nature shaped into a human design, as the poems of *The Wild Iris* are representations of our hunger for what we have named God, nature, love, self. Each of these grows in the mind. Glück subverts the conventional wisdom of much contemporary poetry—regarding the pathetic fallacy, the primacy of imagery, and so on—to make her lyric inquiries into the "nature" of that mind. After all, the flowers don't really speak in *The Wild Iris,* nor is God exactly peering at Louise Glück from behind the trees. Rather, these poems carry out a dramatization of the processes of birth and growth and of those habits of mind which must be exposed and conversed with in order to be better known. In the book's final poems a serene and strengthening wisdom settles in. The figure of God calls down in "Sunset":

"My great happiness / is the sound your voice makes / calling me even in despair." But it is as if Glück's human speaker collects and claims as her own the previously divided voices. In the final stanza of "The White Lilies" the voice could be God's, the gardener's, the lover's, or the garden's. They are, of course, one and the same:

> Hush, beloved. It doesn't matter to me
> how many summers I live to return:
> this one summer we have entered eternity.
> I felt your two hands
> bury me to release its splendor.

The predominant stance in the work of Eric Pankey and Louise Glück is inner and contemplative. The kind of knowingness they reach is singular, though its purpose is certainly connective. Linda Bierds's poetry contains virtually no such self or singularity. Her work and her intelligence are plural, other-centered; experience and story, rather than idea and meditation, become her means to sustained thought and derived understanding. She wants to represent history rather than myth. She does not intend the kind of philosophical distillation that Pankey and Glück seek—though, like them, she resists the self-satisfied and anecdotal lyric popular today. She is not a lyric poet, though her work is certainly lyrical. Her metier ranges from the narrative poem to the dramatic monologue, wherein experience, action, and voice are the best representations of meaning and philosophical design.

Both Pankey and Glück attempt to distill the clutter of imagery into a clearer, abstract intelligence. Bierds also suspects that the image, by itself, may not yield accurate sightedness or understanding—even though she fills her poems with minutiae, facts, and phenomena. One of her sustaining projects is to dramatize moments of discovery, invention, or recognition, and often her characters must analyze the unexpected images before them in order to see truly. In "In the Beeyard," a man and his daughter approach their winter hives:

> She lowers her ear to the deep hummings.
> Like mummies, she thinks of the cloaked rows, like
> ghosts. Then salt pillars, headless horsemen

turned white by some stark moonlight.
In a flurry the images reach her,

their speed almost frightening, splendid,
as if the myths and fables of her life are a blizzard
drawn suddenly to her, drawn suddenly visible. . . .

Like a cloud of bees, these images dazzle and scare the daughter; instead of discrete and lasting impressions, they yield "myths and fables," representing through their many metamorphoses the possibility of an underlying, perhaps even archetypal, significance.

Throughout *Heart and Perimeter* Bierds places her characters in just such critical and transformative circumstances. Like many poets currently, she pursues an anecdotal method, narrating events that are intended to become representations of meaning. But unlike most, she eschews autobiography and personal confession—and the minor, diary-like epiphanies often the result of such self-study—and undertakes instead a fascinating investigation of historical characters in the midst of discovery, invention, travail, and hence of dramatic understanding. Not one of this book's twenty-six poems is spoken, as it were, by Linda Bierds or someone very much like her; not one occurs "now"; and not one offers less than a stimulating look into the human compulsion to understand, as personified by the likes of Whistler, Tolstoy, Nancy Hanks Lincoln, Schumann, Tom Thumb, or a thirteen-year-old boy who painted borders around Audubon's canvasses of birds. Musicians, painters, scientists, explorers—the figures in these poems seek that particular moment of innovation or clear-headedness, that "brief harmony, brief melding of truth and illusion," as Bierds describes it in "The Helmet of Mambrino." The poem that perhaps most directly represents Bierds's method is "For the Sake of Retrieval," in which three deep-sea explorers search for "the lost *Titanic* // and find instead, in the splayed beam of a headlamp, / silt fields, pale and singular, like the snow fields / of Newfoundland." Full of rich description, nonetheless the poem resists a precise grounding, just as the unearthly, changing seascape seems to the divers "filled with the music of Bach or Haydn" as well as with "boiler coal, / a footboard and platter." Bierds's poems seem both beautifully and perilously "awash" with shifting particulars.

Reading Bierds's poems is a treat of oddities, arcana, and assiduous learning. These stories derive mainly from historical figures of the nineteenth and early-twentieth centuries, as if Romantic adventurousness and Victorian gadgetry provide her with her most engaging scenes. Her characters are doers and makers, like Wilbur Wright in "The Wind Tunnel," who are driven to act out and test their theories or beliefs, who go eagerly "Head first in the grace" of experiments, dangers, and innovations. We discover much in these poems—about dance notation, music theory, tunneling under the Thames, prototype running machines ("bicycles without chains"), balloon flights, beekeeping, and so on. Bierds is not casual about her information or material, either. A reader might actually *learn* something here. For instance, again in "In the Beeyard":

> the orchard outside has slowly chilled,
> snow on the windbreak, deep snow on the hives
> in their black jackets. The honey is warm,
> and the hive walls, and the domes of bearded wheat straw
> tucked under tarpaper rooflines.
>
> To nurture this tropic climate, the bees
> have fashioned a plump wheel, clustered body to body
> on honey cells, chests clicking out a friction, a heat—
> faster, slower, in inverse proportion
> to the day's chill—while the hives
> keep a stable ninety degrees. . . .

And to complement her poems' absorbing content, Bierds's writing itself is typically distinctive, concentrated. In a single three-line sentence, describing the natural color of honey, Bierds demonstrates her fondness for tight alliteration, hyphenated phrasing, and extended lineation as well as her ability to make crisp imagery and a memorable voice:

> Clover-rich, lugged close to the thorax and twirring heart,
> wax-capped, extracted, the viscid liquid
> is not gold at all, but the color of cellophane, ice.

❖

Bierds's method derives most directly from Norman Dubie, I suspect. Not only sharing his curiosity for historical facts and a penchant for narrative tension, Bierds also shapes her poems in ways similar to his. She writes in long, uneven lines and equally uneven stanzas—creating a ragged, proselike density—and often applies enjambment to lines and stanzas alike. She doesn't rhyme or count beats, but her writing is nonetheless lyrical and marked by complex figuration. Her sentences are typically long, intricate, full of detail. Her poems are spoken in a voice which shares with Dubie's a notable, unselfish inquisitiveness. Given the remarkable range of subjects, characters, and incidents in her poems, in fact, I find it a little curious that Bierds doesn't do more to vary her poems' prosodic routines. So many unusual things happen to so many people in her work, yet the poems are formally similar, often close to the same length—approximately fifty lines— and with no especially compelling organic reasons for their comparable shapes or sizes. With more formal variety or technical pressure, Bierds might even better represent the richness of experience and understanding already so admirably embedded in her poems' content.

There are many ways to think, to *know*, in a poem. Pankey and Glück pursue a contemplative, introspective poetic, preferring the kind of understanding derived from compressing image into idea, by distilling experience into parable. Bierds chooses to dramatize the more particular, critical moments in the lives of others, so we might, for ourselves, determine how to invent, discover, create. All three poets bring to their work a decided and sustained thoughtfulness. Given their other differences, it must be especially significant that the quality all three of these gifted poets most admire is clarity. Beyond the clutter of imagery, beyond the mere "precision" of sensual awareness, these poets hunger for the kind of knowing which unites disparate impressions and moments into knowledge. Bierds's "Wanting Color" describes this clarity through Sergei Prokudin-Gorskii's early experiments with color photography. Both her poem and his experiment describe an act of synesthetic transformation, a vision and a music most clear:

> Wanting color, I have fashioned a spectrum box:
> three filters—cyan, magenta, yellow—

three shutter-clicks in the distance of a sneeze,

then three separations placed

over one another, like the notes of an A-chord,

and the world is as clear—focused—

as the crow to my left

troubling the hens for a pearl of grain.

Plainness and Sufficiency

The plain style is essentially a mode of religious discourse. William Bradford introduced his *Of Plimouth Plantation* by claiming the traits of humility, piety, and sincerity to be implicit in his "plaine stile, with singuler regard unto the simple trueth in all things." He represents a stern Separatist zeal for clarity, that direct touch from God which endows its recipient with the special "true" grace of the chosen, "as by the Scriptures we are plainely told." Indeed, in early America, to write *any* kind of poetry was to undermine the sincerity of plain and useful communication. One of the bases for Bradford's persecution of Thomas Morton (he of the fateful Maypole) was because Morton was a poet, proud to "*shew* his poetrie" and therefore prone to "haveing more craft then honestie." American poets ever since have sought to trade in the plain style for its obvious related effects: poetry in a plain style sounds genuine, unaffected, somehow more sincerely encountered and expressed than the artificial adornments of baroque styles, where in Pope's words, "True wit is nature to advantage dressed."

Let's make no mistake: the plain style *is* a discourse, rather than a "found" utterance or purified expression handed straight from the gods or from experience, and so we must regard it rhetorically, as a style as purposeful and contrived as the most ornate expression. The American lyric mode over the past thirty years has employed the plain style extensively, and it has come under attack lately because many poets forget that it is a rhetoric, not a natural expression or mode of pure experience. The popular first-person, anecdotal lyric has lately been troubled because its poets

On *Psalms* by April Bernard, Norton, 1993; *Incontinence* by Susan Hahn, Chicago, 1993; *Devolution of the Nude* by Lynne McMahon, Godine, 1993; *Erasures* by Donald Revell, Wesleyan/New England, 1992; *Apocalyptic Narrative* by Rodney Jones, Houghton Mifflin, 1993.

often seem to believe that sincerity, honesty, and experience are sufficient virtues in themselves, without the necessity of artistry or "craft." Hence, humility becomes simplicity, clarity becomes easiness, and rhetorical sincerity devolves into a desire to be liked. The lyric mode will survive and flourish if it is able to be adaptable, pliable, inclusive of elements from other poetic manners, absorbing the rhetorical suggestions of such modes as narrative poetry, speculative poetry, and dramatic poetry. My suspicion is that even now these subgenres are inadvertently providing for the invigoration of the lyric.

Of the five writers addressed here, April Bernard clearly approaches the most pure lyric stance in her second book of poems, *Psalms*. Not just her title but many of her book's other elements—its rhetoric, forms, and imagery—suggest a religious sensibility limned with the plain style of a faithful revenant. Except for the book's last piece, a ten-part prose meditation titled "Lamentations and Praises," each of the book's thirty poems features "psalm" in its title. Bernard's poems seem elemental, ancient, impersonal:

> Today the prayer came like blood upon my lips:
> Give me courage not to hate,
> Take the sweet taste from the violent thought,
> Give me charity for my stammering heart,
> And let me on your wind pass one dreamless night.

These beseeching lines from "Psalm of the Wind-Dweller" demonstrate the rhetorical character of Bernard's method. The "give and take" of these supplications suggests a litany or the formal repetitions of prayer, and the archaic "upon" connects further with the dignified conventions of religious discourse, as does the syntactic inversion of "on your wind."

The speaker of *Psalms* is a wanderer, a pilgrim ranging over unfamiliar wastelands. As in "Psalm of the Sleeping," Bernard's traveler is faced with alien landscapes as well as with nebulous relationships:

> Here catastrophes of grey, high ceilings of grey, the sky flying away
> on great wings of grey, receding
>
> As still the low, muffled mist of water trundles in

Once there was a woman who just kept walking, head down,
though she lifted it long enough to tilt Minoan eyes
and we moved, suddenly, as if to follow.

One of Bernard's most chilling effects derives from haunting scenes such as this. Her searcher seems willing to undertake dangerous journeys and to make perilous contacts in order to gain spiritual insight, much like a mythic hero facing the gods' challenges in the underworld. Some of her prayers, with the purity of song, demonstrate the speaker's trepidation in undertaking her pilgrimage ("If I wandered with bloody feet on this bitter night / and asked for God, / I would be afraid to find him"). Elsewhere her entreaties bespeak a darkened, severe humility, her desire to be humbled ("Come down upon me now, O wrath implicit in that wall of black"), and they show her abiding, faithful posture ("I find myself permanently in an attitude / of supplication and gratitude, haunched upon this new world"). The images drawn in these poems are, like W. S. Merwin's in *The Lice,* ghostly, primitive, fundamental as water, stone, and earth, and like Merwin's they are both disturbing and familiar, as if remnants from a prior time, archetypal, charged with spiritual resonance.

But "this new world" that she mentions in "Psalm of the Historian" also refers to the compelling, denser second layer of Bernard's poetic landscape. Alongside or, like a palimpsest, atop her archaic and hieratic scene is another one—companion, concurrent, and contemporary. Bernard ironizes the reverent plainness of her poems by this developing, modern locus:

Why does the man on the radio play only strings today?
Sawing away on geometry puzzles, as if c
sat up straight between c sharp and b natural.

Why is every crooked smile held dear,
every half-devil on the street welcome to my kiss?

O villains, O violins, net me about like a caught fish
Hold me in the wash of the sound, trail me in your wake

Always already I am drowned
in the cold and salt of all I have left undone

Here in "Psalm on the Eve," as elsewhere, contemporary elements antagonize Bernard's soulful "prior" details, as the plain, beseeching rhetoric of the prayer tangles with idiom and slang. Bernard identifies the usually repressed doubleness of her method in the mournful "Always already," as she translates the Poststructuralist *toujour déjà*. The condition of being here *and* there—and consequently *neither* here nor there—provides the dominant desire and repercussion of *Psalms*. For both the pilgrim in her search for God and the poet in her wish for pure or originary language, this predicament results in an eternal deferral of any contact with the ideal. Something has "always already" preceded any attempt to locate the "first cause"; the world changes even as she tries, as in "Praise Psalm for the City Dweller":

> See how the young men of the city weep and fall upon
>   one another's
> shoulders, see how they turn their shining faces away
>   from us who stand
> encumbered by the changing sky

Like the psalms of the King James Bible, like Whitman's spiritual verse, Bernard's poems often employ a long, proselike line whose rhythm is nonmetric but incantatory. Her phrasing, however, is more tight, obsessive—her method more associative and highly elliptical. Her voice is an impersonal echo of ancient scripts, and yet it bears a hip, ironic currency: "There is no God, Mohammed is his last prophet, and my car / is a lozenge of salt," she laments in "Psalm of a Dark Day." Besides Merwin, the Psalms, and Whitman, I can detect in Bernard's work the severe, elemental demands of Louise Glück and the mercurial anxieties of John Ashbery. *Psalms* is only her second book of poems, and it is, I think, best read as a whole; it's got a chilling, cumulative quality. Separately, some of these poems may be cryptic or fragmentary. Even still, I am convinced of Bernard's considerable skill and engaged by her original, demanding vision. Hers is an ancient, spiritual search in an urban and profane world. That's her magic—the faithful one's agony—that each moment of our lives bears the remnants of its own history, at once focusing, vanishing, evolving. In place of hope or salvation, as here in "Song for the Bereft," she urges herself finally to embrace and even adore the evasive nature of things as the most constant circumstance of our lives:

It seems we are all looking for another
to have and hold and lose once more.
Loss proves you once had.
And who could discard that thin blanket,
raggedy wool chewed up with holes, useless against the wind,
but which you clutch to your breast like salvation itself?

Susan Hahn's *Incontinence,* also a second book, approaches an equally severe lyricism. Like Bernard she represents a kind of latter-day Romanticism in the scheme of her poetic. But where Bernard directs her lamentations and psalms to the spiritual world, trying to divine its absented origins, Susan Hahn probes the corporal ailments of a physical existence that is equally beset and aggrieved. To her the body's condition may be taken as a symbol of the spirit's well-being or discomfort, and in this she seems to take some of her method from the Confessional poets. Her confessions, however, are almost entirely bodily, presenting a pathology of illnesses, expulsions, and diseases. This is not a poetry for the weak of heart. The pure directness of her style results in a continual blunt confrontation with the tortures of body and, hence, of mind:

Gnarled hairs, one after another,
are enough to yank.
I don't require a hank
to feel my head a bruise
to pamper. Doctor, sometimes
I dream I snip
my nipples with manicuring
scissors. I let my husband use his
tongue to ruin each

thing I say to him,
while I pretend it doesn't matter.
You say I need a brain scan
to discover what is wrong
but I'd rather keep these thoughts
between me and my pen and paper. . . .

These lines from "Masochism" characterize the strident world in *Incontinence*. Extremely personal, often painful, occasionally grotesque, Hahn's poems mediate between corporal diseases and the dis-eased extremes inherent in our loves, our madnesses, and our smaller daily fevers. Her lineation reminds me of Sharon Olds's purposeful, ragged, "humble" techniques, but Hahn establishes a further layer of obsessiveness through her tight, bedeviled recurrences of sound. The uneven iambics seem pulse-like, perhaps a little bit mad, and the frequent internal rhymes ("hair," "after," "another"; "hank" and "yank"; "snip," "nipples"; "scissor," "matter," "discover," and "paper") begin to haunt the reader like a whispered mania.

Hahn doesn't present these poems, though, as the personal diaries of a psychopath or hypochondriac. Rather, as "Virgin" demonstrates, her intimate exposures are raids into the poetic—rather than finally the medical—domain:

> Before the trespass
> of ink no eraser can scratch out,
> before the race to command
> impossible stanzas and the dream
> of rhythms . . .
>
> > before you and I
>
> and any knowledge
> that we would ever be
> read about, page and pen
> were at peace; before
> the arrow arched
> into the bull's-eye of the unspoiled
> place, this sweet tissue
> remained unmarked.

Stitching together tropes about writing and technique, as well as hunting and the loss of sexual innocence, she marks and exploits the body with surgical precision in order to explore the peripheries of the personal lyric. She wants to take poetry to the most tangible and sensual extremes. It's often uncomfortable and yet as often results in a poetry of generous, piercing honesty, as if (to rewrite Bradford) it's by the *body* we are "plainly told."

Another result of Hahn's method is the distinctive relationship between speaker and reader. The speaker is ever aware of her own presentation. Like dramatic monologues exposing secrets to the audience, the poems are a deliberate performance of ills, positioned alternately as surgeon, patient, the experimented-upon, and the willing case study:

> The metamorphosis of the flea
> from harmless egg to adult
> and its hunt for a host
> remind me of us. How I craved
>
> the inflammation—the fierce dream
> of the piercing. I can count the times
> I ripped down past the surface
> of myself.

We're invited to examine the discomfitures of the body as we would the machinations of a metafictional text. So, despite the "sick heart," the "broken fine bones / of [the] soul," "the oozing crust that surrounds" the infected spirit, our considerable pleasure derives in part from our heightened awareness of the artifice of this poeticized body, both *corpus* and corpse.

April Bernard doubles her poetry's effect by pitting the elemental and organic against the urban and ironic. Hahn as well is able to complicate her stance by similar means. She follows and praises the cyclical nature of the seasons—February with its "odor of heavy winter / coats, red bleeding hearts" or Indian summer when "I cool, then rise to the heat / again, to the candlelit sun"—and the similar recurrences of the body with its "pageant[s] of blood," marking menstruation, and its absences of blood, signifying pregnancy and menopause, when even "the pen [has] nothing to bleed." But the body of Hahn's work, like Bernard's, is also transitory. We measure our lives by seasons and cycles, but we must nurture these lives by artifice and deviation, by kidney dialysis where "artery and vein / connect," by surgeries where "my torn /paper gown [becomes] privacy's poor / joke," by transplanted organs where, at least, we may feel "the strength of the ways / we are all attached." The balance between nature and artifice, between the "pure" ancient world of the spirit and the harrowing modern situation, becomes precarious but necessary as a means for our continuation and our practical salvation. Poetry for Susan Hahn is a monitor to help us maintain our systems of good health and right minds.

April Bernard and Susan Hahn both describe two poles of the plain style—from the highly spiritual to the ironic—with subjects ranging from the imperiled conditions of the contemporary soul to the infirmities of the contemporary body. Lynne McMahon's lyric tactics are far less pure, less intensely private. The work in *Devolution of the Nude,* her second book, is more akin to songs of praise than to the lament or the complaint and more hopeful of the durable possibilities of joy. I detect the clear-spiritedness of Elizabeth Bishop in McMahon's work and, even more, the rich, knobby, densely textured discernments of Marianne Moore, who figures prominently in several of these poems, both for her slightly obsolete decorum ("And though we may laugh at Marianne / Moore's remark—'I like the nude,' she said, / handing back Kenneth Clark's book, 'but / *in moderation*'—it is us / we find / swathed in bedclothes," McMahon writes in her title poem) and for her distinctive, vivid ingenuity, "her wildness of language, even at the absurd level of automobiles," as McMahon calls it in "Utopian Turtletop":

> The car was finally named Edsel,
>   Turtletop being perhaps too diffident, and Utopian
>   unrealizable, and therefore expensive,
>   and a gracious Marianne Moore
>
>   conceded to a gallant Henry Ford.

McMahon's lyric style is, like Moore's, not plain, not stripped to its essentials, but densely figured. There are few direct allusions or extended conceits in Bernard's and Hahn's new books, but McMahon often turns to these devices to provide coherence and shape for her busy poems. Shelley, Hopkins, Whitman, Odysseus, Byron, the Brontes, and Mrs. Gaskell are among the many literary figures who visit these poems. McMahon's use of figuration is neither highbrow nor off-putting. Rather, her impressive proclivity for allusions provides a common and practical, if well-educated, grounding. The title of "Reading Virgil" leads directly into the opening lines:

> From this ledge of sun where I sit, black shirt burning,
>> looking up sometimes into the wells
> of dark the living room preserves, I can see
>> how the venetian lights,
> striping the floor, hinge a passageway from this world
>> to the next
> where *The Georgics* instructs the sill's terrarium
>> in seed-time and in flower.
> How easily my guide telescopes into the dwarfed
>> dimension. . . .

The playful doubleness of these details—the "venetian" blinds, the nearby hovering "shades," a journey to the other world (Hades? the window *terra*rium?)—enriches this poem whose speaker imagines herself, like a new-age Dante, guided by Virgil through the perilous dominions of television, where a "cardiac evangelist" preaches the salvations of vegetarianism. "If you can't / be a vegetarian . . . then eat the vegetarians / of the sea—clams, oysters, scallops," he proclaims. Yet McMahon's speaker worries, aware of the contaminants threatening even the "purest" of foods, and cites the poem's mentor:

> But those
>> opalescent mouthfuls
> wobble against the tongue like sheeps' eyes in Virgil,
>> swollen with plague and death to eat.
> "As storm-squalls run across the surface of the sea
>> Disease comes, not killing sheep singly."

This poem also indicates the second of McMahon's extended frames of reference—popular culture. *Devolution of the Nude* offers an invigorating, cheering mediation between elements of high "art" culture and the icons of kitsch and commonness. Though, as she claims in "Little Elegy for the Age," "We've sworn off nostalgia / this time for good, no more recounting the sixties / and those astronaut hairdos giving way to a wilderness / of plaits and frizz and blond Marianne Faithfull falls," it's also true that these poems situate us by means of our highest as well as our lowest forms of play, tossing Elvis, cool sunglasses, and Barbie's Ferrari into the same toybox with Dante and Randall Jarrell. This is another means by which McMahon complicates the conventional territories of the lyric. In a mode whose purest tendency is to step away from worldly or crude matters, essentially to stop time altogether in a binding lyric instant, McMahon compounds that instant with the artifacts of domestic life—the convenient, the synthetic, the sentimental—to connect the past and the current and finally to argue against the hierarchic values of high and low. In "Artifact" a lost plastic nipple is rediscovered during the speaker's packing to move, and while it is "artificial, / lint-wrapped from its long hiding, / and bug-traveled," it inspires McMahon's wonderfully connective imagination to invoke Freud's object lesson in mother-substitution, Wordsworth's intimate vanishings ("unlatching // the mother from her child, the child / from his unconscious"), and even "Napoleon, falling again and again at Josephine's breast." It's a delight in poem after poem to follow McMahon's surprising, inventive designs, at once fabular and familiar.

Her final revision of lyric purity stems from McMahon's subtle narrative strategies. Not that she's a narrative poet, following the strictures of chronological order and overt plot development, but rather she veers from the more static lyric instant by overlapping scenes, times, and actions. There is narrative coherence to her poems. This is partly the result, I think, of the many figurative connections that her poems make, but also of her desire to unite aspects of history—literary, cultural, and familial. McMahon weaves devoted and poignant chronicles of the domestic fable, from her speaker's current situation as an adult, a wife, and a mother back to her own childhood, as in "My South":

> Look at Mrs. Austin,
> my mother would say whenever we whined for something
> we couldn't afford,
> To Mrs. Austin a bottle of Pepsi *whenever she wants it*
> is wealth. . . .

> it's surprising how clearly
>   I can still summon
> the picture of that woman and her garage, how Pepsi,
>   even after thirty years,
> has the power to provoke in me a twinge,
>   not of pathos,
> exactly, or nostalgia, but something like historical
>   consciousness. . . .

Like Moore, McMahon is proficient at constructing formal textures to correspond to her layers of reference, story, and figure. By all of these means—technical and thematic, allusive and commonplace—Lynne McMahon's *Devolution of the Nude* is an invigorated, important variety of the lyric mode.

Erasures, Donald Revell's fourth book of poems, continues his movement away from the traditional lyric poem toward a more transgressive, politicized lyric matrix. His lyric is now the lyric of history, of critique, of Postmodern politics. Like Susan Howe's or Charles Bernsteins's Language texts, Revell's new collection explores the wilderness of American history, its connections as well as its rips, absences, and superimpositions. Revell is important for his linkage of a mainstream lyric style with the sensibility of the experimental, subversive, purposefully marginal Language text. His new poetry is difficult, but not unreadable as Howe's sometimes is; it's politically acute but not prosaic or pedantic as Bernstein's can be. He's as associative as Ashbery, as inventive as Creeley, but he is his own poet, original and solemn.

Erasures is driven by a deliberate, sustained paradox. The book's primary tone and stance is anxious, its rhetorical designs most closely related to the jeremiad. Revell's fear and warning is that history's powerful imperialism will obliterate the distinctions of the ordinary, the peace of the tolerant, that it will redetermine itself in behalf of the brandishments of power. In "The Next War," Revell envisions this frightening future:

> When it is tired, when there is no music,
> history turns to its extremes, rehearses

the scene of the dagger, murder in a room

with no exit, locked from the inside. . . .

Racial and ethnic strife are as we taught them.

We rehearsed our enemies,

our hands buried up to the wrists in them.

The words they use will be familiar.

Their bodies will be young, transparent

inexhaustible choreography

when there is no music, locked from the inside.

Despite this fear of erasure, of totalitarian mastery, Revell incorporates a number of stylistic absences and dissociations in the poems themselves. Hence the body of his poetry becomes both gathering place and battleground, where the dissensions between history and vacancy, and between meaning and oppression, are enacted.

In Michael Wigglesworth's "Day of Doom," first printed in 1662, and in Cotton Mather's late-century, shrill premonitions of ruin, the American imagination found its first vital voices of alarm and revival; the Puritan Great Awakening would conclude in the mid-1700s with Jonathan Edwards's powerful but finally obsolete sermons. Puritanism failed because it refused to move—a fatal fact, given the stronger American tendency to explore, exploit, and enjoy. But this early period provides Revell with an allusive richness; it's one of his recurring models:

. . . I name a city under my breath, feeling

its cold altars retrograde inside me.

Jerusalem. The Pilgrim ziggurat

taller than history and greeny now

like a woman above her sex and crowned

with aspirations that are all flowers.

In "An Episode of the Great Awakening in New England," the archaic Separatist tower recalls John Winthrop's vision of a "Citty on a Hill," but now it is overgrown with Modernist richness (here in the allusion to William Carlos Williams's wild asphodel) and with the larger sensual forgetfulness of nature. But of course these seasonal, born-again promises also naively prefigure their own decay. The speaker sees in this paradigm the potential for his own spiritual blight. His doubts about "election" are not Puritan but political, exposed on the Calvary cross, "the high places" of urban expansion:

> The revivalist finds his driveway in the dusk.
> I love that man. His doubts are my doubts.
> Am I elected to only one life
> or is there a flower without watchfulness
> beautiful to everlasting
> in recombinant cities warm as summer?
> Can I live beyond the prices that I pay
> out of my heart to the upward circuitry
> of the New Jerusalem's ziggurat?
> Exposed on the high places for delight,
> the spring's revival sees into the valleys,
> forsythia, dogwood and early apple
> seeing the vanguard of a great darkness.

In Revell's poetry the rhetoric of the religious jeremiad is intensified by the discourse of politics, economics, and social anthropology. The lyric moment is made ironic by its position within a larger cultural matrix. The forces at work on the individual imagination are devastating: the inanities of mass communications threaten our solitude and sanity; the ever-watchful eye of government sees into our erotic and imaginative privacies; nature is distorted into an emblem of materialism, of advertising jingles; and the innocent brutes of the future expel us from our own lives, as in "The Deposed":

> They come to power tomorrow.
> By the unpated hulk, behind a rail,
> beneath a bulb, their rostrums
> come to power tomorrow
> when sky no longer recites the sky
> but rates of exchange and blue anthems.

The weight of these subjects and the catastrophic power of their collisions provide the gravity and complexity of Revell's method. These poems are (all but one) only a page or two pages long, and yet they witness the contemporary world—the threats of domination; the rise of surveillance; the loss of solitude, of eros, of safety, the post–Cold War angst—with a seriousness that seems more like Kundera and Camus than the common lyric.

The accruing pressure of this book is its strength. As with Bernard's *Psalms* and Hahn's *Incontinence,* I believe *Erasures* is best read as a cohering document rather than a separable miscellany. Taken together, these poems best demonstrate Revell's method. We can hear the cacophony of machinery, of dread, of chaos amid the poems' forceful demands for integrity. The dissonance of the poems gathers strength in numbers. What appears as a surreal dislocation in a single poem is, recurringly, a powerful and purposeful association: "His voice is a perfume / sprayed into shafts of sunlight, a smell / of flowers burning too fast. . . ." The ominous synesthesia of this early poem, "Jeremiah," is compounded into a further, political composite in "Last":

> The unsigned architecture of loneliness
>
> is becoming taller, finding a way farther
>
> above the horizontal flowering
>
> of the Cold War, the peonies
>
> and star asters of wild partisanship.

In fact, while *Erasures* may seem at first dissociative, its ultimate impact is direct and clear. Its syntax and voicings are surprisingly close to the plain style. A simple extrapolation might find that the theological doubts and sufferings so "plainly told" by the late Puritans have transfigured into the late-day political alarms of Revell's work. He can be as clearly aphoristic, can deploy language as mnemonic and plain, as Edwards or Wigglesworth (or Franklin or Thoreau, for that matter), as in these lines from three different poems: "Faith chokes the world with his memorials. / Unbelief chokes the world with his nakedness"; "Who rejuvenates the martyrs / rejuvenates the tyrants. / Best governs who least grieves"; and "The romance of every ideology / torments the romance of another." The stern and shattered vision of these poems and Revell's occasional use of prose as coun-

terpoint to his poems' conventional lineation are formalized by his unam-
biguous syntax and by his frequently conventional use of decasyllabic blank
verse. *Erasures* is not about erasure but memory—about the intense pres-
sures put to bear on the contemporary spirit and the capacity of the lyric
poem to contain and resist the damages done to us in the name of power.
Erasures is an awakening.

Rodney Jones writes like nobody's business. And, given the parameters
of this particular essay, he writes on a vector whose destination is far from
the plain style. He often strays a good distance from the traditional lyric mode
itself. *Apocalyptic Narrative* is a full-blooded collection of thirty-two grandly
realized poems, many of whose strengths seem like combinations of the
achievements of the previous books—the textural pleasures of McMahon,
the perilous warnings of Bernard and Revell, the corporal gravities of Hahn.
Apocalyptic Narrative also takes as its campaign to articulate a sense of *fin de
siècle* peril. With warnings and oaths, Jones is acute in his observations of
worldly politics, as in "Fun in El Salvador" or "A Story of the South Pacific,"
but just as canny about local decline, as in "Progress Alley":

> How did I miss this isthmus of old bricks between the Shelter Workshop
>   and the Dominion Bank,
> This bumpy lane, not even a street now, but pot-holed and tar-streaked
>   and smeared with the indiscriminate droppings of pigeons?

But even amid the "festering [of] some old rage," there is also something
wonderfully, deliberately enjoyable about Jones's style—it's here in the rich
invention, energy, and detail of these poems. Whatever his other, occasional
positions or triggers, Rodney Jones's abiding theme is poetry itself: "Not
the song, but the humming after the song, / The barrier, the quiet knowl-
edge, called for and unspoken." And the breadth of his attention is as wide
as any poet's currently writing—from songs of play and praise (for his new-
born son; for "the Beatles, W. C. Fields, and Bessie Smith"; for "my love,
my mother, my one daughter, my song") to the most wrenching laments
for the indigent, the hungry, the overlooked.

Jones's sympathy, his intelligent wholeheartedness, is one of his most
remarkable gifts, as his fascination with the lyric frame—flexible, adaptable
—is his most prevalent concern. His spirited experiments with the lyric

mode may account for the variety of his poems, their abundance, their leaps, their "unbreakable" grasp. He titles this book a "narrative" but seldom abides by the demands of plot, chronological sequence, or full character development. Whatever narrative elements Jones employs, he undermines them with the paradox of his title's other word: if the lyric's impulse is to step outside of time, then an apocalypse is a terrifyingly appropriate occasion to dramatize a lyric stoppage, where continuity is sabotaged by cataclysm. Jones tells stories, but in fits and starts and always in the service of a meditative incentive.

In his book's most fully narrative poem, "The Bridge," he opens with a dramatic episode in a style reminiscent of James Dickey, as he describes

> a small man
> I knew in high school, who, seeing an accident,
> Stopped one day, leapt over a mangled guardrail,
> Took a mother and two children from a flooded creek,
> And lifted them back to the world. In the dark,
> I do not know, there is no saying, but he pulled
> Them each up a tree, which was not the tree of life
> But a stooped Alabama willow, flew three times
> From the edge of that narrow bridge as though
> From the selfless shore of a miracle, and came back
> To the false name of a real man, Arthur Peavahouse.

Jones instantly turns the poem away from a straight narrative toward a denser, speculative complication. In the passage above, his dramatic additions ("I do not know, there is no saying," "which was not the tree of life," "the selfless shore of a miracle") announce the more complex focus of the poem, a drama clearly beyond the story's drama. Jones strips away the plain reality of the narrative by a series of negations: "These fulsome nouns . . . Are not real"; "There is no name for that place"; "the creek is not real and the valley is a valley of words." We see it's not a "real" story that Jones wants us to "believe" but the deeper grief of the lyric—its artifice, its "unreality"—whose own swirling movement is suggested by the "roiling water" where the family's third child must remain "Shrugged . . . in the unbreakable harness." "Arthur Peavahouse" could not save the last child, and the reality of his heroism is ruined by this ultimate failure. The speaker articulates a further collapse ("Many times I have thought everything I have said / Or thought was a lie, moving some blame or credit / By changing a name") and thus truly names the paradox underlying all of *Apocalyptic Narrative*—that our history, our lives, and our language are better described as a field of ruptures, dissociations, and misrepresentations than as a linear or narrative continuum.

Jones complicates his lyrics by narrative inclusions. But he turns as frequently to the rhetoric of drama, of social oratory, as in the long-lined manner of C. K. Williams or a good preacher; he exposes his own rhetorical tactics as piercingly as Jorie Graham; he sings as freely as Gerald Stern, and is as mournful, as faithful, as exuberantly additive; and he *thinks* with a transparent mixture of detail and intelligent abstraction, as in his long, tender poem "The Privacy of Women," arguing that "the age of men has passed":

> So much of the prose of duty
> Has us scrawled in the margins: slow nights at the shipping docks,
> I thought of Lawrence,
>
> his star-crossed, improbable, symbolic lovers—
> They are not our story,
>
> who burn briefly in that moment
> That is shipwreck and rescue.
>
> I was not chosen for any loveliness
> But chose loveliness.

His vision and technique are more than large enough to contain these methods and still be his own. Who else could be so ingenious and so blasted at once? Consider these lines from "Fun in El Salvador," as the speaker finds himself working in Salvadoran cotton fields after "twenty years jabbering in schools":

> Behind us, stolid as Job, lovelier than Montana,
> The rivulets of the sleeping volcanoes
> Hung like the pleats of drawn curtains.
>
> I suppose that just behind there, behind the coffee,
> Bitter and innocent children were hurting each other

With all manner of weaponry.

On hundreds of channels and in thousands of periodicals

The week before, no more than thirty kilometers to the southeast,

Drunk *guerilleros* or government soldiers

Drove out into a pasture with bazookas

And took out twenty-one imperialist or insurrectionist cows,

Depending on which reports one believes.

The hard humor of these lines keeps at bay, barely, the terrible approaches of brutality, the constant knowledge of calamity and pain. Jones's equally constant awareness of his own position in the history of these poems is an essential ingredient in their shrewd, sinuous rhetoric. In "Romance of the Poor," for instance, he admits his exploitation of the "poor people in Springfield [who] go to Dayton to be miserable in style." His usurpation of their plights is necessary to the making of this poem, but he realizes that their lives are not improved by the poem he writes:

Tonight the steaks frown up at me through the odor of blood,

And the poor need no help from poems to limp down the alley

    and up into the van.

They glide to Dayton. They check in to the Club St. Vincent de Paul.

Whatever it is, it is not much that makes a man more

    than a scrap of paper

Torn out of a notebook and thrown from the window of a bus,

    but it is more than nothing.

If he holds himself straight up and does not take the life

Next to his own, give him that much. Leave him to his joy.

Give him that much and more. Writing like this is, well, like magic. Rodney Jones's subject seems to be everything—what it means to be fully, vibrantly alive in this world—though his compulsion is finally not so much to make a point as to make a poem. And he is one of the best, most generous, and most brilliantly readable poets currently making poems in America. His chronicles are both widely cultural and deeply personal, capturing the torpors of contemporary America alongside the agonies and blessings of a single mind's will to create. In addition to the poems discussed here, I believe many others in this collection ought to achieve the stature of small masterpieces—"Contempt," "Grand Projection," "Ecology of Heaven," and "Speaking Up" among them. From the example of Jones and the four other poets discussed here, I cannot help feeling encouraged to believe that the lyric mode is far healthier, more vital, more fully engaged than many would have us believe. It plainly suffices, in all its varieties, as one of our most accurate monitors of the state of our well-being—and of the threats thereto.

Line by Line

A poem's inexorable bearing is downward, to the bottom of the page, to its end, to stillness. Prose is more languid, drifting laterally, with leisure, nudged downward only by a right-hand margin. It spreads like water over wide earth, looking for small cracks. A poem is a waterfall, tumbling. But to defer or delay its downward-falling fate, a poem may construct and then usurp any number of impediments—from lengthened or heavily end-stopped lines, stanza breaks, and rhyme to the more rhetorical techniques of meditation, speculation, or song. The story, we know, the narrative, is already written in the poem's descent.

Rough and uneven, the poems in Donna Masini's first book, *That Kind of Danger,* often prefer a rather dramatic velocity downward. Impatient, unstopped, they hurry like the clamorous, fast locale of their most frequent setting, New York City. In "Nightscape" the speaker's wired insomnia provides an effective narrative cause to connect with the city's exposed nerve ends, its incessant speed: "It's not only my lights that hum in this city / through the arc of night / at two a.m. when I'm up again, waiting." With a broadening sweep from the vantage point of her window, she extends the poem's reference in all directions, upward, outward, downward:

> Upstairs a man knocks his wife to the floor,
>
> drunk again, no light in her
>
> but the heat of their angers spark and fall
>
> to the windows below.
>
> Under nodding streetlights junkies trade shoot waste,

On *That Kind of Danger* by Donna Masini, Beacon, 1994; *Fresh Peaches, Fireworks, & Guns* by Donald Platt, Purdue, 1994; *The Tulip Sacrament* by 'Annah Sobelman, Wesleyan/New England, 1995; *Orders of Affection* by Arthur Smith, Carnegie-Mellon, 1996; *Rough Music* by Deborah Digges, Knopf, 1995; *Worldling* by Elizabeth Spires, Norton, 1995.

> the Chinese waiter pees in the lot,
>
> the taxi driver lights a cigarette, waits for his fare,
>
> the policeman slams his car door, runs for a beer.

Effectively, the shorter and unstopped lines of this passage suggest the sudden, fateful violence of the adjacent domestic scene, and then the longer, end-stopped lines allow the speaker's perspective to extend and to collect a widening catalogue of other "rootless insomniacs," until it seems to the speaker—and reader—that no one is sleeping in the rowdy city. Masini's ambitious pacing often appropriately results in this kind of narrative hurry, but it can also indicate hasty composition. The verbs "spark" and "fall" in the third line above ought to agree with the clause's subject "heat," not "angers," the object in a prepositional phrase, and the phrase "trade shoot waste" is awkward at best, since each of these three words could be any number of parts of speech. Still, the speaker continues with forceful momentum, "chew[ing] the cords of [her] own unraveling hungers," to achieve a further connection within the cityscape of raw nerves. In the poem's final figure, she gathers these many people, this noisy, widened urban scene, back into the domestic, "as though night itself were a big house."

That Kind of Danger is Donna Masini's first book, winner of the Barnard New Women Poets Prize. This poet has an admirable, spirited skill, the ability to capture by turns the energy and momentum of the city and then to examine the tender yet also the often troubling mysteries of the family fable. This is the other, complicating side to Masini's poetic, in which the crashing city is balanced by a compassionate sense of belonging wrought from the speaker's familial relationships: with the husband in the lovely "For My Husband Sleeping Alone," "a gentle man, a man who could fall / in love with a difficult woman"; with the mother in the remarkably complex "My Mother Makes Me a Geisha Girl," who "works me over, licks / the tip of the Maybelline liner, marks / a black arch across my brow, adding / the years, filling in what she knows / should be there"; and with many more—sister, grandmother, relatives, neighbors galore. Often Masini's family poems bear a formal composure, the lines spreading wider or stopped with closed phrases and punctuation, more stanzas to defer the tumble downward, to permit more chance for meditative deliberation.

These are the tactics of such strong poems as "Today for the First Time I Listen" or "Girl, Gingerpot, Tree." Masini can write well in both situations —the speedy, rambunctious urban narrative or the more intimate family lyric—though sometimes she succumbs to a predictability in her treatment of subjects and in the forms she uses to treat those subjects. She is better at rendering description and impression than circumspection or idea. Sometimes, too, she flashes her influences rather obviously, as in "What Drives Her," where the stamp of Sharon Olds shows in "She knows if she can / get to the, / just to the, / just to the, oh / she is everyone. . . ." I wonder whether these problems might have been lessened or eliminated by a more judicious selection of poems, cutting the less effective or overlapping instances from this sizeable book. What I find most original in *That Kind of Danger* are the occasions when Masini resists the expected—the rush and sprawl of the city, the private clarities of family—and arrives at more formal irony or surprise in her work.

"When I Understood" is such an example, an intimate poem in which the speaker's mother "could not name the place" where her cancer is growing, "*down there.*" Here Masini presses the poem itself powerfully downward, as if to contradict the speaker's own desire—the desire, of course, to make time stand still, "to go back," and thereby to postpone or even eliminate the growth of the mother's tumor. What she wants, to heal her mother, is in direct tension with what she says:

> When I understood my mother
> might have something in her
> *down there*—she could not name the place—
> *growth*—she could not say the word—
> it is growth, after all, she fears
> (how she must hate the way
> her plants grow from their roots out,
> pushing against the windows,
> their flat heads pressing to leave)
> when I understood I felt her
> at the other end of the phone. . . .

This first sentence continues for another twelve lines. Masini extends her imagery, too, for these plants pushing outward prefigure Masini's other subsequent details of growth—nature's flower, the mother's cancer, the speaker herself who knows she was her mother's first "blood and tumor" as a growing fetus: all of them unstoppable. Fewer than a third of these forty-three lines are themselves end-stopped. The whole poem is one unstopped stanza. The long, complex sentences unwind with unyielding speed, so fast they seem to stutter, revising themselves, adding on. Neither poem nor nature can be held in check, though the speaker tries to imagine them so. Masini borrows the intense pace of her city poems to dramatize this striking personal crisis. In this moment and in other such poems in *That Kind of Danger*—by turns horrible, erotic, passionate—Masini's best work finds its fulfilling utterance.

Donald Platt offers us an even more pronounced variety of tempos in his first book, winner of Purdue's Verna Emery Poetry Prize. *Fresh Peaches, Fireworks, & Guns* finds much of its narrative where Masini found hers, in family correspondences juxtaposed with wider cultural involvements. Platt extends the linear techniques that Masini exploits as well, writing sometimes in even longer lines, sometimes in even shorter lines, often using caesuras and indentations to discover the appropriate, revealing pace for his work. Part of this variety is adventurousness, I suspect, and part is apprenticeship, a search for his most effective style. He knows the effect of the slender, heavily enjambed poem, and in "Kaaterskill Falls" employs the trope of falling water, spilling music, and erotic passion to demonstrate that technique in (mostly) two-beat lines:

> Love, our bodies
> are spring runoff
> hustling down
> a thawed streambed
> pouring over
> bald boulders, riff
> of white water
> like fingers among
> sixteenth notes. . . .

This poem—this single sentence—continues for forty more lines, only three of which conclude in punctuation. It's a breathless rush of gravity and passion, like the quick movement of hands over a keyboard, toward the water's "applause" against the "still stones" at the end of the fall.

"Kaaterskill Falls" is a skillful enough poem, though its occasion and its metaphoric realizations are finally rather familiar. In fact, I can usually estimate the larger successes in *Fresh Peaches, Fireworks, & Guns* according to the length of their lines and/or shape of their stanzas. Platt is at his most inventive and dauntless in poems of longer lines and shorter stanzas rather than in poems of shorter lines and longer stanzas. Most of the poems abiding by this second strategy are located in the middle of the book, and most of these are family narratives, anecdotal, confessional, rural, tender, but not altogether remarkable in their discoveries or rendering: "Grandmother's Quilt," "Short Mass for My Grandfather," or the sequential "Everything We Wore," which features, again, eight poems deriving from childhood and adolescence. If this were all that *Fresh Peaches* offered, I might still find this a relatively admirable first book—throughout, Platt is a careful, passionate lyricist—but richer in promise than actuality.

But Platt's more powerful skill finds its fullest expression in the book's initial and concluding poems. The title poem, "Aria for This Listening Area," "Kore," "High Fidelity," and "Welcome Hardings' Clocks & Music Boxes" are among the best poems I've read lately in a first book. In each of these cases Platt has developed a line and stanza of considerable tension, slower, more probing, composed either of long, unfolding lines or short but shattered ones. Here he complicates the kinds of awarenesses his family poems proffer:

>   Language, not
> geography,
>   is where we live.
> Tennessee's
>   a way of talking.
> I listen for
>   the idioms
> that mean I'm home.

The dismantling or frustrating of the tidy line corresponds to Platt's narrative disruption as well, for he has learned that language, not locale, is the poet's residence. In his best poems, curiosity replaces nostalgia or comfort. Later in "Aria for This Listening Area," as if revising the simpler treatment of falling water in "Kaaterskill Falls," he asks: "is speech more / a river that loves / switching beds / in a flash flood?"

In his best poems, too, Platt's voice seems larger, more spacious, ranging from witty good humor to speculative social critique. He is able, in the title poem, to navigate in just a few lines from the intricacies of "the dissonant opening bars of [Mozart's] string quartet / in C major" to "the roadside sign / I saw on Rt. 29: // Fresh Peaches, Fireworks, & Guns." This strong poem shows Platt at his finest. He discloses the primary aspect of his technique, additive and aural, as he listens for a "a different kind of order, // the same principle / of musical composition" that drives the surprising twists and inclusions of great music as well as the cacophonous order of the roadside stand. In "High Fidelity," for instance, he listens as hard for Glenn Gould's humming and grunting, in a kind of deep structure beneath the music, as he does to the "glitter of arpeggios" of Gould's Bach performance. And in "Fresh Peaches, Fireworks, & Guns," he turns an even more scrupulous ear to the language of cultural cruelty and violence just beneath the surface of conversation, as the poem powerfully strains to contain this most unlovely of human musics:

> Mozart,
>
> there is no music
> for this moment. I have only the taste
> of peach juice mixed
>
> with the grit of words I can't spit out,
> nigger, 12-gauge,
> Georgia, Jesus, poontang, Ground Blossom Flower,
>
> all these gutturals
> grinding against each other as if words were stones
> under a stutterer's

tongue, which keeps on stumbling over each syllable
until silence,
our final sentence, be said.

Here, as in several other poems, Platt deploys his most successful visual structure. These unfolding triplet stanzas gather and hasten by turns, allowing him a dramatic space in which to build his narratives as well as to meditate on them, to unpack the layers of meaning within experience. The irregular pace provides a kind of technical suspense. Platt presses his language more originally in these poems, embracing oddity and discomfort as well as gracefulness. This form gives him more room to sing and more room to think.

Of the three first books I consider here, 'Annah Sobelman's *The Tulip Sacrament* is the most uneven. By that I mean it displays a wide range between its strengths and its frailties, but also I mean that its forms, its visual prosodies, are the most shattered or fragmented. Sobelman's preferred formal structure features extremely long lines alternating with short ones, arranged in stanzas of only one or two lines apiece, radically enjambed, frequently indented. Like Jorie Graham or Jane Miller, who may be her most direct influences, Sobelman heightens her language, or the self-consciousness of her language, with frequent italics, dashes, parentheticals, halts, and asides: *"pardon my italics,"* she dares us in one poem. It's very hip, self-knowing, like a long wink—an ambitious blend of Language poetry, jazz, diary entry, and painterly apprehension. When it works, this is a rejuvenative poetry, full of richness, lyric opulence, and resourceful surprise. But it can be too artsy in places as well, at times indulgent or unshapely.

"Absolute Gravity, Time, the Clarinet" nominates several of Sobelman's favorite patterns of imagery. Though in another poem she only nebulously defines "physics and science as a kind / of elliptical genetic dash and still softer // bits of strong / violet white stuff," she does often turn with real depth to the operations of physics as well as of both classical and jazz music. In this poem, for instance, she constructs a many-layered narrative whose central trope seems to be breath itself, the density or pressure of the air, but which also extends to black hole radiation, the radio music of a clarinet—a wind instrument—and the speaker's grandmother puffing away at a stifling cigar. As the air in the house blackens, the speaker seems to choke and blink:

since air is being pressed out of almost

    everything, the clouds, their loud
    sound *scuttering*—I am in my house—Though Stephen

Hawking insists that after the universe's collapse time won't get to start

reversing itself after
all so we won't get to see lightning

before we smell it black ions colliding with summer locust silt

    backwards—My grandma's breathing on her short

cigars—Though clouds keep dropping, the barometric

    pressure is low. But the clarinet playing "Up the Lazy
River" on the radio is sounding pleased

since it's being touched with so much passion. . . .

The syntax is a dense clustering of theory and image, one thing pressed into the next before it's resolved. The active visual structure of the poem seems a successful equivalent of the speaker's good-natured attempts to keep the conversation flowing despite the nasty air. She finds relief at last in a wonderful hyperbolic leap. From her place within the thickening center, she imagines the smoke beginning, ever so slightly, to dissipate like the slight leaking of radiation from within the great density of a black hole. It's her promise of "escape":

. . . since the black

    hole also has
    a temperature, "Up

the Lazy River" may be perfectly made for the clarinet, *especially*
    the further

and further out you go, she insists through her clouds of cigar smoke

which physicists now think
might be somewhat elastic in that breach because

look,

I said, beginning to breathe

> somewhat deeper, *the escape of radiation makes*
> *the singularity less black,* though time in there is supposed
> to be very long. . . .

It's a pleasure to see such playful skill, such effortless combining of the personal and the intellectual. Just such juxtapositions are Sobelman's strength, as she recognizes in another poem: "I am the *no /* and the *yes,* the friction you've been longing for." "Bitter Bird," with its tighter, stricter lineation, "My Odessa" and "My Grandma and the Sack of Potatoes" (both of which again feature one of her presiding spirits, the grandmother), "Coming Home and the Mouth," "Possible Margins of Error and Variation in the Matter Stream," and the title poem are all among the best, most daring work in *The Tulip Sacrament.*

The poems are less evocative when the technique becomes predictable or when the elements seem juxtaposed for the sake of oddity. Her additive method can seem prolix or capricious. She repeats the tripling pattern of "Absolute Gravity, Time, the Clarinet" in a number of other poems, mixing three unlike elements in "Of Gravity, Menses, Tomatoes" and "When the Devoted Rats Come to Hide Themselves in My Breasts." Her ability to transform the usual into the remarkable can, at times, tend to the precious, as in the title and text of "The Pigeons Have Decided Not to Wound the Sidewalk." And finally, the improvisatory edge of her forms seems flat or indulgent when reused too often, when her unique forms are merely transferred from poem to poem rather than invented for each occasion. But this new poet is full of ambition and verbal richness. Her work will continue to sharpen as she learns when to expand and when, as she says herself in "The Tulip Sacrament," "the cutting cuts out some [of the] drift."

I have been looking forward to a new book from Arthur Smith for a long time. What a patient and precise writer he is. Eleven years after his Starrett Award–winning volume *Elegy on Independence Day,* published by Pitt, finally we have his second book, *Orders of Affection.* His work is sharply contrasting to the open, expansive formulations of 'Annah Sobelman, for here is a severe craftsperson. In fact, his work is slimmer, more pruned, more selective, than that of any of the three previous poets. Perhaps this is due in part to the most current period style. Many younger poets seem driven by an ambition for inclusion, largeness, a sort of rhetorical size, where virtually any kind of experience or information or language is poured—sometimes quite haphazardly—into the poem. Smith, however, hones, selects, and broods. He's nostalgic, plaintive, and like his forefather James Wright, beautifully plain.

Nostalgia can be a numbing demeanor in poetry. But *Orders of Affection* locates its back-looking, Romantic anxieties in circumstance and necessity rather than in sentimentality or any lack of imagination. This is the deepest secret of Smith's book and the site of its substantial dramatic tension: the nostalgic urge in these poems is not willed or wished for, but inevitable:

> Every night as I prayed God would kill you
> In my heart, and every morning
> The moment I awoke,
> And all the day between,
> For twelve months, one full year, I ached for you,
> And then it stopped.
>
> Not, of course,
> All at once, and not as though, overnight,
> The weeping willow bleeding leaves
> Near the bedroom window
> Were more vibrant, or the scent of hyacinths
> Bunched in the planter
> More coy than cloying. . . .

The source of the speaker's memorial lament is the death of his wife, and her absence—her presence—underwrites virtually every poem in this book, whether a particular poem admits or tries to avoid that fact. Even when, as "Every Night I Prayed God Would Kill You" asserts, the ache for her has "stopped" and the speaker begins to notice more of the "vibrant" pleasures of the world, she continues to haunt the speaker in more subtle if equally disturbing ways. Smith tells us this is the doubled terror of such a loss. The pain brought about by the lover's omnipresent absence may begin to fade, yet the second loss, the loosening of memory, has its own dread and grief:

That's when
It stopped enough for me to see
The tree leaves bathed in light,
And the feisty bluegill butting heads,
And, like plucked strings, the sprung cattails
Thrumming in the river's wash,
And a variable wind, and, over it all,
A fine mist that both soothes
And, bit by bit, erodes—small comfort,
This cooling off, this bearing down,
This wearing away.

This death provides a context for every loss, every elegiac occasion, in *Orders of Affection.* Smith is a subtle poet of lament and sorrow. Even in "the least of things" his imagination sees a contest between decay and continuation, corruption and beauty. In one of the book's best poems, "The Least of Things," Smith's speaker pauses to "admire / The evening primrose." His first impression of the beautiful "pink, water-colored wildflower" bears as well a sense of loss: "Its petals so diaphanous . . . so fragile / Being looked at seems / To bring on its withering." This poem is located near the book's midpoint and signals an important transfiguration in the narrative of *Orders of Affection,* for here—midway in the poem—Smith learns from another of his poetic forebears the difficult instruction of nature's "restless revising": "This is what frightened Whitman: / Out of all indifferent decay / Indifferent beauty springs." The speaker "come[s] back to" the primrose to see in its withering also a larger persistence:

> it surfaces
> Through the cream-colored froth
> Of meadow foam
>
> Spilling out over the hillside,
> Which, this closely, is beautified entirely
> By the minions of corruption.

Whether he is "walking on down to the wreckage" of a brakeless truck or passing through a century-old cemetery in "Late Century Ode for the

Common Dead," the speaker carries with him the intimate presence of loss and its power both to destroy and to transform.

A careful maker, Smith "orders" his poetry with a variety of formal techniques. He reapplies in some of these poems a strategy of construction frequent in *Elegy on Independence Day,* shaping his language into regular stanzas of from two to six lines, often indenting alternating lines. The effects here are multiple: a lateralizing of the dramatic momentum, a sense of visual rhythm or regularity, a deferral of the inexorable. These effects do not result in increased speculation—Smith is not interested in philosophizing—but rather in lengthened occasions for the performance of song or lament. And to complicate this technique there are many other poems in *Orders of Affection* in which Smith allows himself to relinquish some control or regularity; many of these poems are plainer, looser, constructed in irregular long stanzas which appear, at first, less adorned or crafted. I feel again the gentle presence of James Wright, turning his own formal mastery toward humbler shapes. Here Smith's poems begin to move more vertically. Here too he turns away from the regular short stanza to the verse paragraph, closing each classical strophe when the sentence or the larger rhetorical instance resolves or ends. Among the book's finest works are poems in this category: "Outdoor Theater," "Beauty," "Bad Luck," "Harmony," and "Untitled Canvas," whose first stanza seems an apt capsule of Smith's art:

> I've been home from the gallery
> Since late noon, and all this time,
> While the swamp oaks have been rowing
> Through the blown rain,
> I've been thinking of a canvas
> In which one of the masters
> Lets it be known
> Life is sad.

Deborah Digges's third book, *Rough Music,* features poems of a linear and stanzaic construction related to Arthur Smith's freer forms. She too shapes some of her poems into regular, frequent stanzas, but most of her poems, lyric and lonely, are unbroken by stanzas and uneven in line length, though they also bear a distinctly formal inflection, a kind of rhetorical dignity. I have admired this poet's considerable growth since the publication of her first book, *Vesper Sparrows,* in 1985. While she did not always project the personal or familiar impulses of this book into wider spheres of connective consequence, she was already gifted with a moving Romantic melancholy and a direct but graceful lyric voice. Her 1989 volume, *Late in the Millennium,* demonstrated a poet for whom family narrative and intimate disclosure had become forcefully balanced by historical or social attachments as well as by meticulous attentions to syntactic and imagistic complexities. And now *Rough Music* gives us a powerful, fully realized writer in whose work we find a shattering lyric severity:

> Little left of me that year—I had a vision
> I was strata, atmosphere.
> Or it was that the host entire coded in my blood
> found voice and shrieked, for instance,
> at what we now call *roads*
> and I must maneuver freeways, bridges with these inside me
> falling to their knees beating the ground howling.
> One might well ask why they'd come forward—
> fugitives flushed from a burning house. . . .

Compared to the more buoyant graces of *Late in the Millennium,* this new work is lonely, darker, more mournful. The central, suppressed narrative involves a broken relationship, a lost lover or spouse, as prefigured by the "burning house" in "Rune for the Parable of Despair" above. While not often overtly revealed, still this loss is inscribed onto every gesture and detail in the book. In Arthur Smith's new book the lover is lost to death, but in *Rough Music* it's the relationship itself, not the lover, which has died. "Spring" most directly exposes the speaker's grief: "I can't find your hair among my clothes / nor will the birds this spring / where you loved to groom yourself / in the sunlight." Instead, as the speaker returns to the metaphor of the distorted or ruined house where "furniture [is] shipwrecked in a field," she is resigned to carry out a spare ceremony of forfeiture: "My shadow lies down with the memory of your shadow / in this house without a roof, this room whose floor is grass." The language of this poem may be clear, sparse as loss. Yet the ritual enacted becomes powerfully complicated when Digges fuses the act of lovemaking, lying down, with that of burial. With a subtle echo in the above passage, too, she summons a kinship with Dickinson's "Because I Could Not Stop for Death," in which the grave is also the marriage house and the earth grows pregnant with loss: "We paused before a House that seemed / A swelling of the Ground— / The Roof was scarcely visible. . . ."

Throughout this book Digges writes without self-pity or blame, without the rehearsal of confessions or accusations which one might find in a poet of lesser character; the poems instead reach for increased self-understanding, for discipline, strength. Ruins and runes abound, as in "Tombs of the Muses," where "fucking up the world's the least of it," as gangs of teenage boys inscribe the wall of a freeway underpass with their own presences or rough music— graffiti, obscenities, and finally their own "tags": *Chek, Alert, Sparo, Abuze, Atone.* Digges's selective, obsessive art provides a series of frames with which to contain grief and to "atone" for disaster or destruction with discipline. The whole book moves through the structure of a calendar year, and the arrangement of poems suggests a journey through an underworld of wrecked cities, local displacements, and remembered loves. The conjured presences of Darwin, Anna Akhmatova, and Freud, among others, also provide solace by their models of "tortured beauty" or belated fulfillment. Ultimately, *Rough Music* is a story of returning to oneself, of stepping back into time with renewed, connective sympathies.

"Nothing made of fear alone can last / like nothing made exclusively of happiness," Digges writes in "Christmas Rain," balancing her two lines with these extremities of experience. "[E]ven grief seeks some proportion," she says elsewhere, and the technical strategies of her work seem proportionally suited to lend another dimension of struggle and composure to the narratives therein. Most of the poems push vertically, in single stanzas, toward the bottom of the page, yet her rhetorical formalities defuse that downward demand. Digges uses long lines to delay or contest the pace of her immediately shorter ones, detains many lines by punctuation, stops them further with clear changes of tone, and even when enjambing her lines, provides a sense of deliberation or extension by breaking those lines at the most finished rhetorical point—often at the ends of major clauses or phrases. These tactics result in a poetry of dignity and studied care:

Then came the day even the water glass felt heavy
and I knew, as I'd suspected, I grew lighter.
I grew lighter, yes.
Say, have you ever fainted?
Such a distinct horizon as you are raised
above your pain—
And after forty years they entered Canaan . . .
Don't tell me about turning from what might change you.

This is, I suppose, free verse, and yet Digges commands the prosodic choices of free verse with such expertise that her poetry often proceeds with the formal control of the ode or the metered lament. The poems balance their drive downward with a crafted lateral composure, a type of free verse at the opposite end of the spectrum, for instance, from 'Annah Sobelman's improvisatory expansions. Digges's new book is exacting and forceful. Its demands on itself are severe, yet its rewards are the large kind won from the ordeals of difficult fate: "There is a sadness older than its texts / that will outlive the language, / like the lover who takes you by the roots of your hair."

Elizabeth Spires's new book, *Worldling,* features poems more traditionally formal, forged, and finished, than those of any other book considered here. The twenty-eight poems which comprise *Worldling* are models of grace, of patient articulation, of balance; even the book's structure, two sections each with fourteen poems, in a kind of double sonnet, is well-made and sensible. After all, Spires's is a poetry of Neoclassical shapeliness rather than of a more Romantic, organic design. The first section of *Worldling* is about the company of women—mothers, daughters, friends. Even with her most expansive gesture in a later poem like "The Bodies," in which all the "naked, disproportionate, lush" bodies of women in the sauna are "like orchids blooming out of season," Spires exercises a poised control. In this catalogue of generational connections, she echoes Whitman's linked sleepers while crafting a more restrained enthusiasm:

I see them, row upon row, the rank and file
of generations moving without pause:
—the bodies of the young girls, the willows,

complete unto themselves, androgynous;
—the great bodies of the mothers,
circled by their little moons, adoring;
—the mothers of the mothers,
the old wise ones, ponderous and slow. . . .

Body of the world! Body of flesh!

Such discoveries have been made before in contemporary poetry, but they have been more often rendered in open forms, in great declarative inclusions. Her exclamations above notwithstanding, Spires's spiritual and formal sympathies are more likely to be with Sara Teasdale, Mona Van Duyn, or Eavan Boland than with H. D., Marge Piercy, or Sharon Olds.

Among the most tender poems in this book are those about pregnancy and birth. Placed at the book's beginning, these poems trace the mother's anticipation of her unborn child "swimming / her small strokes inside me as I swim." "The Summer of Celia" bears a Wordsworthian sense of memory, but Spires blends into this intimate scene a subtle, disquieting irony in her echo of Yeats's dramatic lines from "Easter 1916" ("All changed, changed utterly: / A terrible beauty is born"):

Speak to me, Celia. Speak. Speak.
Before birth erases memory and suddenly

you are taken from me, then given back,
wrapped in the white gown of forgetting,

changed, utterly changed.

Elsewhere the speaker, in dreams, in "expectant" preparations for the child's arrival, waits in a kind of rhythmic pause, "neither here nor there." She knows it is not only her child's life being created but her own as well, her self as mother—that she must be patient, steady, like the "white stone on the beach . . . the wordless white stone of my life," for her child shortly will arrive on "wave after wave" of pain, delivery, and presence. Spires constructs these poems with plain, graceful supervision, using a few favorite patterns of imagery (of water, flowers, gardening) and a soft-spoken language to

announce the new life, "greeting her days with ceremony." By the first sec-
tion's end, and the child's first birthday, the speaker accompanies her small
family once more to a watery edge, this time to a beach on Cape Cod:

> Yes, it's easy after a few weeks here
>
> to believe we know this place, to feel it's ours,
>
> but if we drew a picture in the sand and signed our names,
>
> it would all be gone by tomorrow, the way we'll be
>
> when we pack the car at dawn and drive to Baltimore.
>
> Still, three children do just that, raking out
>
> giant letters and hieroglyphs in the sand. . . .

In "Fisher Beach" we see again the important act of language-making, of
inscription—with its double notation of presence and prescience. This
naming, even on sand, provides an analogy for the poet-mother's work as
well, to "defy, or underscore, the transience of our stay."

The poems of *Worldling* are remarkable not for this poet's ability to
render a newness of trope, a startling image, but for the resonant beauty of
their familiarity, like small archetypes. In lesser hands, I suspect, some of
this material might be unimaginative or trite. Spires's is an art of sanity and
continuity rather than of transgression. Disruptions, dangers are threaten-
ing to the well-being of the family, in fact, and this anxiety provides an
additional tension within the poems of the book's second part. In "Clock"
the intrusions of war, the accumulating damages of history, tick on the
death clock of London's Imperial War Museum:

> 963385 . . . 963386 . . . 963387 . . .
>
> The dead must be counted, their numbers tallied up,
>
> to rise like ghosts, or stars, into the unimaginable
>
> night of the new millennium. . . .

Even the returning rhythms of water, so life-giving in part one, now have
the capacity to blind or discourage. In "Good Friday. Driving Westward"
the speaker feels a *fin de siècle* anxiety in her passage through "the rain, rain
that will not end" and through the ceaseless anxieties of daily life—phones
ringing, the omnipresent need of others. As she retraces John Donne's

spiritual quest in "Good Friday, 1613. Riding Westward," Spires accounts for her own fears, which are personal, soulful, and deep:

> Daily, I turn my back.
> The suffering of others more and more
> like television. Do I drive East? West?
> Do I suffer? Shall anger be divine?
> Uncorrected, I steer. Swerve
> on a slick patch. Lose control.

Fear of the loss of control is the parent's fear and can be the poet's. It is Spires's nightmare, the force against which her poetry does battle. It may be due to the more harrowing, enlarged context of the second section, or it may be the remarkable grace of the individual poems, but among her finest works here are two poems of nearly perfect technical rendering, "The Rock" and "The Great Sea," wherein Spires creates an almost mythic contest between steadfastness and the fluid, uncontrollable movements of time. These are notably plain poems, surrounded in this section by more fully drawn or anecdotal lyrics. The formal and spiritual control they exercise reaches an exceptional serenity as the poet applies, with nearly symbolic depth, her two most haunting images—again, of water and the sturdy rock within it. "For a day and a night," she writes in "The Rock," "I sat on the rock, / and the sun went down / and the sun came up, // and the tide rushed in / and the tide rushed out, / and I was the center, / the fixed still point."

Once again Spires's speaker "[holds] fast / to the rock of my life," in a protective embrace against chaos or againt the loss of "will" in a chaotic "world." Sometimes the two-beat lines of these quatrains rhyme, and sometimes the rhyme is more an echo of meanings ("up" with "down," "in" with "out"). The rhythmic pace is tidal, elemental. These perfectly measured quatrains anticipate the same structure in "The Great Sea," near the book's end, where Spires most fully embraces the perilous condition of flux. This change, this "choosing [of] change," derives neither from concession nor defeat but rather from her understanding that the "great sea moves within us, beyond us." In this large, simple gesture Spires links the maternal and the spiritual. The spare landscape seems appropriate to the speaker's sense of existential balance and courage as she gives herself to the inexorable fluidity of things. Even the solid, closed stanzas become like water-tight vessels on this tide:

> A starless night. No moon.
> A gull, several gulls, wheeling
> overhead, their cries reminding
> me of those I have left behind.
>
> But I do not grieve. All
> that I need is here: a sail white
> as morning, a sheeted bed
> I won't sleep in. Not tonight.
>
> On the horizon, a pale glimmering.
> I sail toward it, knowing
> the sea enfolds and destroys.
> But the sea holds.
>
> The wind touches my face.
> Or, there is no wind
> and I drift, becalmed,
> free to forget and remember.

The subtle three-beat line, the echo of rhyme, the rhetorical gravity are further examples of Spires's art of control. Such writing is her method of resistance against all that is shapeless, shrill, or hurried. It is, as well, the repeated knowledge of *Worldling*. With craft and devotion, perhaps we will make something so well it will float on the waters when we have gone.

PART FOUR

Probable Reason, Possible Joy

Probable Reason, Possible Joy

When Henri Coulette died in 1988 in his native California at the age of sixty, he left behind two published books of poems, a finished but unpublished collection, many pages of uncollected or uncompleted poems, and a small but very devoted readership. Even though his first book, *The War of the Secret Agents,* appeared to some acclaim in 1966, garnering for its author the Lamont Prize, his work never quite caught on with the poetry-reading audience; *The Family Goldschmitt,* released in 1971, hardly even reached that audience. The editors of *The Collected Poems* point out that *The Family Goldschmitt* was, "through an inexcusable error," shredded in the publisher's warehouse after its initial distribution and was never reprinted.

Throughout the three decades of his mature writing, Coulette wrestled in his work with such disappointments, discouragements, and discomforts. It's little wonder. He was a rigorous, driven formalist, indeed something of a latter-day Neoclassicist, often writing in the most exacting traditional prosody during an age of free verse, an age when deep-image mysticism and a nearly institutionalized Romanticism were the more likely poetic stances. In one section of his witty, clandestine "The War of the Secret Agents," Coulette could be delineating his own strategy for self-sufficiency and survival, the *ars poetica* of a formalist horrified to be stranded among the primitives:

> The lost addresses of the soul are these:
> the great estate
> with mermaids at the gate

On *The Collected Poems of Henri Coulette* edited, with an introduction, by Donald Justice and Robert Mezey, Arkansas, 1990; *Pieces of a Song: Selected Poems* by Diane di Prima, City Lights, 1990; *Naming Our Destiny: New and Selected Poems* by June Jordan, Thunder's Mouth, 1989.

or the cold-water flat with wolves—
wherever loneliness like a disease
or a wildflower evolves . . .

or where, powerful, irresponsible,
you turn away
from what the others say,
and—like a mirror come to life—
make of duplicity the single rule,
and use it like a knife.

One of Coulette's dominant recurring tropes—the knife, the sharp
instrument wielded as a tool to create and hone and also as a weapon to
protect—here literally assumes its two-sided function. Fusing reality and
its mere or mirror reflection, forging out of doubleness a "single rule"—
that is, a principle as well as a straightedge—the speaker sharpens his self-
imposed seclusion into an instrument to enable him to endure as well as
to make art from his longings. "The tongue," he asserts in a later poem,
"The Black Rose," "is what we strop our words on."

For Coulette, who finds himself aesthetically and temperamentally
abandoned in the present, the project of poetry is then to create durabil-
ity, to make what will last beyond the merely fashionable or current. His
obvious intent is to exploit the traditional elements of rhyme and meter
and the typically Neoclassical implements of wit, reason, and style in order
to craft an object of lasting beauty. Here is a poet, after all, who in one
poem turns the human heart into a diamond in order to provide the body
with a more clean, durable core. In his best work, such as "The Fifth
Season," he is precise as stone, compressed, graceful, even refined:

It will be summer, spring, or fall—
Or winter, even. Who would know?
For no one answers when we call
Who might have answered years ago.

The harvest will be in or not;
The trees in flower or in rime.

Indifferent to the cold, the hot,
We will no longer care for time.

Mortal, of ivory and of horn,
We will become as open gates
Through which our nothing will be borne,
By which all nothing now but waits.

It will be summer, spring, or fall—
Or winter, even. Who will care?
We will not answer when you call,
For nothing, nothing echoes there.

This poem is typical of Coulette's best art. It is a gorgeous lyric, formally exact, reminiscent in some ways of Dickinson and of Robinson in his more compressive moments. The final quatrain echoes and then adjusts the rhetorical structure of the first quatrain, turning the first question's conditional tense into the final question's future. Further, by the end, the speaker has himself transformed from caller into listener, not so much passing beyond worldly time but rather finding such measurement only partly useful. Like the four seasons, turning on themselves in cycle, the poem's four stanzas also complete their circuit only to conclude in lovely paradoxes: arrival at stillness or sameness by means of motion; a concluding emptiness, a "nothing," whose presence is nonetheless tangible, perceptible as an echo. Even in a poem whose primary tone is melancholy, Coulette insists on making room for quiet punning and witty multiplicity, for his trees are triply alive: literally ("in flower"), memorially (in the decay and renewal of nature's inevitable "rime"), and poetically (sustained by his own "rime" or rhyme).

Neither is Coulette afraid to apply his sharp standards to current events in order to find, even among the chaos of the present, the materials for his art. He focuses his attention, by turns, on the Viet Nam War, on an X-rated bookshop that goes up in flames, as if by internal combustion or autoerotic overheating ("The pornographic bookshop— / It's caught itself on fire!"), and on the era's numerous political assassinations, as in "A Short History of the Sixties":

Bang! Bang! Bang!
And always in the head,
Click, and we're watching TV:
The Plane, the Widow, the Mass.
We drive with our lights on.

His inflections generally range from melancholy to wit, from amusement to wry precision. Sometimes, however, his voice and his attitude toward his surroundings turn cynical, even bitter, as his tongue sharpens past precision into severity or meannness. In two epithetic lines he can dismantle the work of a colleague: "Sixteen thousand lines, give or take sixteen— / And no two lines that you can read between." His occasional machismo (which also hints at a latent homophobia) shows up twice in the wittily titled but despondent "Bitter Suite"; the fourth of these six epigrams is "The Gutless Wonder":

Dapper I perceive:
Clothes upon a peg:
Nothing up his sleeve,
Nothing down his leg.

Elsewhere we suffer with him through the strains of alcoholism, the loss of love, and the nagging fear of oblivion. His most unbecoming moments are often also his most human, exposed, where reason breaks down into fury or grief.

Donald Justice and Robert Mezey have restored for us the work of an important voice of the past three decades. His work may be especially relevant to readers now, when many are returning in their affections to formal prosody and to Neoclassical aesthetics. The editors here have been generous in their selections, including Coulette's major work as well as many of his more minor writings. The result is a disarming collection, the life's work—sometimes brilliant, sometimes obviously flawed—of a classicist, a scholar, a poet driven toward perfection yet relentlessly nagged by doubt and loneliness. Once again, in the final section of another series of epigrams, Coulette reiterates for us his sustaining preferences. Here and elsewhere, it's as if he felt compelled to rehearse his own epitaph, typically surrounding himself with the small, private pleasures of his daily habitat:

A one-eyed cat named Hathaway on my lap,
A fire in the fireplace, and Schubert's 5th
All silvery somewhere on a radio
I barely hear, but hear—this is, I think,
As close as I may come to happiness.

For Henri Coulette the beauties of art and the familiar comforts of grace
and wit provide more lasting companionship, and sharper insight, than
mere happiness.

It's hard to imagine a poet more radically contrary to Henri Coulette
than Diane di Prima. California must be a big place indeed: di Prima lives
up the coast from Coulette's Los Angeles in San Francisco, where (as the
biography printed in *Pieces of a Song* states) she is "writing and teaching at
San Francisco Institute of Magical and Healing Arts. Continuing to study
and practice Tibetan Buddhism, as well as magic, alchemy, and healing."
If Coulette is a lonely Neoclassicist, struggling to shape experience into a
reasonable beauty, then Diane di Prima is a wild, woolly, sometimes unac-
countably daffy inheritor of Romantic zest. Her career in poetry has its
most fundamental recent grounding in the aesthetics of the Modernist
experimentalism of Pound and H. D. and follows through to the Beats and
the Black Mountain group; like Gary Snyder she turns these influences
toward a more mystical, natural Romanticism. Where Neoclassicism most
values the elements of wit and reason, Romanticism is readier to contain
the irrational impulses of magic, mystery, and sensation. Diane di Prima
beckons them with a smile. Her poems are loose, open-ended, informal
(tonally as well as technically), sounding at times like tribal chants, at times
like nonce improvisations, and elsewhere like prayers. She's as likely to be
exasperating as inspiring, but I admit to finding her brash energy and her
willingness to find wonder and joy in the world refreshing.

The second section of her poem "Deer Leap," from a sequence entitled
"Loba," speaks clearly of her desire to maintain a direct connection to the
mysteries of the natural world. Having observed her "little Brother" hold-
ing still for a moment while he drinks at a brook, she continues:

Wonder is light
at wood's edge, falling

reflecting green, wonder
is open space where the forest
closes itself, and nothing
protects or shelters.
Outside the forest, no law
shelters the beast of the wood.
No law outside where wonder
sings limpid, glances
sideways. Let us go then
love, where light
twinkles in the gap
between the Law
and ourselves.

Where T. S. Eliot's Prufrock issued a like-sounding invitation, asking his would-be lover to journey through the maze of city streets and museums as through his own paralyzed subconscious, di Prima's poem steers toward an act of imaginative freeing, toward wonder, toward the primitive laws of nature, and toward union with the wild things in the woods, far more reminiscent of Galway Kinnell or James Dickey than of Eliot. Her most lovely and lyrical writing typically concerns such desires—to touch the heart of mystery and possibility, to become more naturally uninhibited, to reach a place where nature will "let us be what we are." So the poem concludes "mid leap," precisely at the point of the self's giving-over to natural fate, when the speaker has transformed from singular to plural. This is an act of unification but also of necessary acceptance that the aboriginal woods contain both beauty and annihilation:

let us be what we are, mid leap
let us fall or rise
on the breath the Will
                    yields to.
there are eyes
under all the leaves, there are

lynxes, yes
       & the whisper
of passing shadows, but wonder
is there where boundary
breaks against itself
       & the Law
shivers & bursts like diamonds
       in the heart

I am sometimes less convinced or less fully engaged by di Prima's more social and secular poems. Among exclusively human goings-on, her tendency is toward the flakier side of Beat Romanticism, with its hip phonetics and often facile, surprisingly inflexible politics. Her "Short Note on the Sparseness of the Language" is a little narrative about two lovers' decaying relationship. But "wow man" is all they manage to utter "when [they] hit the mattressrags." The flatness of their voices suggests not only the flattening of the relationship but also the hollowness, the insufficiency, of their ability to relate to each other. It suggests as well their inability to recount the depth of the story to us, as the final lines confirm:

wow man I said the day you put me down
(only the tone was different)
wow man oh wow I took my comb
and my two books and cut and that was that

The poem tries to attain the terseness of a Robert Creeley poem, but I find the brief, nonchalant language merely tiresome, more pathetic than cool, more inexpressive than meaningfully sparse. It is bereft of any real figurative resonance; it suggests no special import in its sketchy details. Even more disappointing, the poem is a feeble literary paradigm, if indeed its purpose is to provide us with an acting-out of its arch, literary title. If its desire is to represent irony or to dramatize a certain Imagist aesthetic, its result is closer to mere sarcasm or flat happenstance. Perhaps it is true that the poem's limitation stems partly from the immaturities of a young writer. It falls early in the present collection, which does seem to be arranged in rough chronology. But the editors have not assisted such understanding; they have neither dated the poems nor designated in which of di Prima's many individual collections they may have appeared first.

My complaint about "Short Note on the Spareness of the Language" is not to say that di Prima cannot write about politics or culture. "The Practice of Magical Evocation," despite its rather loopy title, is a significant state-ment of feminist poetics and selfhood, and di Prima is sometimes convinc-ing in her many poems written in sympathy with Native-American culture, ritual, and perception. It is characteristic of a Romantic sensibility to turn for guidance toward primitive, archetypal, and tribal practices. Di Prima's fascination here—in her many prayers, chants, and spells—perhaps better signifies her active criticism of the more conventionally modern or urbane ways of living.

The real secret to di Prima's best work, however, lies in her occasional ability to integrate all of her otherwise separate impulses. In what is surely her most fully realized achievement, the long sequence "Loba," she pushes her poetry past the charming or easy—perhaps the most damaging tempta-tions of a Beat aesthetic—and past the exclusively natural. The she-wolf provides di Prima with a fierce, elemental, female hero: a rapidly moving per-spective able to maneuver from ecology and politics to erotics and religion, a perspective alternately predatory and nurturing. The ambition of the sequence is to contain as much as possible, including elements of Buddhism, Christianity, and Romantic naturalism, and to employ a wide-ranging rhetorical variety—narrative tales, lyric chants, visionary prayers, hallucina-tions. Here, loping through antique mythology ("I chant / a voice like angels from the heart / of virgin gold, / plaint of the unicorn caught in the bound-less circle") as well as through recent cultural history ("who walked across America behind gaunt violent yogis / & died o-d'ing in methadone jail / scarfing the evidence"), di Prima finds her most memorable voice and her most significant visionary stance, wholly if ideally American in its equality:

> that she is black, that she is white
> that you always know who she is
> when she appears
> that she strides on battlements, that she sifts
> like stones in the sea . . .

that there is anything about her
which cannot be said
that she relishes tombstones, falls
down marble stairs
that she is ground only, that she is not ground
that you can remember the first time you met
that she is always with you
that she can be seen without grace

that there is anything to say of her
which is not truth

These lines from "Some Lies about the Loba" strain to contain the multitudes that Whitman envisioned. If Henri Coulette's Neoclassical work suffers at the point where severity tightens into stinginess, di Prima's challenge—the point of her successes and failures alike—is to contain, accept, and still be able to discern.

Occasionally I feel about Diane di Prima's poems the way I do about June Jordan's—that she writes poems as if poetry were sometimes rather far down on her list of interests. That is both compliment and complaint. Jordan is obviously devoted to the poetics of politics and judgment; she's a poetry activist. Her aesthetic includes not only the casual or democratic sensibilities of free verse but also the bald, repetitive, encantatory powers of oratory. Hers is a persistently spoken poetry, whose closest contact with song is the chant and, occasionally, the heavily stressed, feigned naivety of the blues, as in "Winter Honey," where "sugar know / ain' nothin' run me for my money / nothin' sweet like winter honey."

Coulette is representative of some of the ongoing influences of Neoclassicism in American poetry, and di Prima charts the development of at least one strain of Romanticism. June Jordan reminds us that while these two aesthetics have comprised the dichotomy of Western philosophy and literature for thousands of years, they are incomplete in expressing the more various cultural heritages of this country. Jordan's prosody may derive primarily from the free-verse liberties of Romanticism, and her decidedly non-transcendental, socially aware sympathies may align in intriguing ways with Neoclassical worldliness. Still, Jordan's most immediate tradition and her most notable accomplishment correspond with her development of a distinctly African-American poetry. Much of her power stems from her antagonisms—intended or not—with the two more predominant forces in our poetry. That's why I said earlier that though her interests do not seem to reside wholly in poetry, I find that stance to be critically valuable. For Jordan, to adopt the techniques of a Western aesthetic is to risk forgetting the history of an African past—and an importantly African present:

> What kind of person would kill Black children?
> What kind of person could persuade eighteen
> different Black children to get into a car or
> a truck or a van?
> What kind of person could kill or kidnap
> these particular
> Black children:
>
> > Edward Hope Smith, 14 years old, dead
> > Alfred James Evans, 14 years old, dead
> > Yosef Bell, 9 years old, dead. . . .

"Test of Atlanta 1979" exemplifies the sternest and most blunt qualities of Jordan's poetry. It is expressly unpoetic, ungarnished; it is virtually prose in lines. Yet the power of its testimonial rhetoric, the plain and undeniable fact-making embedded in the poem, produces a voice capable of moving beyond mere shock, blame, or stupor into an accumulating indignation leading toward action. Jordan's well-chosen title to this volume reiterates one of her most urgent tasks: to name names in order to rehearse the details of one's past, to identify the face of one's oppressor, and to actively take part in the creation of one's future.

Imagine the liberating importance of naming for a culture whose identity has for centuries been refigured or erased by a more dominant or controlling one. There are names abounding in *Naming our Destiny:* in titles ("A Richland County Lyric for Elizabeth Asleep"); in dedications (to her son Christopher, to Jane Creighton, to Adrienne Rich, or in "commemoration of the 40,000 women and children who . . . presented themselves in bodily protest . . . at The United Nations, August 9, 1978"); and in the characterizations within virtually every poem. In Jordan's important "Fragments from a Parable" the nominal and spiritual transformation of Saul to Paul provides a paradigm for another crucial naming: the naming or recreating of oneself. As if directly to confront the paradox of an artist—the desire to be original while employing the received technique and traditions of one's art form— Jordan opens her poem in purposefully tentative fashion:

> The worst is not knowing if I do take somebody's
> word on it means I don't know and you have to believe
> if you just don't know. How do I dare to stand as
> still as I am still standing? . . .
> Always there is not knowing, not knowing everything
> of myself and having to take whoever you are at your
> word. About me.

Elsewhere in *Naming our Destiny* the trope of nomination produces a push toward responsibility and duty as well as a sense of kinship or sympathy; in "Fragments from a Parable" the drive to name participates in the fundamental process of self-identity. The speaker must invent herself, must give birth to herself not only as artist but as person. Ralph Ellison's terrible figure of invisibility must be surmounted through distinct verification: "She seeks to authorize her birth." To authorize is to certify as well as to transcribe. Jordan's speaker moves from the distances of third person ("And this is my story of Her. The story is properly yours to tell. You have created Her, but carelessly. . . . Your patterns deny parenthood; deny every connection suggesting a connection; a consequence") into the immediacy of first person ("I am. // My name is me"). The subsequent narrative reimagines her birth and childhood, and the speaker continues to confront the pressures which attend her race and gender: "My father loved the delusion he sired. The fundamental dream of my mother, her unnatural ignorance refreshed him. . . . He said to my mother many nouns." Finally, the speaker seeks to move beyond even her own creation: "Let me be more than words: I would be more than medium or limestone. I would be more than looking more than knowing. . . ." The poem concludes in an act of personal liberation, having served as a vehicle for self-creation.

The issues of race and self-reliance (artistic and otherwise) are not the only political topics to which Jordan returns persistently. She speaks searingly in behalf of the hitherto silenced or subjugated: women, the poor and hungry, the imprisoned, the politically tyrannized in Nicaragua, the enslaved in Manhattan. I can think of very few contemporary American poets who have been so willing to take on other people's troubles. Decidedly, this is not the poetry of a sheltered, introspective confessional, not the work of a tidy scholar or a timid dormouse. Jordan's variety of poetic stances enacts her drive to connect and represent, for in addition to her principal mode of delivery—the poet talking directly to an audience—she also speaks through a number of other characters in persona poems, giving sympathetic articulation to lives, idioms, and concerns beyond her own. Like Carl Sandburg, she makes public art out of public occasion and the available word, and she does so with confidence and conviction.

While I admire the task of such writing, such purposely unartistic or democratically accessible art, I do nonetheless tire of some elements of Jordan's work. It is finally hard to read page after page by somebody who is always right. The six-line poem "Some People," for instance, offers us only the assertion that "Some people despise me be- / cause I have a Venus mound / and not a penis." There is no narrative drama, no figural development, no creative discovery, no tension created by the poem. Such work may articulate a feminist corrective, but it is certainly inadequate as a poem. It's more like a sound bite, a facile commercial for rightness. Especially when her tone steps over from witness to blame, or when her accusations don't seem grounded within the body of the work itself, Jordan's voice resounds with self-righteousness and sanctimony rather than urgency:

They said they were victims. They said you were
Arabs . . .

Did you read the leaflets that they dropped
from their hotshot fighter jets?
They told you to go . . .

I didn't know and nobody told me and what
could I do or say, anyway?

Yes, I did know it was the money I earned as a poet that
paid

for the bombs and the planes and the tanks
that they used to massacre your family

But I am not an evil person
The people of my country aren't so bad

You can't expect but so much
from those of us who have to pay taxes and watch
American tv

You see my point;

I'm sorry.
I really am sorry.

Here, in "Apologies to All the People in Lebanon," sarcasm, obvious irony, and feigned helplessness prevent the poem from becoming a more serious indictment of American brutishness. The result is something closer to the sentimentality of mere or obvious correctness. Jordan's more powerful social critiques occur in poems which implicate her speaker more personally in events. "Poem about My Rights," for instance, is explicitly about the relationship of personal experience and general history-telling. The trope of rape operates as a figure for both individual and social damage, as the poem moves from the speaker's regret that "I can't do what I want / to do with my own body because I am the wrong / sex the wrong age the wrong skin" to France where "they say if the guy penetrates / but does not ejaculate then he did not rape me" to the literal and political rape of Namibia and its citizens by South Africa. The speaker becomes both a voice of specific indignation and a voice of more wide-ranging, accumulating rage: "I am the history of rape / I am the history of the rejection of who I am / I am the history of the terrorized. . . ." In a serious pun on her own title, the speaker asserts her own "right"—her legal and moral liberty as well as her correctness—as the poem concludes in another important act of verification and naming:

I am not wrong: Wrong is not my name
My name is my own my own my own
and I can't tell you who the hell set things up like this
but I can tell you that from now on my resistance

> my simple and daily and nightly self-determination
>
> may very well cost you a life

"Apologies to All the People in Lebanon," quoted earlier, provides an example of my second complaint about Jordan's work: her occasionally rather wearying approach to technique. It is sometimes as if design and prosody are incidental bothers to her, things to be quickly dispensed with, rather than integral and integrated parts of the whole poetic effect. This is often an inevitable result of a public poetry whose primary foundation is oral rather than visible or written. Even while I can rationally explain the purposeful raggedness and homeliness of her work as a visible resistance of the conventions of power implicit in Western poetry, I still wish she were willing to apply more formal pressures to her material. In "Ghazal at Full Moon," for example, she ironizes or complicates her work by a juxtaposition of technique and subject matter. Borrowing the Mediterranean form originally designed to celebrate love and drinking, Jordan uses its independent couplets paradoxically, not pastorally, to represent the variety of cultures vaguely named by the term "Indian"—from the "dead man" on the obsolete nickle to the cultures of Guatemala, Pakistan, and elsewhere. Much of the poem's power and tension derive from the formal progression embedded in the closed couplets as well as from the speaker's accumulating sense of injustice done to many cultures wrongly named and blurred. In other poems, though, I often feel that Jordan's work reads too easily, as if she can't be worried by technique when there is so much other real work to do.

Even given my complaints, Jordan's work is a reminder that poetry might yet be a viable and persuasive form of social corrective, that its more oratorical modes may have the capability to mobilize as well as inspire. Her project is especially whelming, given her ethnic as well as artistic fidelities: she requires of herself, and invites us, to review some of the most basic assumptions about myth, identity, and influence that writers as various as Henri Coulette and Diane di Prima more willingly inherit and more generally take for granted. Together, these three Californians suggest the depth, difference, and significance of current American poetry. The point for us is not to elect one of these three voices over the others; it is to learn how to listen to them all.

On Restraint

I am not concerned here with artistic timidity, moral constraint, or polite decorum—that is, restraint as puritanic virtue—but rather with tactics of restraint which allow us to gauge a poem's opposite pole, its power and passion. Even Walt Whitman is at his most persuasive when his enthusiasms are informed by subdued counter-pressures. In "Crossing Brooklyn Ferry," those ominous, looming "dark patches," which accompany his confessions of secular guilt, temper his later transcendental encouragements to "flow on . . . with the flood-tide." The poem's polar forces—obliteration and regeneration, liability and acceptance—are held in a system of checks-and-balances. The result is precarious and powerful. Other poets use different methods of restraint: Dickinson with her severe, compact technique ("After great pain, a formal feeling comes—"); Bishop in her very stance, what Jeredith Merrin calls an "enabling humility." Restraint can ironize, enable, even sustain a poet's great passions and wildness.

Ted Kooser is the most restrained of the five poets I consider here, if restraint also nominates characteristics like compression and control. A critically undervalued poet, Kooser is a joy to read, even if, every now and then, he may be a little *too* restrained. His touch is so light and his poems generally so compact that occasionally there doesn't seem to be enough passion or material at hand. But after all, much of the power of Kooser's work is accretive, since for decades he has been constructing out of individual poems a long, sustained, and important life work in the manner of E. A. Robinson's Tilbury Town, Edgar Lee Masters's Spoon River, or Richard

---

On *Weather Central* by Ted Kooser, Pittsburgh, 1994; *A Wedding in Hell* by Charles Simic, Harcourt Brace, 1994; *Imperfect Thirst* by Galway Kinnell, Houghton Mifflin, 1994; *Song* by Brigit Pegeen Kelly, BOA, 1995; *Chickamauga* by Charles Wright, Farrar, Straus and Giroux, 1995.

Hugo's Great Northwest. Throughout his new *Weather Central* Kooser's individual poems are evocative, often perfectly realized, even as they also become part and parcel of his larger project, the creation in poetry of a distinctly Midwestern social text, as in "Lincoln, Nebraska," where

> . . . there
> is something beautiful
>
> about a dirty town in rain,
> where tin cans, rails,
> and toppled shopping carts
> are the sutures of silver
> holding the guts in,
>
> keeping the blue wound closed,
> while over a pawnshop, the plain
> wet flag of a yellow window
> holds out the cautious welcome
> of an embassy.

Kooser is highly selective in the amount and type of material he includes in a poem. Only seven of the fifty-eight poems in *Weather Central* are longer than a page; the longest, "City Limits," runs to forty lines. He is a devoted chronicler of the Midwest, but so careful, so meticulous, that even his most modest poems ring with pleasing recognitions:

> It is morning. My father
> in shirtsleeves is sweeping
> the sidewalk in front of his store,
> standing up straight in the bow
> of his gondola, paddling
> the endless gray streets of his life
> with an old yellow oar—
> happy there, hailing his friends.

Here in "The Sweeper," and throughout this book, recognition and connection are Kooser's recurrent longings—the connective goodwill of neighbors and families, the connections of the images themselves. Notice how he activates the poem's only metaphor exactly halfway through this poem with "in the bow / of his gondola, paddling," where a plain description of the father's movement turns into the stroke of a gondolier, the absolutely familiar touched with a wistful exotica. He is uncanny in selecting such right-seeming metaphors, but he is also a realist, an Imagist writing haiku-like verse, whose tropes are rarely dramatically transformative but rather clarifying. He wants us to see things more sharply. He connects his deliberate images with a kind of restrained, respectful sanity, like "Aunt Mildred" who "picked up a pencil stub and pinched it hard, / straightened her spine, and wrote a small / but generous letter to the world."

Kooser rarely refers to himself in his work, and then hardly ever in first person. This kind of restraint is particularly striking in a period when so much poetry is, to parrot Hawthorne's Zenobia, so much "Self, self, self!" The closest Kooser comes to self-portraiture may be the image of the blue heron in the book's first poem, "Etude," where the first-person speaker watches "a Great Blue Heron / fish in the cattails, easing ahead / with the stealth of a lover composing a letter." He sees in the bird's actions and its "blue suit" the reflection of a businessman who "holds down an everyday job / in an office" (like Kooser's own occupation as an insurance executive):

> Long days swim beneath the glass top
> of his desk, each one alike. On the lip
> of each morning, a bubble trembles.
> No one has seem him there, writing a letter
> to a woman he loves. His pencil is poised
> in the air like the beak of a bird.
> He would spear the whole world if he could,
> toss it and swallow it live.

The letter is a figure for the kind of lifelike text Kooser seems to strive for in his poems. The final sentence with its sudden, dramatic feat is even more effective given this love poem's delicate restraint.

Midway into *Weather Central* we encounter the image of the heron again, in "A Poetry Reading," though by now he's "an old blue heron with yellow eyes," a poet opening his "book on its spine, a split fish." These mere hints are among the most directly self-revealing moments in the book. Kooser reserves his more emotional involvements for his characters, as in the tender "Four Secretaries," where all day, like ordinary sirens, they "call back and forth, / singing their troubled marriage ballads, / their day-care, car-park, landlord songs." Again like a poet, the speaker here is separated from the cohabitants of his office because of his position. His distance seems to sharpen his sympathy:

> And their sadness—how deep and full of love
> is their sadness when one among them
> is hurt, and they hear her calling
> and gather about her to cry.

Kooser is a poet of deep passion for the daily, workaday world, but he is more interested in human behavior than in the buried motivations for such. He is a reporter, not an editorialist.

With their chiseled lines, perfectly balanced stanzas, unfanciful imagery, and cleanest of syntax, virtually every poem in *Weather Central* is a model of the plain style. But here's a paradox: some of the traits of this style (its transparent inflections and dialect, its invisible craft) may be impediments to appreciating the unique gifts of this plain-spoken Midwestern poet. Yet I think Kooser's a central poet. Poems like "Weather Central," "Another Story," "A Ghost Story," "Fireflies," "In Late Spring," "Snakeskin," and any number of other splendid poems here ought to find their place in the representative anthologies of our time. Kooser documents the dignities, habits, and small griefs of daily life, our hunger for connection, our struggle to find balance in natural and unnaturally human worlds.

A far more acclaimed and much-awarded poet, Charles Simic plays the Romantic to Kooser's Realist. They were born in 1938 and 1939, respectively, and have published a dozen volumes apiece. Each is masterful at plain-spoken rhetoric and impeccably tight free-verse techniques. Each is skilled at creating memorable individual images as well as coherent patterns of metaphor. Miniaturists, each exploits the short poem to great advantage; only two of the seventy poems in *A Wedding in Hell* are longer than a page, thirty lines being the longest. Simic employs many of the same strategies of restraint that distinguish Kooser's poems.

But Simic's metaphors transform where Kooser's clarify:

In the frying pan
On the stove
I found my love
And me naked.

Chopped onions
Fell on our heads
And made us cry.
It's like a parade,
I told her, confetti
When some guy
Reaches the moon.

"Means of transport,"
She replied obscurely
While we fried.
"Means of transport!"

Simic likes to wink at us "obscurely," as here in a poem that opens with the most restrained of rhetorics but the oddest of metaphors. Lovers as potatoes, or cuts of liver? "Transport" takes us into the surreal, as many of his poems ferry us from the familiar to the entirely alien, from the mundane to the holy, or from the dim to the philosophical (or vice versa). As he professes in another poem, "'I'm crazy about her shrimp!' / I shout to the gods above." Simic is a Postmodern Romantic, a mystic grinding his forehead into the stones though he knows that God is dead and buried, a believer who asserts the transcendent moment but who also perceives that transcendence is likely to send us to the kind of place he describes in "Pascal's Idea": "It was terrifying / And I suppose a bit like / What your heaven and hell combined must be." Poem after poem insists on these kinds of metamorphic changes. I like to amass Kooser's poems, letting them gather in a larger social scene, but I prefer Simic's a few at a time. Too much similar magic at once exposes its tricks.

To American audiences part of Simic's charm derives from his Continental-sounding images and cosmopolitan sensibilities. If he has a riddler's sense of humor, he can also don the Romantic's blackest cape. He recalls Kafka's great European absurdist masterpiece "The Hunger Artist" in the prose poem "Voice from the Cage," where caged animals act out their existential agony: "Sorrow, sickness, and fleabites are our lot. . . . Even the lion doesn't believe the fables anymore. 'Pray to the Lord,' the monkeys shriek." Even the freakish speaker has "dyed [his] hair green like Baudelaire." This contorted display of grotesqueries, like a "circus of quick, terrified glances," is repeated in many poems. Toothless monkeys, "chickens living in a rusty old hearse," a gorilla suit with "silly angel wings," a white cat "picking at the bloody head of a fish"—such often feral malformities are the shadow-images of the faceless soldiers and anonymous "refugees crowding the roads" who also populate Simic's poems. Expatriation, the brutal repetitions of history, the chaos of broken walls, of failed faiths, drive the speaker in "Explaining a Few Things" underground, like Dostoevsky's "sick man." Once again, armies and animals are Simic's companions:

> Every worm is a martyr,
>
> Every sparrow subject to injustice,
>
> I said to my cat,
>
> Since there was no one else around.
>
> It's raining. In spite of their huge armies
>
> What can the ants do?
>
> And the roach on the wall
>
> Like a waiter in an empty restaurant?
>
> I'm going to the cellar
>
> To stroke the rat caught in a trap.
>
> You watch the sky.
>
> If it clears, scratch on the door.

As crisp and plainly spoken as Kooser's documents to the commonplace, still this poem is a world and an age away from Lincoln, Nebraska.

Charles Simic has been writing like this for a long time, sharply, seriously, with a rhetoric of restraint but with a vision of haunted strangeness. Still, I think his talent is growing, as his poems continue to deepen, subtly but surely. The poems of *A Wedding in Hell* are more emotionally absorbing than the work of his famous books of the seventies, such as *Dismantling the Silence* or *Classic Ballroom Dances.* "O dreams like evening shadows on a windy meadow," he sings in "A Wedding in Hell," "And your hands, Mother, like white mice." His plainness makes these surprises, these pointed and surreal mutations, all the more powerful.

Galway Kinnell is another brand of Romantic altogether, as broadly sweeping and declarative as Simic is furrowed and allegorical. He's Whitman to Simic's Baudelaire. And like Whitman's, his tactics of restraint are far fewer and more subtle than either Kooser's or Simic's. I don't think *Imperfect Thirst* is Kinnell's best book, but this poet has such command that his average poems are often better than most other poets' best; and to be sure, there are gems in this book to more than compensate for the disappointments.

Kinnell's gift has always been to mediate between the visible, substantial world and the inutterably spiritual or mystical, and the approach he takes in his greatest poems, like "The Bear," "The Last River," or any section of *The Book of Nightmares,* requires giving over the body's self to the regions of mystery and otherness he identifies in "There Are Things I Tell to No One": "I believe, / rather, in a music of grace / that we hear, sometimes, playing to us / from the other side of happiness." It's an all-or-nothing poetic, Romanticism at its purest, whose procedures are dramatic and self-obliterating and whose tactics are typically the opposite of restraint. Some of this passion still resides in Kinnell's new poems, though the presiding aesthetic of our age is anything but transcendental-friendly. (Is the end of *every* century marked by Victorian-like decoration, cultural prudery and resentment, a foregrounding of the historical, the rational, the scientific?) Frequent critical discouragement with the later work of James Dickey, James Wright, W. S. Merwin, even Kinnell, may be only partly the poets' culpability and partly because of the bearing of criticism away from the Romantic. Even Kinnell seems sometimes skeptical of his Romantic leanings.

Imperfect Thirst is a well-balanced book, with five poems in each of the five sections and an introductory "proem." Kinnell has always counted carefully, shaping his wildness with that particular form of order. It is uncanny, for instance, how many of his superb poems have seven sections: "The Porcupine," "The Bear," "Memories of My Father," "Another Night in the Ruins," all ten of the *Nightmares,* many more. But then, fine music is also mathematical. And music is the condition to which Kinnell's aesthetic aspires in *Imperfect Thirst*. One of the best works in this volume, "'The Music of Poetry,'" is at once a love poem and a catalogue of the values of Romanticism. We find the speaker in the middle of his own lecture "at a podium . . . on Bleeker Street," trying to come up with a "unified theory" of poetry:

> that the music resulting from any of the methods
> of organizing English into rhythmic surges
> can sound like the music resulting from any other,
> being the music not of a method but of the language;
> and after proposing that free verse is a variant
> of formal verse, using unpredictably the acoustic
> repetitions which formal verse employs regularly. . . .

Begun with pseudo-scientific detachment, his explanation soon finds more satisfying answers in "the humpback whale's gasp-cries," tribal rituals, and the songs of "clasped lovers." Where Kooser's and Simic's love poems are models of compression, Kinnell's poetry is additive, an accumulating pre-scription of virtues. Its eventual goal is "to let the audience hear that our poems are of the same order as those of the other animals / and are com-posed, like theirs, when we find ourselves / synchronized with the rhythms of the earth." Kinnell's other, more hidden model is Whitman's "When I Heard the Learn'd Astronomer." (Whitman's hermit thrush also adds its song to Kinnell's here.) In both poems the speaker rejects the jargon of the academic in favor of a solitary, direct connection with nature. So the praise-worthy traits of Romanticism—seclusion, animal knowledge, primitive practice, disengagement with the scholarly and public, erotic naturalism—provide Kinnell with the components of this *ars poetica*. The poem ends as the details of his talk fade, as his social discourse decays, as his mind drifts into a reverie "causing me to garble a few words / and tangle my syntax," all at the thought of his "beloved [who] may have / put down her book and drawn up her eider-down" before sleep. She is another example of the natu-ral, Romantic hero: "I imagine I can hear / her say my name into the slow waves / of the night and, faintly, being alone, sing."

Other poems in *Imperfect Thirst* search for similar articulations: "bleats," cries, "excruciated singsong," gasps, "wolf's howls," and all other manner of natural, alogical communication. It's part of Kinnell's argument with the structures of culture and sense. Usually his critiques are effective, but some-times, as in "Holy Shit," they just don't work. A deconstruction of the oxy-moronic interjection "holy shit," this seventy-nine line poem begins with more than three pages of epigraphs, in historical order, drawn from religious sources, and all about defecation; Plato, Saint Bernard, Chaucer's Pardoner, the *Shacharit,* Whitman again, and Jung are among the conjured voices. But Kinnell is not always an effective satirist, and the poem, which consists of examples proving that living things (as opposed to "the gods") shit, seems merely too witty and self-satisfied to succeed as a brash acceptance of a simple, natural function: "The white-tailed deer stops and solfs her / quarter-notes the size and color / of nicoise olives onto the snow." It wants to be the kind of radical, audacious, ultimately political confrontation that Allen Ginsberg can sometimes bring off, but it remains oddly constrained.

Other poems in *Imperfect Thirst* suffer differently. "Parkinson's Disease" attempts to answer the impossible question, "Could heaven be a time, after we are dead, / of remembering the knowledge / flesh had from flesh?" But it strains with philosophizing and with its many rhetorical gestures of con-nection to Sharon Olds's poems in *The Father.* Readers will find poems to love and poems to flip. "The Deconstruction of Emily Dickinson" shows Kinnell's satiric humor at its most topical and flexible, an anthologist's dream, and the restrained tenderness of "The Cellist" and "Neverland" suit-ably balance the fabular grace of "The Striped Snake and the Goldfinch" and the "wild fiery" joy of "Flies."

A bird flies through almost every poem in Brigit Pegeen Kelly's new *Song.* The relative newcomer of this group, Kelly won the 1994 Lamont Prize for this superlative second book of poems, which follows by seven years her Yale winner, *To the Place of Trumpets.* She's a deliberate writer, though like Kinnell she is also a Romantic of the more transcendental flavor, and so her birds like "flame-flung arrows," her swans and finches, even her crow like a "lord of highness," provide not only the models of song for a human voice aspiring to otherness but also seem to bear communications from beyond. Jonathan Edwards, in his tract of Puritan typology, *Images or Shadows of Divine Things,* declares that "Ravens are birds of the air that are expressly used by Christ as types of the Devil. . . . The raven by its blackness repre-sents the prince of darkness." While Kelly's birds are not so conclusively symbolic, still they seem to indicate types of providential suggestion, like

accompaniments or spiritual equivalents. They are a language to be inter-
preted, a celestial music to be learned.

Kelly's title poem is a good example of her method in the twenty-seven
poems of *Song*. About a group of boys who have stolen and killed a girl's
pet goat, hanging its severed head in a tree and leaving its body beside some
railroad tracks, "Song" is a clear narrative with a denser, fabular mystique:

> It was harder work than they had imagined.
> The goat cried like a man and struggled hard. But they
> Finished the job. They hung the bleeding head by the school
> And then ran off into the darkness that seems to hide everything.
> The head hung in the tree. The body lay by the tracks.
> The head called to the body. The body to the head.
> They missed each other. The missing grew large between them,
> Until it pulled the heart right out of the body, until
> The drawn heart flew toward the head, flew as a bird flies
> Back to its cage and the familiar perch from which it trills.
> Then the heart sang in the head, softly at first and then louder. . . .

The grief of separation articulated in the goat's bird-like song finds itself
repeated by the girl, who looks everywhere for her lost companion, as well
as by the boys, whose guilt ultimately will manifest itself in song, again
embodied by a bird: "They would / Wake in the night thinking they heard
the wind in the trees / Or a night bird, but their hearts beating harder."
Kelly suggests a number of tragic falls from grace—the destruction of
youthful innocence, a parable of brutal rape, the forced cleaving of "head"
from "heart." She severs the word tragedy itself, whose Greek origin *tragos*
literally means "goat-song," after the type of masks worn by actors at the
feasts of Dionysus. Like Kinnell, Kelly proposes that song may be the most
revealing and instructive source for understanding an event that might
otherwise remain both an enigma and a secret:

> There
> Would be a whistle, a hum, a high murmur, and, at last, a song,
> Not a cruel song, no, no, not cruel at all. This song
> Is sweet. It is sweet. The heart dies of this sweetness.

Throughout *Song,* Kelly pushes for these kinds of resonant moments of direct contact with mystery and passion. Her style conveys a similar, grave tension. In these passages from "Song," the dense allusion and the riddling nature of things seem balanced by Kelly's restrained voice and brief, direct sentences. In turn, her short sentences are contained within very long lines—typically between twelve and eighteen syllables—which are also heavily stressed by as many as eight or nine accents. This slow, thick movement is never burdensome, due in part to Kelly's voice, underspoken, whispered, amazed.

In "Song" meaning unfolds by association and music. "Dead Doe" is even less linear, a shattered narrative revising its own progress and vision. More than in any other poem in *Song,* here Kelly opens up her dense lines and stanzas, her tight syntax, in a kind of wide-eyed horror. Even the poem's first line conveys a give-and-take rhetorical hesitation: "The doe lay dead on her back in a field of asters: no." The poem's ostensible mission is instructive, as the speaker tries to explain to her son what they have seen. She is guide and explicator, but she is also protector, and her hesitant, revising rhetoric seems designed to shield the child's innocent eyes, only slowly revealing the figure of death, both shocking and transfiguring:

> The doe lay dead on her back beside the school bus stop: yes.
>
> Where we waited.
> Her belly white as a cut pear. Where we waited: no: off
>
> from where we waited: yes
>
> at a distance: making a distance
> we kept,
> as we kept her dead run in sight, that we might see if she chose
> to go skyward. . . .

In her effort to explain the presence of death to her son, that their "waiting might . . . be upheld by significance," the speaker measures her own maternal role against that of the dead doe: "The doe lay dead: she could / do nothing: // the dead can mother nothing . . . nothing / but our sight." But sight, of course, leads to vision and revelation. Again Kelly deploys her figure of birds as a signal of spiritual or providential import:

The doe lay dead: yes: and at a distance, with her legs up and frozen,
   she tricked

                our vision: at a distance she was
                    for a moment no deer

at all

but two swans: we saw two swans
          and they were fighting

     or they were coupling
        or they were stabbing the ground for some prize
          worth nothing. . . .

And this is the soul: like it or not. Yes: the soul comes down: yes: comes into
the deer: yes: who dies: yes: and in her death twins herself into swans. . . .

The astonishing double transfiguration—the doe into swans, the swans
into the soul—is Kelly at her finest, her most adventurous. The poem's
shifting centers, its alternating "yes" and "no," its modulations between fact
and figure, the body and soul, all set up the final metamorphosis of the
poem. As the soulful swans were "mothered" by the single figure of the doe,
so does the speaker mother two souls, hers and her son's: "and we are not
afraid as we watch her soul fly on: paired / as the soul always is: with itself:
/ with others."

There is not a weak poem among the twenty-seven poems in *Song*, and
not one sounds like anybody else's. Her talent is great and her embrace is
large, from the singular determinations of familial belonging to the most
metaphysical explorations of history, faith, and language. She is not an
ecstatic poet, but one for whom mystery and adventure are best approached
in humble, if certain, song. Her power hums and broods rather than bursts.
Kinnell catalogued his bold Romantic *ars poetica* in "'The Music of
Poetry'"; Kelly reveals the graceful restraint of hers in "The Music Lesson":
"the lesson's / Passion is patience."

Charles Wright uses large, summary abstractions the way most poets
use images. His images alone sustain the oblique storylines of his poems.
These tactics are the reverse of most other poets. *Chickamauga* is an essen-
tial collection of poetry from one of our most original poets, a lyric mas-

ter who continues to adjust and refine his complex poetic. Like most of the other poets here considered, Wright is a Romantic, but he is more expansive than Simic, more speculative than Kinnell, and more lavish than Kelly. Readers of Wright's work will here rediscover his wide range of influences and allusions: Southern idiom and landscape; Italian art and culture; Continental surrealism; Oriental detail and clarity; as well as jaunts into Vorticism, Imagism, and Futurism (as he quips in one poem addressed to Charles Simic, those "who don't remember the Futurists are condemned to repeat them").

Almost nothing ever happens in a Charles Wright poem. This is his central act of restraint, a spiritualist's abstinence, where meditation is not absence but an alternative to action and to linear, dramatic finality:

> Unlike a disease, whatever I've learned
> Is not communicable.
> > A single organism,
> It does its work in the dark.
>
> Anything that we think we've learned,
> > > we've learned in the dark.
> If there is one secret to this life, it is this life.

As here in "Mid-winter Snowfall in the Piazza Dante," Wright's speaker is nearly always physically static and rhetorically circular. He sits in his backyard "rubbing this tiny snail shell," he watches "the hills empurple and sky [go] nectarine," he eats "*gnocchi* and roast veal" at a *caffe* in Florence, and he ponders. We might understand something more of Wright's aesthetic by noticing that "sitting" and "reading" are the primary participles in the titles of the first sections of this book, while "waiting," "watching," and "looking" come at the end. In the middle (and all the way through) he is talking and talking. The eye becomes a voice. Even given his bounty of allusions and references, I think Wright's truest forebear is Emerson, whom he never mentions. In "Circles," perhaps his most difficult and lovely essay, Emerson could be prescribing Wright's revolving imagery and rhetorical stance: "Conversation is a game of circles. In conversation we pluck up the *termini* which bound the common of silence on every side." Wright's voice throughout *Chickamauga* is conversational—never lax, never dull, but also never spoken in the larger oratorical tone of Kinnell. If Wright seems continually to muse to an intimate friend, he also knows that the winding destination of language is also its extinction, that the real meanings—personal as well as historical—are ultimately "not communicable." Emerson in "Circles" concurs: "And yet here again see the swift circumscription! Good as is discourse, silence is better, and shames it."

There are precious few contemporary poets in whose work I find as much sheer wisdom as in Wright's. He is fearless in his use of grand generalities, as comfortable with "O we were abstract and true. / How could we know that grace would fall from us like shed skin, / that reality, our piebald dog, would hunt us down?" as with "Snip, snip goes wind through the autumn trees" ("Waiting for Tu Fu"). "Blaise Pascal Lip-syncs the Void" *begins* with the kind of summary realization at which most other poets' work strains to arrive: "It's not good to be complete. / It's not good to be concupiscent, / caught as we are / Between a the and a the, / neither of which we know and neither of which knows us." Like Wallace Stevens, echoed in these lines, Wright treats the general (an "a") as a type of distinct particularity (a "the"). The abstract is as tangible and stimulating as any concrete detail. Emerson once more in "Circles": "Generalization is always a new influx of the divinity into the mind. Hence the thrill that attends it." Still, however thrilling, the operations of language ultimately persist in baffling Wright's desire for transcendence, as he says in "Looking Outside the Cabin Window, I Remember a Line by Li Po": "We who would see beyond seeing / see only language, that burning field."

Wright's affinity with Emerson is also apparent in his rhetoric. Emerson is invariably effective at the level of the sentence, but his paragraphs are often monuments to circular structure or to impressionistic meandering. That can be pretty damning for any essayist attempting philosophical stratagems, less troublesome for a poet of Wright's skill and orientation. Wright is a master of the sentence, and his own circular movement in both the stanza and the section seems well-tuned to his thematic faith that "I remember the word and forget the word / although the word / Hovers in flame around me." Both Emerson and Wright glean considerable rhetorical power by varying the structure of their sentences, migrating with ease from the elongated compound-complex sentence to the clipped aphoristic kicker. I hear Emerson and also Franklin in pronouncements like these: "Ambition is such a small thing"; "Prosodies rise and fall"; "Words are wrong. / Structures are wrong"; "This text is a shadow text." His diverse syntactic arrangements reinforce Wright's doubled persona, both ambitious and humble, and his very long lines are suited to contain his sentence variety. If Wright's language can seem too opulent or his line too thickened on occasion, veering toward the over-lavish, this quality is more frequent in *Zone Journals* than in *Chickamauga*. More often, the rich, flexible syntax is an apt partner for Wright's questing imagination.

I can, in fact, think of no other recent poet who can successfully deploy very long lines in such utterly non-narrative poems. In "Sprung Narratives," the book's longest poem at nine pages, Wright again refers to one of his masters as he alternately reveals and conceals his own strategy for story. Gerard Manley Hopkins's sprung rhythm, that endlessly strange and accurate self-description of Hopkins's metric idiosyncracies, of course provides the trope for Wright's more extended application. Where Hopkins says that "the stresses come together," making a dense, nearly overlapping rhythmic pressure, Wright also suggests that memory is much less a narrative line than a series of bumping, elliptical shards, merging into and abandoning each other. The poem shifts through many possible plots and settings— Wright's childhood, Italy in the 1960s, his seventeen years in Laguna Beach, his return "home" in Virginia—and yet, all along, Wright extinguishes story in favor of image, image in favor of abstraction: "Who knows what the story line / became. . . . The world is a language we never quite understand, / But think we catch the drift of." He urges himself toward a continued temperance, his deepest act of restraint: "Returned to the dwarf orchard, / Pilgrim, / Sit still and lengthen your lines, / Shorten your poems and listen to what the darkness says / With its mouthful of cold air." Wright's ascetic discipline is an instruction and an aesthetic. The whole world seems to orbit in a kind of meditative, slow circle around Wright's grave influence. That's the brilliant paradox throughout this big, powerful book. In a poetry where nothing ever happens, everything is possible.

Romantic Melancholy, Romantic Excess

The Romantic lyric in current practice comes in many modes: the dissociative inventions of John Ashbery, the anxious meditations of Louise Glück, the radical disassembling of a Romantic self of T. R. Hummer. The rhetoric of these poets is striking, dramatic. Yet most critics of contemporary poetry agree that the recent Romantic lyric is more typically spoken in a wistful, plaintive, or melancholy voice, neither rising to eloquent pitch nor scavenging the depths of the vulgar. Its fundamental method is the plain style, its frequent mode the personal anecdote.

Yet how odd: the nineteenth-century Romantics located melancholy through a kind of lyric excess or extremity. Who but Poe with his manic spondees and trochees ("Leave no black plume as a token of that lie thy soul hath spoken! / Leave my loneliness unbroken!") could describe his own poem thus: "Beauty of whatever kind, in its supreme development, invariably excites the sensitive soul to tears. Melancholy is thus the most legitimate of all the poetical tones"? Who but Keats, in the great "Ode on Melancholy," could dramatically claim "Ay, in the very temple of Delight / Veil'd Melancholy has her sovran shrine, / Though seen of none save him whose strenuous tongue / Can burst Joy's grape against his palate fine . . ."? How far they were from the wistful strains we are now accustomed to hearing.

Linda Gregerson has come far from her own skillful, if melancholic, first book, *Fire in the Conservatory,* published in 1982. Her early poems

On *The Woman Who Died in Her Sleep* by Linda Gregerson, Houghton Mifflin, 1996; *Loosestrife* by Stephen Dunn, Norton, 1996; *The Wellspring* by Sharon Olds, Knopf, 1995; *The Marriage in the Trees* by Stanley Plumly, Ecco, 1996; *Sun Under Wood* by Robert Hass, Ecco, 1996.

flexed their considerable rhetorical muscles for occasions that frequently might have called for less—bad weather, a card game, reconsiderations of Renaissance history or its tropes. By no means must poetry always be wrung from extremity, but Gregerson's first book evinces more commanding tactics than context. *The Woman Who Died in Her Sleep* bears no such tentative potency. Rather, with harrowing depth and exacting clarity, the poems in her second collection seem wrought by the stringent demands of the largest passions—profound love, horrible fate. I sense so much life lived between these two books (and such patience) and find so much excellence as a result.

Gregerson is an eminently reasonable poet who has crafted an art to confront the demons of extremity. Her persona—variously parent, social commentator, scholar—laments that "the world's a world of trouble," and her reasonable demeanor seems often insufficient defense against the invasions of breast cancer, the contagions of familial harm and abuse, and the related social diseases of warfare and political cruelty. The outrageous growth of disorder threatens the speaker's security. In "The Bad Physician" the figure of cancer provides for this larger scheme, and the experience of recovery bears as well the intimate knowledge of loss:

> The beautiful cells dividing have
>> no mind
>> for us, but look
>
> what a ravishing mind
>> they make
>> and what a heart we've nursed
>
> in its shade, who love
>> that most
>> which leaves us most behind.

This stanza form is Gregerson's favored construction throughout *The Woman Who Died in Her Sleep*. Staggered triplets allow her work a kind of deliberating momentum—the pace of serious thought unfolding—and, as well, allow ample opportunity for the catching of one's breath. Her long sentences, coupled with the many outrages of body or spirit, might congest the poetry, but the form gives the syntax and ideas room to unpack. Gregerson often ironizes her flexible form by other internal strategies. Here, the inevitable grief of being left "behind" seems most piercing since she has prepared its closure in the prior rhymes of "mind"—twice—and, even more cleverly, in the medial "shade," after which follows a small, final triumph of perfect iambic pentameter.

If a formalizing wit provides one antidote to the horrible, then tenderness marks another. One of Gregerson's favorite subjects, the family, appears most pointedly in a number of poems about cultural damage. In "Bunting" her child's awakening from a nighttime chill prompts Gregerson's speaker to a profound connection with the televised image of "child after child in the chalk / embrace / of chemical death" in footage of the Iraqi/Kurdish war. Soothed and "protected," her own child "believes that someone's / in charge / here," but the speaker fathoms the terror of sanitized images where "not one [is] dis- / figured by what brought them here, / by death / throe and the bland assimilations / of the evening news, by lunatic cal- / culation or malevolence, which launched the gas, / by money, which made it. . . ." Nothing except the whim of fate differentiates her from "the man / in the dust / and the child in its unearthly / beauty, still in his arms." Her conclusive lines that all of us are "rocked . . . in the arms of the state" illustrate Gregerson's great ironic skill. The image of the soothed child, duplicated by the image of the dead child similarly "rocked," is both beautiful and horrible, and the omnipresent sponsorship of the state—the American media, the Iraqi military—provides in frightening finality the fact of vulnerability that we all embody.

The vulnerable, the abused and infirm, the innocent—these are figures of the Romantic hero of the nineteenth century, and they are Gregerson's as well. In "For the Taking" the speaker's "golden sister at eight and a half" suffers the sexual abuse of a "bad uncle." Though the child was her uncle's "piece of luck, his / find, / his renewable turn-on," Gregerson finds here her model for another kind of connective awe. She witnesses the conversion of rage to forgiveness in the example of the sister herself: "we // were deaf and blind / and have / ever since required of her that she // take care of us, and she has, / and here's / the worst, she does it for love."

Like the prior Romantics, Gregerson visits her heroes in their lonely struggles. Unlike them, she finds potential for recovery in the efforts of the collective as well of the individual. The many examples of cultural membership in this book—the family, the neighborhood, the country, the societies of art, the precincts of conscience—clearly represent threats to the self, as the "bad uncle" does, but they also can provide, like the sister, a means for preservation.

Linda Gregerson's is an art where reason and extremity undertake their large battles. Poison seeps into our basements, moral and imaginative corruption leak through our televisions, and our bodies are a war front where unrestrained "growths" threaten our well-being. Gregerson's impressive achievement is as large as her subjects—more like the large, public renderings of catharsis in Classical tragedy and comedy than the milder epiphanies we are used to reading. Throughout *The Woman Who Died in Her Sleep,* the severity of the poetry is due to such dramatic cruelties of fate and, occasionally, to such large recoveries. This is a wise, probing, beautifully composed collection of twenty-one poems, relentless in its subjects, yet neither hyperbolic nor resigned to melancholy. For Gregerson, understanding is the deepest ally of forgiveness.

Stephen Dunn more directly risks the perils of melancholy in his new book, *Loosestrife.* To be frank, he writes a kind of poetry which, by lesser poets, often shakes me with tedium these days: plain-spoken, in an easygoing method of personal anecdote, homely in its formal strategies, wistful in tone. His strategies may seem initially easy to imitate. How many pale emulators are there, whose work says little more than, "Hey, I'm a guy, I understand sports, not women, and I have feelings too"?

Of course this is entirely unfair to Stephen Dunn. He is wonderful at what he does. I look forward to his books with great eagerness. He brings important news, and warning, from the nearly paralyzed districts of American suburbia and middle-age: "Mornings I used to walk the dogs / by Nacote Creek, months before their deaths, / I'd see the night's debris, the tide's vagaries, / the furtive markings of creatures desperate to eradicate every smell not theirs. / I understood those dogs, who had so little / of their own" ("Loosestrife"). Dunn is wonderful because, unlike many, he writes with powerful and astute ironies: a deep sense of terror yet a resonant spiritual investment; an available, charming voice capable of great intimacy or confessional revelation.

Loosestrife is Dunn's tenth collection of poems in twenty-five years. He's perfected a kind of facility in his poetry, journal-like and precise. But *Loosestrife* seems to me a darker book than his others, and the flower of its title, the purple loosestrife, is a pertinent totem. This plant was imported in the last century from Europe, with the best purposes of providing a rugged, beautiful flower to household gardens. Yet, like kudzu, it has become a contagious invader, hated by gardeners, taking over suburban wetlands as a natural predator, invasive and unrelenting. Just so, Dunn's terror is of a similar invasion into privacy and coherence:

> Last night on Chestnut Neck Road, vandals
> used baseball bats on the mailboxes,
> selectively it seemed, and our house
> was broken into while our old, deaf dog
> guarded his sleepfulness.

The invasion that Dunn fears is material but also emotional, and his reaction in "Responsibility" is a suitable ironic compound: "Oh, vandals, / I can understand, but will not forgive you." To be broken into—such is the householder's fear. And such is the lover's. In "After Making Love," we see the inevitable rupture of privacy even in these most tender gestures: "No one should ask the other / 'What were you thinking?' // No one, that is, / who doesn't want to hear about the past // and its inhabitants, / or the strange loneliness of the present. . . ."

The most revealing invasions of Dunn's cosmos are those brought about by self-knowledge. "After Making Love" completes its progressive arc by moving from the lover's encroachment to the self's own. Again the figure of the invaded house provides Dunn with fearful, familiar grounding: "Some people actually desire honesty. / They must never have broken // into their own solitary houses / after having misplaced the key, // never seen with an intruder's eyes / what is theirs." What such self-knowledge exposes in Dunn's poetic neighborhood—and ours—is likely to yield shame, guilt, meagerness of spirit. The symptoms of this disease are Dunn's most acute subject. Many of the best poems here examine related maladies: "Power" with its explication of shame; "Tucson"'s fascination with violence, where "you won't get hurt / unless you need to get hurt"; and the exploitation of intimacy in many more.

Caught in the middle of such forces is the self. Not surprisingly, the self's own fractured edifice finally spills its contents, as in "Named": "He'd spent his life trying to control the names / people gave him; / oh the unfair and the accurate equally hurt. // Just recently he'd been son-of-a-bitch / and sweetheart in the same day, / and once again knew what antonyms // love and control are. . . ." Being opposed has become Dunn's trademark circumstance—that is, being resisted or contested, as his many poems of invasive damage establish, but also being doubled, being composed of contrary wills or fates. Rather than succumb, Dunn has learned to make art from his providence. In "Poetry" he claims the "middle" region which is both his home and his temptation: "Yet it helps as well / here in the middle, somewhat amused, / to have a fast red car / and a winding, country road"; and in "Ars Poetica" he identifies more fully the source of his powerful, contradicting clarity: "I'd come to understand restraint / is worthless unless / something's about to spill or burst." Stephen Dunn shares such circumstances with legions of contemporary Americans, taunted by comfort, uneasy in our own homes due to pressures within and without. Yet he is unusual, and his work is important, for the clarity and depth of articulation which make us confront ourselves and our fates "because you can be what you're not / for only so long."

If Dunn shows us the sources of our melancholy, then Sharon Olds commits them. I can think of no other poet whose individual poems I like so much yet whose books I like so little. A powerful, individual poem about a father's agonizing death is one thing. The tedious redundancies and gross fascinations of *The Father* are another. Even her best-selling *The Dead and the Living,* full of terrific poems, becomes a rhetorically dubious book; it establishes a ratio of victimizations that equates the Jews' extermination by Hitler to the speaker's martyrdom by her family. I suspect that much of Olds's influence and power draw precisely from the widespread sense of victimization that permeates our culture. As a generation of readers turns to Dunn for his representations of guilt, the once-intact household now fractured, so the same generation of readers has sought Olds for her speaker's alternating tenderness and strength, perhaps also for her advocacy of the martyr and victim. Men and women alike feel forgotten, unheard, misrepresented, and her poetry often articulates our lonely silences.

The Wellspring provides a number of good poems, yet its successes as a book are doubtful. Its narrative and thematic progression yields an oddly static and idealized Romantic self, though its chronology intends to trace that self's growth. I mean that literally. The four sections represent Olds's notions of one human's development: birth and childhood; adolescence, first love, the discoveries of sex; parenthood; adulthood, death, and transcendence. This is neither a daring nor a dubious construction, except that Olds risks especially large matters by her ambitious projections. In "My Parents' Wedding Night, 1937," for instance, she visits the site of her mother's loss of virginity ("She was naked with a man for the first time, / the intricate embroidery silks of her / pudenda moist upright alert"). Often exposed, the parents find themselves also to blame, as in "The Planned Child," where Olds's speaker "hated the fact that they had planned me." In "Earliest Memory," in a style and syntax identical to her other poems, she recreates her infant self in a crib surrounded by "light, shade, light, shade." "My First Weeks" muses that "sometimes, when I wonder what I'm like, underneath, / I think of my first two weeks, I was drenched with happiness." Sentimentality aside for a moment, one of the largest questions begged throughout this book is Olds's ready assumption of such a coherent, unchanging, and inculpable sense of self, the same in the womb as in middle age.

I wish I could report that the dramatic sentiments lessen as the book proceeds, but consider these opening lines from "Early Images of Heaven": "It amazes me that the shapes of penises, / their sizes, and angles, everything about them / was the way I would have designed them if I had / invented them." In previous books, Olds has written in remarkably fresh, astute ways about sexual love, yet here too often she seems exaggerated, burlesque. "First" provides us a glimpse of her first experience of giving oral sex:

> I went to him like a baby who's been crying
> for hours for milk. He stood and moaned
> and rocked his knees, I felt I knew

> what his body wanted me to do, like rubbing
> my mother's back, receiving directions
> from her want into the nerves of my hands.
> In the smell of the trees of seaweed rooted in
> ocean trenches just offshore,
> and the mineral liquid from inside the mountain,
> I gave over to flesh like church music
> until he drew out and held himself and
> something flew past me like a fresh ghost.

The risky figures of the man's infancy and the mother's massage might cohere into a dense and compelling trope—the erotic of the familial body—yet the images seem added-on rather than exercised. Olds's descriptive clarity about the oceanside landscape also is evocative, elemental, but the final images, "church music" and the especially unfortunate flying "fresh ghost," are sentimental and hyperbolic, even funny. Not that sex can't be comic, playful—of course—but I continue to find in these poems a combination of sentimentality and exaggeration, even falsification. This is Olds's most serious shortcoming.

As the book proceeds, we follow the speaker's development from childhood and adolescence into full adulthood, parenthood. If her parents are liable, their privacies exposed, the speaker depicts her own parental experience much differently. She becomes a rather angelic martyr in poem after poem, who tends her children's illnesses ("Finally I fondly remember even Benylin, / Robitussin, Actifed / Tedral, erythromycin," she laments), who patiently plays "Ninja Death" with them, and who finally grieves from abandonment as they move away from home. Even the title of "Forty-One, Alone, No Gerbil" identifies the narrative circumstance and the doleful pathos of the speaker, where a pet's death assumes the dimensions of a child's death or leave-taking: "now I must wait many years / to hear in this house again the faint / powerful call of a young animal."

There are sixty-one poems in *The Wellspring.* Some of them are examples of Sharon Olds's best abilities. "The Source" is a small marvel, a powerful rendering of Olds's magical touch with sexuality, "the deep spring of my life": "it is what I dreamed, to meet men / fully, as a woman twin, unborn, / half-gelled, clasped, nothing between us / but our bodies." Proud and vital, this poem best establishes Olds's ironic, primal scene: before birth yet after experience. The erotic meeting is "where I feel complete," the mythic site where "each one of us is whole." Her vigorous hunger for the body produces a poem whose formal effects seem equally hurried, driven. Radically enjambed lines, alternating long and short lines, complex sentences—rapid breaths, all of them—these are Olds's technical signatures. At best they produce a sense of rush and obligation, of uncrafted sincerity. Yet the improvisatory humility of her rhetoric in a few poems seems considerably less original when all the poems bear similar effects; redundancies of style, voice, technique conspire in *The Wellspring* more often than they cohere.

In form, stance, and theme *The Wellspring* is less than its strongest parts. It does not satisfactorily ironize its positions nor bespeak the daring, troubled scene of personal and historical juxtapositions of Olds's best earlier work. It is a domestic romance—like the four other books here—but while this speaker's parents have mistreated her and her children have abandoned her, she herself bears little sense of guilt or wrongdoing and undergoes surprisingly little change. It's not so much that Olds's tone is melancholic. Rather, that's how I feel after reading this book.

Stanley Plumly is a Romantic lyricist of such depth and fidelity that he seems as much a figure of the nineteenth as of the twentieth century. Plumly's beloved models—Keats, Whitman—seem as proximate as any other characters in his new *The Marriage in the Trees:* "Now the oldest surviving poet still alive / weaving with the audience that gossamer, / that thread of the thing we find in the voice again," he writes of Whitman's omnipresence in "Reading with the Poets." Like the other books here, *The Marriage in the Trees* recounts many of the dominant commissions of the traditional Romantic lyric: the primacy of the individual; the coherent solace of nature; the primal intelligence of the young, the infirm, the socially-misfit, the lover. These have been, and remain, Plumly's trademark subjects.

Yet there are many brilliant surprises as well. With thirty-nine poems, and longer by twenty pages than any of his five previous collections, *The Marriage in the Trees* shows Plumly's widest range of tones and stances. Since his 1976 *Out-of-the-Body Travel,* I have loved the obsessive, severe melancholy of Plumly's art. Here I am delighted as well by a new and developing sense of humor. Even the circumstance of "'Woman Drowns after Slipping from Floating Refrigerator'" marks a departure for Plumly—into the bizarre—and his meticulous perceptions now include the playful: "Next to polio, McCarthyism, / communism and premarital sex, / refrigerators were the paranoia / of parents who could afford but didn't / understand the closer other distances / of deep dry wells, sewer drains, the swallowed / empty fall in the middle of nowhere / down a mine shaft or a god's open grave. / It was national news to be buried // alive and saved." Plumly's signature descriptive gifts are sharp and remarkable. A single image can shine, as "Light rain coming down the color of keys." But again, I am especially pleased by the inventive exactitude of these two characterizations in "Alms":

> Her friend
>
> is thirty and touches every line
>
> she crosses in her step-and-a-half
>
> steps since her stroke, as if
>
> she'd been struck on her whole
>
> left side by lightning: she fades
>
> in and out of talking and lets
>
> the man she lives with—twice
>
> her size and boiled at birth
>
> in anger—speak for her.

More people show up here than in any other Plumly book. In fact, I wonder whether the absence of a lover-figure in this book has provided Plumly with imaginative access to more of the rest of the world. Keats, Whitman, and Conan Doyle coexist with paramedics, a "dwarf with violin," neighbors, "war veterans in regalia," and of course the abiding, contradicting presence of parents. In "Drunks," a longer prose poem, Plumly examines the effects of a father's alcoholism, "a dance, pathetic yet magical"; the figure of a mother haunts the book, as in "The Last Parent," who "wave[s] goodbye, the ocean-liner's melancholy size towering like Manhattan." Vanishing presences are accounted for, remembered, by their natural counterparts, trees and birds. *The Marriage in the Trees* is a life-list of losses, as in "Souls of Suicides as Birds" ("Jack Butz, whose Vietnam wound was total, /

like a lightning scar, lived for as long / as is possible in Piqua, Ohio, and be alive; / and Jerry Hart, star athlete, died of Aids: / one is a Purple, one a Boat-tailed Grackle"). The names and characteristics of trees and birds become this spiritualist's taxonomy, for nature accompanies each human gesture, loss, and passion: "Doctoring, then witchery, then / love—nothing we tried would work. / More apple trees that grew nowhere / but down. More maples spilling sugar. / More hawthorns blazing out, telling truth" ("The Marriage in the Trees").

Stephen Dunn's rhetoric of natural ease derives from his familiar voice; Sharon Olds's radical enjambment enables her sense of the passionate rush. The relative, powerful severity of Plumly's poetic is the result of his distinctive syntax. His tone may be melancholy, but it is also rhetorically charged—more Keats than Bishop, more Dickinson than Robinson. His greatest achievement, I think, is to have crafted such a profound, entirely original lyric style:

> This pyrrhic fire the barn burned down and blew back
> into the dust-weight of its carbon, that burned the air
> flecked bright with it, above the wheat in flags,
> the barn I spent the summer part-time painting, white
> on white to purify the wood. . . .

Just a few lines and we know it's Plumly—deliberate, intense, furrowed; engaged with the unfolding, complex rigor of work and memory. His particular mode of the Romantic lyric derives from Keats's heightened severity, Poe's estrangement. Many of the poems in *The Marriage in the Trees* provide an additional formal severity, too, in their decasyllabic construction. Such formality can be precise, tightened-down, and it can be playful too. Plumly seems delighted to juxtapose lines as accentually heavy as "Bums ears, burned black, blackhead-encrusted, rubbed" with others as rhythmically deft or light as "Next to polio, McCarthyism. . . ." Each has ten syllables, yet each imparts a very clear tonal and rhetorical distinction. Even memory seems a product of syntax. Plumly's long sentences go in search of recollection, and the zeugma is his favorite figure to get there: "That night was industrial and animal, a burning-off of flesh, the blue clouds' upward drifting . . . ." The parallel structure yields unlike parts of speech, though the rhythmic and alliterative likeness of "industrial and animal" connects them, as in memory. The gerund "burning-off" further extends the grammatical construction and the memory of this nighttime disaster in "Complaint against the Arsonist." The zeugma, like the dense alliteration, adds music as well as a kind of rhetorical anxiety to the narrative itself.

Stanley Plumly is one of our best poets—one of a tiny number—and this is a wonderful book. Perhaps in a shorter version, I might have wished to delete "Panegyric for Gee" (a Christopher Smart–like celebration of a bulldog) or "Human Excrement" (which, like a couple of others, just seems slight) or even Plumly's translation of Canto XVIII of *The Inferno.* And yet they also contribute to the surprising range and variety of this book by a poet whose art and gift are still powerfully growing.

Robert Hass may have the deepest potential for greatness among these poets. Each of his collections of poetry has been produced with care and published over a period even longer than the one in which Plumly's exacting work has been published. *Sun Under Wood* is only his fourth book since 1973, yet already a number of his grand poems seem destined for long lives. It's hard for me to say that this is his best book, since each of the last three has seemed landmark in its achievements. But still, Hass's new volume contains many of his most important works to date, among them "Faint Music," "Interrupted Meditation," "The Seventh Night," and several brilliant longer poems, including "English: An Ode" and "Dragonflies Mating."

One strain of American poetry can be identified by its abundant and obviously exhibited non-American influences. Wallace Stevens, Ezra Pound, John Ashbery, and others depict the distinctive American hunger for things European, the high art of the Continent. Gary Snyder, whose influence on Hass seems substantial, weds an American frontier naturalism with Asian spirituality, and Allen Ginsberg soaks up everything from everywhere. Still, few poets wear their influences more obviously and gladly than Hass. He is something of a buttoned-down Ginsberg, emotionally and formally open, inclusive, enthusiastic, if considerably more ironic. A fine translator of the haiku of Bashō, Buson, and Issa, he is fond of embedding his own distilled formulations within longer poems: "Disaster: something wrong with the stars," he laments in "English: An Ode." The poem concludes with this section, quoted entirely: "So—what are the river stones / that come swimming to your eyes, *habitante?* // They hold the hope of morning." A brilliant shorter lyric, "Happiness," recounts two lovers' relationship as erotic partners and as writers, each practice being a manner of "coax[ing] an inquisitive soul / from . . . the reluctance of matter." The poem finds its surprising closure in a touch of self-exposed, odd tenderness: "*happiness! it is December, very cold, / we woke early this morning, / and lay in bed kissing, / our eyes scrunched up like bats.*" These haiku-like poems-within-poems serve to crystalize or focus the larger emotional scenery of their surrounding text. Not explanations but accompaniments, they depict one kind of discourse with another.

If the haiku provides Hass with imagistic and emotional clarity, then his translations of Dante may represent another, larger aspect of his poetic—a heroic Romanticism that is both allegorical and natural. "Faint Music" recalls some of the best poems from Hass's 1979 volume, *Praise,* in its grace and subject:

> When everything broken is broken,
> and everything dead is dead,
> and the hero has looked into the mirror with complete contempt,
> and the heroine has studied her face and its defects
> remorselessly, and the pain they thought might,
> as a token of their earnestness, release them from themselves
> has lost its novelty and not released them . . .
>   maybe then, ordinary light,
> faint music under things, a hovering like grace appears.

To add a third dramatic influence to his repertoire, Hass draws mightily from his long, productive relationship with the work of Czeslaw Milosz. As antidote or ironic solution to the melancholy of haiku and to the heroism of the Romantic lyric, Hass pursues within his longer poems an analysis of the progress of those texts themselves, a kind of post-Enlightenment social critique. This tactic is his most extended poetic trope, skeptical, self-disclosing, deconstructive. Everywhere the poems describe their progress and methods, reveal their sources, discuss what they do or don't or can't mean. The mother figures into these particular poems with recurrent obsession—her alcoholism, her unsubtle weaknesses. With a knowing wink to us, but also with professorial contrivance, Hass impedes (or rips into) the progress of "Dragonflies Mating":

> When we say "mother" in poems,
> we usually mean some woman in her late twenties
> or early thirties trying to raise a child.
>
> We use this particular noun
> to secure the pathos of the child's point of view
> and to hold her responsible.

If you find this kind of disruption annoying or cloying, then Hass's new book is probably not for you. If such self-conscious and metaliterary intrusion delights you, then *Sun Under Wood* will be your favorite Hass collection. He has never been more allusive, agitated, deferring. The most resonant function of Hass's self-referencing style is revealed in another poem about the mother, "Our Lady of the Snows." Here she is visited "in a hospital drying out," and her young sons must learn to bear their "navigable sorrow." It's as if Hass is commenting on his own tactic of literary referencing: "Though mostly when I think of myself / at that age, I am standing at my older brother's closet / studying shirts, / convinced that I could be absolutely transformed / by something I could borrow." Two important aspects amplify the irony of this statement. The speaker's innocent age undermines the actuality of such transformation, and his adult self-awareness, the sorrow and tenderness of that voice, reiterates the fact. But Hass's methods can be indulgent. He veers toward a kind of textual and personal narcissism at points in these poems. In "Regalia for a Black Hat Dancer," for instance, he may overestimate our delight at witnessing his making of the poem instead of finding the poem intact:

> There ought to be some single word for the misery of divorce.
> (What is the rhythm of that line? Oh, I see. Four and three,

Emily's line!—

> There ought to be some single word
> For the misery of divorce.
> It dines upon you casually
> duh-dduh-duh-duh-dduh-fierce/remorse/pierce/).

If Dickinson's anthem meter haunts Hass or his text-in-delay, the poem is more deeply and importantly shadowed by the mother, asthmatic or emphyzematic, as well as by a brother in a "psych ward . . . coming down from crack." The persistent familial rupture is appropriately signified by Hass's textual ruptures, his revising himself aloud.

Nearly all of the central moments of *Sun Under Wood* are underwritten by shame. Familial breakage—divorce, childhood trauma, adult misconduct —mirrors the shame of aesthetic self-doubt and of textual disruption. "My Mother's Nipples" is a long, fascinating analysis of "displacement," as if a brilliant adult is finally able to absolve himself of the "responsibility" for this particular childhood trauma, the inadvertent witnessing of his mother's breast. The poem becomes a corresponding forgiveness of the mother's own withholding of traditional maternal nurturance. An even more base, corporeal shame is revealed in "Shame: An Aria." Here, caught "reaming out [his] nose" when an elevator door opens, the speaker finds his privacy invaded, and his subsequent "descent" to the ground floor traces a hellish punishment, his public embarrassment. Hass takes this comic episode into surprisingly complex territory, however, in an explication of the socialization of shames relating to the body: "russets of menstrual blood, toejam, earwax, / phlegm, the little dead militias of white corpuscles / we call pus, what are they after all but the twins of the juices / of mortal glory." Ultimately, Hass constructs a fascinating praise-song to shame. He dismisses its sibling "embarrassment" as a mere public response to exposure or being caught, devoid of judgment or moral standing. But shame—that Old World agony—indicates our consciences at work. It is an avenue toward instruction and redemption.

All through *Sun Under Wood,* Hass's ability to convert the comedic to the sublime, the anecdotal to the metaphysical and ethical, the personal to the social, is totally remarkable. This book reaches a level of achievement

Hass has not reached before, a level of achievement that seems to me both unique and significant in contemporary American poetry. It is literary and messy, discursive and lyric. It is risky, large, and hugely compassionate. Hass romances the grotesque and the glorious alike in order to articulate for us the pleasures—the erotic delights, the social critiques, the intellectual renewals—of a life and a text.

PART FIVE

Hieroglyphs of Erasure

Against Mastery:
Adrienne Rich and Philip Levine

When Whitman obliterates his speaker's individuating personality and body in the concluding section of "Song of Myself," the doubled trope of martyrdom and epiphany also signifies an act of artistic mastery, of completion, of transcendental accomplishment. Within the huge cosmos of his poem's vision, Whitman's speaker arrives at last at his own demise, performing and then vanishing into an act of willing self-annihilation: "I depart as air, I shake my white locks at the runaway sun, / I effuse myself in eddies, and drift it in lacy jags." He hovers just long enough to beckon us to follow his lead, out of the body, even out of the poem, into the graces of natural perfection: "I bequeath myself to the dirt to grow from the grass I love, / If you want me again look for me under your boot-soles. // You will hardly know who I am or what I mean. . . ."

American Romanticism—at least in its more transcendental mode— supposes that artistic mastery can lead to spiritual purification, proceeding in part by means of estrangement from the social environment as well as by a "gradual extinction of personality," to iterate Eliot's famous phrase. Perhaps we have learned to doubt the actuality of transcendental leaping, and certainly since the Confessionals we have come to doubt the necessity of a poet's extinguishing of personality for the sake of the poem. But here I would like to confront more fully the issues of social erasure and of mastery, the assumptions that mastery of a vision or of an art form is a desirable, complete, perhaps transcendental end in itself.

Adrienne Rich's new *An Atlas of the Difficult World* suggests grave

---

On *An Atlas of the Difficult World* by Adrienne Rich, Norton, 1991; *What Work Is* by Philip Levine, Knopf, 1991.

doubts, or at least very complicated attitudes, toward the desirability of mastery. In the first section of her powerful thirteen-part title poem, Rich may echo some of Whitman's phrasing but seems specifically to reject the notion of the poet's vanishing or transcending presence and intends, instead, to locate and fix her speaker on the earth:

> This is no place you ever knew me.
> But it would not surprise you
> to find me here, walking in fog, the sweep of the great ocean
> eluding me, even the curve of the bay, because as always
> I fix on the land. I am stuck to earth. What I love here
> is old ranches, leaning seaward. . . .
>   These are not the roads
> you knew me by. But the woman driving, walking, watching
> for life and death, is the same.

Throughout her distinguished poetic career, Rich has been driven to speak for the social citizen, to articulate the abundant pains of the battered public body. Her resolution to remain "stuck to earth" is an acceptance of such duty or obligation. It represents her direct confrontation with imperfection and pain, with worldly "dreck and waste," rather than any desire for the erasures which are the inevitable result of masterful perfection. Her project probes the social design for its abuses, "[follows] the coffins" to represent those who suffer the damages of the powerful, and "[searches] armed streets for the end of degradation."

An Atlas of the Difficult World is one of the more powerful and humane books of poems of recent years, one of the most aching and yet generous. Nowhere does Rich seek the mantle of mastery, and nowhere does she presume to rise beyond the circumstances of bodily and social engagement. The "sweep of the great ocean," the obliterating and transcendental natural force, is simply not part of Rich's domain and dedication. This book's one direct reference to mastery becomes a severe indictment of its effects, both personal and political. In "Olivia" the main character is a white South-African woman, who is both a fundamentalist Christian and apparently an anti-apartheid militant. Rich directly addresses her:

I know the power you thought you had—

to know them all, better than they
knew you, than they knew you knew,
to know better than those who paid
you—paid by them, to move

at some pure point of mastery
as if, in your slight outline, moon
you could dwell above them, light and shade,
travel forever to and fro

above both sides, all sides, none,
gliding the edges, knapsack crammed
—was that it? to lift above
loyalty, love and all that trash

higher than power and its fields of force?
—never so much as a woman friend?
You were a woman walked on a leash.
And they dropped you in the end.

The woman's double identity results in her impossible hovering "above both sides, all sides," so that her commitment is to "none." Her position above "loyalty, love and all that trash" suggests both transcendence and betrayal, and her inevitable circumstance is to be "dropped" by those who have used her, finally marginalized by either social alternative. The "pure point of mastery" concludes here in a betrayal of the individual by the wielders of political power. If mastery results in erasure, then Rich's abiding project is to resist the master.

An Atlas of the Difficult World is a literal mapping out of such resistances. Rich's persona assumes the role of Virgilian surveyor and guide through the treacherous terrain of social experience, although this surface world contains a sufficient supply of underworldly horror and despair:

Here is a map of our country,
here is the Sea of Indifference, glazed with salt

This is the haunted river flowing from brow to groin
we dare not taste its water
This is the desert where missiles are planted like corms
This is the breadbasket of foreclosed farms
This is the birthplace of the rockabilly boy
This is the cemetery of the poor
who died for democracy. . . .

It may be Whitman-like in its expanse and scope; still, Rich's title poem
contains a catalogue rife with particular failures, cruelties, and sacrifices
rather than an encouraging, optimistic list or blueprint for perfection. At
every step Rich refuses to detach artistic mastery from the other associa-
tions inherent in the notion of "the master"—political, genderal, racial.
Mastery blurs or erases detail in its rise above the particularities of social
experience. To resist its temptations is to reject the tacit or purposeful realms
of power and authority that it occupies.

Rich is of course best known as an outspoken representative of femi-
nist poetics and politics. (So much so that I fear sometimes her work is
attended to only to confirm or prove this one political design—though her
poems themselves sometimes lament such exclusive or limiting readerly
expectation.) The concept of mastery does nonetheless clearly connote a
masculine form of power, and much of Rich's intensity stems from her argu-
ment with this paradigm. In another very strong sequence, "Eastern War
Time," the two characters in section five embody the inequitable balance
of power between the genders: "a young girl . . . her ankles greased in vomit
and diarrhea / driven naked across the yard" is eventually sacrificed "on the
operating table / of the famous doctor / who plays string quartets with his
staff in the laboratory." Significantly, the male authority is also a figure of
political and religious persecution, a Nazi doctor who experiments on and
abuses Jewish prisoners. The strongest poems in *An Atlas of the Difficult
World* synthesize the struggles between forms of genderal tension with issues
of racial mastery and slavery, political power-wielding, economic subjuga-
tion, and religious oppression. Indeed, since her 1986 *Your Native Land,
Your Life,* Rich has been increasingly interested in exploring her own Jewish
identity, as in "1948: Jews":

It was a burden for anyone
to be fascinating, brilliant
after the six million
Never mind just coming home
and trying to get some sleep
like an ordinary person

But even in the most explicit religious impulses of these poems, Rich is focussed on—in anger and in praise—the social body. "Tattered Kaddish" is a very human-centered chant containing another occasion of social witness: "Praise to life though it crumbled in like a tunnel / on ones we knew and loved." Always the brutalities of politics preempt any purer, transcending vision or prayer.

For Rich, the masteries of prosody and technique are not separable from political masteries. Her poems are never exactly pretty. Their rhetorical schemes, their ragged patterns of imagery, their persisting voices, their generally rough technical surfaces never incline toward the more sublime poetic choices, since an impulse toward the sublime—in landscape or vision—contains an impulse to transcend the public arena. Instead, she wants to articulate the widest historical awarenesses and obligations, not leading to the embracing, blurring ego of Whitman but rather toward a style capable of unmasterful citizenry: "A patriot is one who wrestles for the soul of her country / as she wrestles for her own being." Her decidedly non-epiphanic endings, her frequent turns toward blunt discourse, her unevenness in lineation, all establish a powerful social poetic whose intent is to resist, obviously to "wrestle" with, the assumed beauties of purity and transcendence. The roughness of her poems embodies the material and social presences everywhere at work in them. In "Two Arts," speaking directly to the occupation of the artist, and perhaps resisting the losses beautifully and ironically "mastered" in Bishop's "One Art," she clarifies the function as well as the formal property of her art: "you have a brutal thing to do."

To resist mastery must entail pain. *An Atlas of the Difficult World* is certainly a painful book; it aches, mourns, laments, and curses. Nowhere does it abandon its commitment to speak for the enslaved and silenced. Rather than transcendental, sublime, or blurring in its destined vision, Rich's poetry is clarifying. Its clarities are those resulting most directly from the clearheadedness of social engagement and exposure. Rich gives us these lines in "Darklight," as if directly and literally to enact her poetic "vision":

> Under the lens
> lashes and veins grow huge
> and huge the tear that washes out the eye,
> the tear that clears the eye.

Rich's new book is a kind of definition, a mapping out of experience into a terrain of political and poetic engagements. Philip Levine's brilliant new *What Work Is* also presents a defining vision, but does so more precisely in terms of economic mastery and subservience. One of the driving passions of Levine's work has been his sympathetic connection to the blue-collar, working-class citizen, the brutalized servant of capitalist machinations. *What Work Is* is his strongest pronouncement of that social contingent. Like Rich, Levine draws much of his force and his motivation from a stubborn resistance of masterful manipulation.

At the center of *What Work Is* is a stunning, seventeen-page poem entitled "Burned," and near the center of "Burned" come these lines, which once again echo and doggedly challenge the Whitman-like epiphany:

> How will you know me?
> I won't be tall or dressed
> for dinner or carrying a dark bag,
> I won't be whistling like a bird
> or your father coming home from work,
> I won't be anyone you ever
> spoke to or fell asleep beside
> or wakened to. I won't take your hand
> or come forward and touch
> your hair or kiss your cheek.

Adrienne Rich begins her long "An Atlas of the Difficult World" by fixing her speaker/guide "on the land," identifying her as wholly social, "stuck to earth." And here, midway through his seared poem, Levine addresses the same issue of identity and recognition: the gesture which Whitman used as an instructive and transcendental figure ("You will hardly know who I am or what I mean") at the end of "Song of Myself." But neither pastoral nor paternal nor erotic, Levine's voice resists the solace of the sublime, denies the omnipotence of the master:

> . . . do you see a shadow?
> It could be the birth we gave
> back to the rain. It could be
> the silence after love or just pain
> without hope or the need to dance. . . .
> It could be
> a whisper, a secret never kept,
> everything your heart knew
> and you forgot. Don't ask.

Up to this point in "Burned," Levine gives us the urban landscape, ruined and ruinous, of "our least favorite city, / the one bombed and burned from the inside / by its own citizens." The central trope in each section of the poem's first half is one of fire, of a scorching wound: "a burned car left in a field / of sassafras"; "I was burned, / she said, and lifted her blouse to show / me"; "tell me what it is like / to enter the fires of your own making, naked, / day after day, until the burning becomes a sweetness." The burned figures suggest the scorched summers in Detroit as well as the hot factories in whose "forge rooms" the workers receive their daily damages, their "hands turned to pig iron." This landscape is hellish but human-made. What the speaker/worker seeks here is his compassion, his capacity to love and mourn, and his renewed commission as a poet:

> Why am I not mourning the tiny death
> of the sparrow. . . .
> When this passes
> how will I know I was and I was alive
> Who will take my hand
> smelling of earth and

burning now to autumnal rust

Who will lead me to the ceremonies of sorrow

who will lead me

Midpoint in the poem, an emerging, slightly unwilling "shadow" enters to serve as escort and explicator. The figure of flame relinquishes its position in the poem and is replaced by this "shadow," this other. It is not spiritual ("If I called you 'my soul,' you'd laugh in my face"), and neither deific nor erotic ("If I went / down on my knees to you as to / a god or a beloved, you'd . . . shake your head"), but rather an embodiment of experience, pain, the self's own center. It replaces the fires of the poem with a gentle, restorative wind, as if to cool the spirit and to supply or replenish the breath. Like Rich's title poem, "Burned" is not a descent into underworldly horror, not an attempt to transcend worldly "dreck and waste," but rather a direct confrontation with a damaging social circumstance. The poem's own song, its memory, its breath, quenches or at least eases the factory's flames. If "to enter the fire / is to be burned," as one character laments, then this reenacted mortification provides the speaker with the compassionate ability to imagine now, as well, "the slow windward motion of the stars. / Late rain falling for hours / between the squat, closed houses."

The people in Levine's poems have been betrayed by the false promise of the American dream. They have been beaten into slavery by the dehumanizing agency of capitalism. As even the more sublime properties of mastery entail an erasure or removal from the public sphere (as Whitman shows), its more utilitarian or practical aspects elicit from Levine his deepest sense of rage and betrayal. His is one of our most resonant voices of social conviction and witness, and he speaks with a powerful clarity. Perhaps his voice contains more capacity for irony or wry humor than Rich's does, as from the tolerance or composure necessary to survive day after day of indignation, but his rage is no less central or persuasive. Levine is also less likely to situate one person against another in his poems and less likely to probe the schisms between the genders or between races. Men and women alike, "the homeless, the fruit pickers / of creation . . . runaway housewives / bored by their husbands, and bored husbands," all are embraced in Levine's representation of mastery and slavery, as if the primary inhuman and dehumanizing fact of American life is the factory and foodline, the poverty of the jobless or powerless worker:

> Take this quiet woman, she has been
> standing before a polishing wheel
> for over three hours, and she lacks
> twenty minutes before she can take
> a lunch break. Is she a woman?

These opening lines of "Coming Close" demonstrate Levine's sympathy as well as his formal subtlety. Like most of the people in *What Work Is,* the woman working provides Levine with a model for craft and hard work. The act of polishing suggests the poet's task, and indeed Levine's poem is carefully fashioned. The half-rhymes are not patterned though they are recurrent, and the line is generally nine syllables long, most often settling into a four-beat pulse. The question he asks—"Is she a woman?"—identifies a formal issue as well. The woman's humanness is imperiled by her work. Her very form, her body, seems qualified by the machinery around her:

> Consider the arms as they press
> the long brass tube against the buffer,
> they are triated along the triceps,
> the three heads of which clearly show.
> Consider the fine dusting of dark down
> above the upper lip, and the beads
> of sweat that run from under the red
> kerchief across the brow and are wiped
> away with a blackening wrist band
> in one odd motion. . . .

The detail wrought by the poet's work of looking could describe the action and features of a machine well as a person. But in order to make such an observation, in order to validate the conjoining "poetry" of such a statement, the second-person character must take his place beside the woman: "you must hang your tie / and jacket in one of the lockers / in favor of a black smock, you must / be prepared to spend shift after shift. . . ." The gift of such sympathy is language, which contains a nourishment as well as a point of contact: "You must feed her, / as they say in the language of the place. / Make no mistake, the place has a language." The woman returns this gesture of earned sympathy with her own act of knowing, gentle connection, which also bears a mark of undeniable difference:

> she places the five
> tapering fingers of her filthy hand
> on the arm of your white shirt to mark
> you for your own, now and forever.

The measure of Levine's sympathy is "marked" on his white shirt, his poet's attire; he refuses to sentimentalize either the woman's circumstance or his own.

What Work Is may become one of the signal books of poetry of our time. Poem after poem confronts the terribly damaged conditions of American labor. Further, Levine insists on attending to the particularities of personality and character, on seeing distinction in the face of blurring abuse, and on demanding the restorative authority of song wrenched out of the pain and grime of such detail. These are the primary materials of his art. Like Rich he resists the social estrangements of a more transcendental poetry, preferring to remain within the cultural community of the worker and victim rather than to rise against or above them in the guise of perfection, of the master. Both of these poets have learned from, and have insisted on amending, the alternately sympathetic and masterful encouragements of Whitman. Not only echoing the "sixty-year-old smiling public man" in Yeats's great poem but also parodying Whitman in the thirty-second section of "Song of Myself," who thinks he "could turn and live with animals, they are so placid and self-contain'd," Levine persists to find subtle promise in the human, in "Among Children":

> . . . not one
> turned against me or the light, not one
> said, I am sick, I am tired, I will go home,
> not one complained or drifted alone,
> unloved, on the hardest day of their lives.

Eleven years from now they will become
the men and women of Flint or Paradise,
the majors of a minor town, and I
will be gone into smoke or memory,
so I bow to them here and whisper
all I know, all I will never know.

The poet's audience here is also his model. And his job, his own brand of work—to invest the future's "majors" with the life-bearing gifts of poetry, humility, and shared mercy—has never been more needed.

The Crux of the Matter: David Wojahn

The poems in David Wojahn's *The Falling Hour* are grief-stricken, lined with peril, thick with loss. Not one of these thirty-two poems is easy to read in any sense, though reading them may yield a paradox: clarity, the integrity of deep feeling, may arise from an art of distress. *The Falling Hour* is Wojahn's fifth book of poems, following most recently from his superb *Late Empire* (1994), and continues a trajectory of impressive growth from his *Icehouse Lights,* which won the 1981 Yale Series of Younger Poets Award.

David Wojahn's poetry is crisis poetry. In "Border Crossings" he applies explicitly this trope of "crossing over" to describe the speaker's citizenship in the doubled world of ancient horror and contemporary disease. Here, seeking a kind of repair, he accompanies a loved one to a rehabilitation center for alcohol abuse. He is compelled by a childhood memory of repair—when he could handily "glue together" a model toy—but must reject that easier nostalgia. He urges himself to "reside in the moment" as he enters this radically "foreign" country with its "zebra-striped gate, / the guards who hold his documents." Throughout *The Falling Hour* the speaker ventures deep into such underworlds of death, torture, and personal agony, relocating from health and sanity to the region where "shame [is] the lingua franca of these lands." He is a Virgil for our distorted contemporary voyages, and this book depicts a life haunted by a search for purpose and clarity, if not solace:

> And he knows his skin is glass,
>
> his mission shame . . .

On *The Falling Hour* by David Wojahn, Pittsburgh, 1997.

and shame the notebook
>and the novels he's brought her,

riffled and shut with a strange
>and final delicacy, and shame
>>the signal that motions him on.

The immediate or local impetus for much of Wojahn's sense of grief derives from the death of his wife, the poet Lynda Hull, whose 1994 automobile accident recurs like a nightmare in these poems. The lover's elegy is one of poetry's ancient and abiding performances; suitably, the dirge becomes one of Wojahn's chronic patterns. In "Dirge Sung with Marianne Faithfull," the speaker is transported by the "dope-sick, booze-sick, heart-sick" voice of the sixties rock singer—herself an icon of the times—to "stroke the damp hair" of his lover: "when I hear her I can only // feel terror; when I hear her I can only / think of you." But if elegy is poetry's oldest lyric melody, then Wojahn brings to bear on it the peculiar contemporary fact of electronic recording, where the voices of the dead haunt not only our dream songs but also our waking silences. The difficult knowledge of *The Falling Hour* is that nowhere are we immune from the omnipresence of the lost. In his powerful sonnet "God of Journeys and Secret Tidings," Wojahn reiterates Rilke's assertion that "Eurydice is better off in hell," where death is both permanent and merciful. The unreal and unrelenting horror of our new technology is that it can play back our losses forever:

And how, indeed, could such beauty be borne,
>except by the shoulders of a god? Here on the dome
of hell it rains, and you are six months' dead.
The answering machine tonight spins down—
February's messages, a half year unerased,
>another mistake to tally. And on them is your voice.

The speaker's losses multiply in *The Falling Hour* with terrible velocity. In "Ode" we are witness to the speaker's "mother at St. Joseph's, & the chemo's slow razoring, / curls fallen, threshed; scalp left patched with a little down; & and not the lasering // Vitalis stink on the fat mortician's hands, comb bestowing my father's final part. . . ." The death of both parents by disease, in such close proximity to his spouse's fatal accident, results in the speaker's nearly benumbed, Poe-like utterance, "Never this, never this, never this." Stunned by horrors, the speaker tries to recall any moment free of grief, any articulatable coherence. But even the language of his child-hood is afflicted, as in "Stammer," where the young speaker tries to "effect the cure" for his speech distress. Throughout *The Falling Hour* other dis-tortions of language combine to become an important trope, as the dam-ages of experience serve to disfigure our ability both to recall and recount. How we speak intractably shapes what we are able to know. Like the sup-port group of "chirpers, gulpers, tic-ers, / 'scat singers'—as in scatological" in "Tractate for Doctor Tourette," the characters in *The Falling Hour* strain for clarity against the individual body and cultural circumstance.

Wojahn's rendering of personal trauma is powerful. But the narration of personal experience is commonplace in contemporary poetry. Wojahn enlarges his art by crossing over from the personal to the political; his sec-ond large subject is historical, the cultural upheavals in recent European and American society. In such collisions of political calamity and personal loss Wojahn finds his most forceful tactic. Even in his first book, *Icehouse Lights,* Wojahn probed his family's central-European heritage. But now, as though to mirror his personal devastations, he is drawn to the most severe cultural allusions. In a nine-part sequence, "The Nightingales," Wojahn rehearses a horrible episode of recent European history, the rise, decay, and fall of the Ceausesçu regime. Mixing opulence and cruelty, singing "of the partisans, stopping to reload // Klashnikovs" as well as of "Thy Palace and Thy Chocolates / girdling strawberries star kiwi fruit, dulcet filling //of Cointreau," Wojahn constructs a powerful narrative through a kind of parataxis—through radical and direct juxtapositions. The sequence con-tinues with a surprising range of poems, from the darkly humorous "Before the Wine and Cheese Is Served," a satire of a contemporary English depart-ment bemoaning that it is "undertheorized," to "The Solitary Voice," a fragmentary narrative which explores both "the market value of repression" and the intimate privacy of masturbation, the shame of exposure: "When I do it I am polyphonic but alone." In such sequences Wojahn recalls Milan

Kundera, with his powerful blending of political and personal jeopardy. For both writers the humiliation of the individual body reflects the shame or corrosion of the collective spirit.

Wojahn's new work pursues a kind of Postmodern application of Romantic teleology. Wordsworth and Emerson depict nature as a method of constructing a self. To the Romantic, nature reflects the soul. Recall Emerson's own proclamation that "Particular natural facts are signs of particular spiritual facts." For Wojahn, however, since nature is a figment of the human cultural sphere, politics must be the most visible evidence— the vocabulary—for the tension between cultural and personal desires, even for our most intimate experiences. And so, not only in "The Nightingales" but in many of the sharpest poems in *The Falling Hour,* Wojahn regards the political in order to portray the collective as well as the personal psyche. The book becomes a valuable documentary, fusing "the president's resignation // and the spaceship that crashed in Roswell, New Mexico" with televised SWAT teams, Walter Cronkite as he narrates Ruby's assassination of Oswald, and a myriad of other episodes from our cultural history. Again, this method is not unfamiliar in recent poetry, but Wojahn's choice and handling of material seems exemplary.

Wojahn's third subject derives from another specific articulation of our culture. Since *Mystery Train* (1990), Wojahn has found inspiration in the lyrics of rock music and in the lives of its musicians, and he continues this investigation in *The Falling Hour.* The primitive colloquialism of rock suits Wojahn's popular idiom, and its cacophonous sounds provide his poems with the melodic equivalent of a collision—again, a crossing over of discordant desires. The poems warn us that our personal voices are as likely to be imperiled as defined by the collective din. At times, as in "Hey, Joe," the rock lyric speaks for us, like a metrical substitution. Here is Jimi Hendrix in performance, who knows the song is both "gallows tree and killing floor":

> He must take both parts—killer and chorus, strophe
> and antistrophe forged from feedback of an amp
> hiked up to ten. *Where you goin' with*
>
> *that blood . . . your hands. . . . I heard you shot*
> *your woman down.*

Other popular-culture media inform the poems as well. Wojahn applies theories and allusions from film, jazz, and television as well as rock. The poems become like a jump-cut video, or a pop collage, a multiple narrative of the personal and cultural. It takes a poet of considerable skill to manage such ambitious, and potentially over-familiar, blending. I wish to quote one poem entirely, in order to demonstrate how effective Wojahn's technique can be:

> The trigger pull of flip-flops on the Bay of Pigs
> Where Danes as pale as canvases by Malevich
> Parade fat torsos on a white sand beach.
> Someone's shortwave blares the Pogues
>
> From Key West or Fort Lauderdale
> As six Yemeni women test the waters
> In the chain mail of full-length Lycra *chadors,*
> The husband shadowed by a beach umbrella
>
> Flaring in the wind with his burnoose.
> A wall divides us from prying locals,
> *Socialismo O Muerte* neatly stenciled
> On stucco topped with wire and broken glass.
>
> Daiquiris by the graves of "revolutionary martyrs,"
> Machine-gun fire of ice in dueling blenders.

Here, in "Resort at Playa Giron (Cuba, 1992)," the social juxtapositions startle us, as Wojahn cuts within single lines from gun triggers to "flip-flops," from "chain mail" to *chadors* made of Lycra. The chewy alliterations heighten the dramatic displacements of things, yet nowhere is the tension among contraries more evident than in his brilliant end rhymes. The political shame of the Bay of Pigs is ironized further by its rhyme with "Pogues," a late-eighties rock band. Similarly, the final couplet's rhyme of "martyrs" and "blenders" pierces with wretched irony, as political turmoil is replaced by hedonistic leisure. As here, Wojahn reconfigures the sonnet form in a number of cases in *The Falling Hour* and employs other traditional constructions as well, especially the villanelle. But while his lineation and stanza forms are tight, conventional, the predominant rhythm of these poems is decidedly non-poetic. He veers away from the traditional poetic meters, even from a kind of graceful lyricism, preferring the rhythm of dense prose.

The Falling Hours is a solemn, exacting book of poems. Wojahn critiques our contemporary culture even as he exploits his own life's crises. He crosses these borders, unflinching, in hopes of clarity and repair. As he writes in the last poem, "Before the Words": "The tablets have been broken / and the tablets now shall be restored."

The Romance of Betrayal:
David St. John

I admit to a ready and predictable boredom with contemporary American poets for whom a vacation to Europe is an occasion to write another poem. Tourists do not make good poets, for the knowledge of a tourist is the knowledge of the passer-by, the consumer-as-voyeur. It is the momentary point of view of an outsider for whom native life and language are exotic and therefore thrilling at a distance, through a wide-angle lens. The poem as postcard. Especially familiar are those trips to France, England, and Ireland, with their nostalgic and pastoral comforts; and Eastern Europe often inspires American poets to wax political and just, judging and chiding from afar. And Italy brings us the grand, baroque solace of high art, Keats and Severn struggling again up the Spanish stairs, gondolas and fresh pasta, great wine, old world clarity and grace. Italy, where they love even their artists.

And where, as David St. John reminds us, they kill them.

This last fact provides the doubled wisdom of St. John's fine book of poems, *Terraces of Rain.* Though it is set entirely in Italy, St. John's new collection subtly and vigorously denies each possible skepticism I have identified in the first paragraph. This poet has travelled to Italy and come back not with an album of snapshots, not with the tourist's appropriations of pre-packaged scenery and borrowed experience, but rather with a complete sketchbook, an artist's patient, complex rendering of love and landscape on one page—and duplicity, loss, betrayal, and murder on the next. His new poems are anything but tourist-like, yet they are Romantic in the old

On *Terraces of Rain* by David St. John, Recursos, 1991.

sense, full of longing, mournfulness, even high sentiment. St. John uses these lyric conventions to express a profound understanding of both the local and the universal collision of love and loss. He has taken as his project to create rather than merely to purchase, to paint rather than to snap an easy photo.

To establish and justify its Italian locus, the book's first poem enacts an appropriate generative paradigm. Where other than on Mediterranean shores might we expect to find a lover/hero returning home from the sea once again to reclaim his birthright and fate? The mythic resonance complicates the specific literal narrative of the poem:

> And the mole crept along the garden,
> And moonlight stroked the young buds of
> The lemon trees, and they walked the five lands . . .
> Sheer terraces, rocks rising
> Straight up from the sea; the strung vines
> Of the grapes, the upraised hands of the olives,
> Presided and blessed. Between Vernazza
> And Montorosso, along a path
> Cut into the sea cliff, a place for lovers
> To look down and consider their love. . . .

As in each of the first five poems in *Terraces of Rain,* this one, the title poem, speaks from a third-person stance, from a knowing and gracious distance; it's one of St. John's many unselfish techniques. Out of the seaside mists begins to take shape a landscape appropriate for an ageless tale, and then out of the initial ambiguities of that imaginative landscape form the details of character as well as the omnipresent constructions of language:

> . . . Signore and Signora Bianchini are having lunch,
> She stops to talk with them, weather being
> The unavoidable topic. Slips of rain, a child's
> Scrawl, sudden layers and pages. . . .

The birth of romance commences at the seashore and pursues its progress through a refining of image, as if a lovers' drawing were taking place before our eyes. Even the weather, the "unavoidable topic," possesses importance and meaning here, for it too is inscribed with the characteristics of language. Throughout these poems, in fact, St. John maneuvers subtly between conventional expectation—"Here, the world's / Very old, very stubborn, and proud"—and a sophisticated awareness of language *as* language. As this poem edges toward conclusion, St. John establishes the book's primary scheme, for out of an antique, Romantic past, out of the provincial Italian landscape, comes an unavoidable doubling of impulses:

> Across
>
> The scallop of bay, the boats began
> Returning to the harbor. Silent. Harsh. Such country
> Breaks the selfish heart. There is no original sin:
> To be in love is to be granted the only grace
> Of all women and all men.

The birth of love is also the birth of failure, loss, betrayal. This attitude toward love and the passionate possession of language is perhaps even truer now than during the ages of Virgil and Dante.

In "Vespers: The Balcony," St. John continues to subvert the conventions suggested by his setting. Here the "light across the bakery windows / Shiver[s] a little with the clouds," and "a soft leaf of rust [is] / Not to be confused with the real / Passage of time. . . ." The artifice of the setting, the suggestion that beneath the familiar lies a more disturbing truth, is reinforced subtly by the actions of a female character "tearing away / The soft, pocked rind" of an orange. Through the fourteen shorter lyrics which comprise this book's first half, St. John insists on establishing the familiarity of Italian romance and then goes on to "tear away" its more sentimental conventions. For instance, in "The Doors" the oak and bronze doors of a twelfth-century monastery not only embody for him purity and faith in "the oldest stories, / Parts of which had always been his life, / His many ancient ways," but also bear the inscriptions of profane temptation. On the wings of a carved angel he sees "heavy veins / Like the fronds of an enormous feathery / Palm, the plumage of a showgirl." The poems in this section move from the innocence of apparency through a variety of erotic and intellectual confrontations toward an increasing sense of decay, loss, or betrayal. At last, in "From a Daybook," the lovers "[leave] it all, crossing the river," as if to enter a sort of imaginative underworld where each natural phenomenon delivers the suggestion, the music, of death:

> The musk of the cemetery
>
> Was like music to the birds
> Who smelled it from miles away
> Its call
>   the spiked
>
> Caskets of the fallen chestnuts
> Split and open on
> The paths between the stones
>
> The tombs   and all
> In all the present was a little
> Hymn to be joined in with . . .
>
> And that was the simple goodness
> He supposed
> That they would be allowed
> As sparrows settled around them
> Like ash or leaves   like silent snow
>
> All the tombs in the world share
> This: you knock
>
> None of the living answer

St. John makes the Italian setting essential to his wise, lovely poems. His deep sympathy for the conventions of antiquity and myth, as well as his meticulous skepticism about the sentiments therein, provide the dramatic tension which sharpens his lyricism. Only in a few places does his touch seem more insistent than natural, as in the opening of "Last Night with Rafaella":

> Last night, with Rafaella,
>
> I sat at one of the outside tables

> At *Rosati* watching the *ragazzi* on Vespas
> Scream through the Piazza del Popolo
>
> And talking again about changing my life. . . .

Perhaps he overemphasizes the charming Italianness of the scene, and perhaps we too readily hear the echo with Rilke's Apollo. But generally these lyrics are beautiful, in the old lyric sense, while at the same time managing to subvert or modernize their own beautiful gestures.

If such double impulses provide the tension to drive the short lyrics in this collection, then they come together even more directly and violently in the book's second section, "To Pasolini," a long sequence of poems about the Italian writer and filmmaker murdered in 1975. Pasolini is for St. John a personification of the forces developed in the shorter lyrics. Pasolini's desire to keep company with, and to protect, the boy prostitutes and petty criminals in the slums of Rome, where he was finally murdered, makes him the sad, perfect embodiment of the romance of betrayal. St. John's lovely eight-part sequence traces Pasolini's art, his lifestyle, and his death, through a variety of narrative modes. The figure of Italo Calvino begins the tale—"Italo says you cruised / Every night of your life—that test / A man makes in the dark"—and then turns the story over to St. John. In "1984," St. John confronts his own haunting by Pasolini:

> A young woman I didn't know turned to me. . . .
>
> > and what could I say
> When she asked about you, whom I'd never known?
> Yet something took me over, the way
>
> In a dream one suddenly feels at home
> In even in the oddest circumstances. I talked
> Endlessly, just the two of us alone,
>
> About those last few days before your death,
> Your murder. . .

In telling the story, he witnesses a sort of imaginative ghosting by Pasolini, another "resurrection of the mist."

Having conjured the figure of the artist in "1984," St. John follows with "Una Vita Violenta (1955)," a reenactment of Pasolini's own haunting of a "typical Roman slum / Where half of the sons end up in jail or dead." Throughout this sequence St. John reinvigorates the Italian tradition by composing in graceful terza rima, a relatively easy prosody in Italian, extremely challenging in English. Here specifically, as if in tribute to Pasolini's own powerful artistic skills, St. John intensifies the terza rima by compressing its qualities into the related form of the villanelle. The obsessive repetitions enact the inevitable finale of these lives:

> In the park, given head
> By some prosperous client, they roll him,
> Or become one of the few in his bed,
>
> Living longer this way, staying fed
> And clothed, even having a little fun
> Before going to jail or ending up dead.
>
> They're all my boys, Pier Paolo said,
> From the streets and the gutters and the slums;
> So many to save from the Tiber's cold bed—
>
> Then God divides: These to jail, these dead.

The boys' poverty, the either/or fate they personify, is echoed in the limitation or willed poverty of the poem's form and represents as well Pasolini's desire to "Never forget what it meant to be truly poor," as St. John writes in "Love for the Dragon."

The Passolini sequence is remarkable and fresh for contemporary poetry. St. John's lyric and narrative skills are sharpened by formal method and by his mournful wisdom, and the figure of Pasolini provides a necessary focus with which to document his notion that "History is blood." For St. John the sentiments of romance must be tempered by the fact of betrayal, as for Pasolini a life of art tragically ended in violence. "Hotel of Ash" describes this doubled ending, of Pasolini's life and of romance itself. The desire for forgiveness embedded in confession results not in pardon but merely in deposition, in witness:

The Angel of Forgiveness is reasonable,

And waiting. Waiting for this silence
To be broken, for the boy at the dresser
To begin his story of concluding violence.

He shrugs and, as if still without a care,
Lights another cigarette. The breeze
From the window mutters in the ashen air;

Angel-breath, mirror-fog: the man's pleas
As the board smashes against his head—
The Alfa no longer purring like the sea . . .

The boy continues until Pasolini's nearly dead,
Then gets into the lean gray car
And backs over him, then forward, across his head.

Now the boy lifts his eyes to this horror
Of himself: the mask of the dead angel
Hanging before him in the blowing mirror. . . .

The sentimental landscape which provided the setting for the book's first poems, with its seaside cliffs and originating mists, is at last transfigured into the locus of treachery, a reflection of smoky horror.

Terraces of Rain is a very fine book of poems. Its Italian setting is altogether appropriate, even necessary, for St. John's project—both to embrace and to amend the conventions of sentiment. In an age of increasing fustiness in poetry, St. John's poems are wonderfully large-hearted, full of longing and sadness. They are unabashedly lovely, but modest and gentle, too. Indeed, the whole book seems to have been made by people who still love books. Its elongated shape takes the form of a sketchbook, and Antoine Predock's ten full-color drawings—of Italian villages and landscapes—seem perfectly suited to the intimate, observant, meticulous proclivities of David St. John's poems.

Hieroglyphs of Erasure:
Albert Goldbarth

Erasure derives from the Latin verb *eradere:* to scrape, scratch out; to raze. But what might the critical trope of my title have to do with one of contemporary poetry's most enthusiastic writers, a writer who is a virtual assembly line of poetic exhibitions, whose work verifies the mass (and mass-appeal) quantities of popular-cultural production? Throughout his career Goldbarth has been a prodigious maker of comedics and thick tracts alike. His strategy is to amass information, from the most mundane and eccentric to the most astute. His motive seems anything but erasure.

Yet in this book of poems, *Adventures in Ancient Egypt,* Goldbarth has been able to confront the poet's demon knowledge: that the poem is ultimately an unwriting of its own desires. Language erases the world it seeks to represent. The circumstance which occasions Goldbarth's most overt elegiac impulse is the death of his speaker's mother. Never before in his work has Goldbarth so pointedly provided a sustained context for his wit, grief, and skill. In the narrative of maternal loss, Goldbarth articulates his deepening sense of writing-as-loss.

Adventures in Ancient Egypt is comprised mainly of five sequential poems, long, difficult, dense, and as tonally diverse as anything he has done before. To be sure, he still goofs and clowns around:

> The scenario is: I'm six, and an invincible Venusian army of robots
>
> swarms the city, easily conquering its human defenders with (guess what)
>
> death rays shooting like 1954 home-movie-projector lightbeams
>
> out of their boxy heads, in *Target Earth.* In *Devil Girl from Mars,*

On *Adventures in Ancient Egypt* by Albert Goldbarth, Ohio State, 1996.

the eponymous leather-fetishy siren of outer space attacks
accompanied by Chani, stomping hunk-o'-hardware robot
extraordinaire, whose particular laserlike sizzle disintegrates
a tree, a barn, a village truck, and a villager.

But these many delightful "scenarios" are addressed by an inexplicable (for Goldbarth, the inexplicable must be sheer torture) sorrow and devastation. Even here in "Meop," which is part of the longer sequence "Ancient Egypt, Alpha Centauri (a dozen poems of recombinant timelines)," Goldbarth immediately amends his dashing comedic momentum with a newfound skepticism:

                         No oratory
dissuades these invaders, no pitiable stare. And if this
somehow all sounds comic in my cavalier retelling, I
assure you it wasn't, then—no, it was set to exactly
my level of terror then: we're born instinctively knowing
an enemy awaits us, and the world provides it a series of faces
keyed to match our ageing understandings.

The "ageing" of Goldbarth's "understanding" of terror is precisely the issue in *Adventures in Ancient Egypt.* In *Popular Culture, The Gods,* and other recent books, he exploited the points of collision between the comic and the solemn, and between the fabular or mythic and the personal. But never before has Goldbarth been so confessional, so vulnerably self-exposing, as in *Adventures.* In earlier work his personal gestures were oblique, heavily disguised by playful energy and by allusive (and elusive) references to popular culture and history. But in "The Route" he shifts toward an increasing and maturing intimacy, triggered by sorrow:

In Chicago, my mother is being carried by cancer
over the threshold of a next world,
and she fights it, but she goes
an inch a day, and with such pain
as only miles could measure, only an odometer
of suffering.

The aging of his mother, the destination of that aging as death, leads directly to the speaker's own maturation. His imagination witnesses and suffers the wisdom of loss. Up to this point Goldbarth has seen language as generative, life-making, the turning of nothing into something by acts of poetic magic; language is alchemizing to him. Now he must come to grips with the insufficiency of his own faith in language, for his poetry, his "oratory," cannot "dissuade" the coming "invasion" of death.

Of course this book does not mark Goldbarth's first venture into the elegy. *Popular Culture* (1990) was underlined throughout by a corresponding loss at his father's death, but there Goldbarth seemed much more indirect. This current book is explicit, stark, and more beautifully disturbing. He demands our attention to his blunt grieving. In a later section of "Ancient Egypt, Alpha Centauri (a dozen poems of recombinant timelines)" Goldbarth seeks to assure himself—and us—that, among all the verbal fire-power and stratified historical allusions of which he is so enthusiastically fond, we do not miss the point. This section, curtly entitled "What the Poem Is Actually About," traces a history of writerly misapprehensions and read-erly misconnections—from a Fred Chappell review of Robert Dana's poetry, to an "epistolary history" of artists' letters from the seventeenth century—and is followed by a hilariously fictive parody of Coleridge and Wordsworth at McDonald's, arguing about mortgage payments. "There are clues—there are a few clues / to the contents," he prods, impatiently but with ironic humor. It's a little lesson in reading, meant to assist "some reviewer / [who] stumbles through darkness," and its purpose is to assure that, this once, we are clearly attuned to Goldbarth's subject.

I have never seen Goldbarth so passionate, so willing to be exposed, and I find the result, here, to be remarkably effective. His work has always had great personality, and now it has great personalness as well. "What do I know of Ancient Egypt?", one of his poems asks, and the tacit echo that the book makes is, "What do we know of each other?" To Goldbarth, answering one question also answers the other, and his task is therefore exploratory, discovering, documenting, a task driven both by distant fascination and intimate love.

If the theme of this book is related to the poet's occupation—to find a language so vital and appropriate that it lends a kind of immortality to its subject—then Goldbarth situates himself as excavator, searching for the nearly lost, nearly forgotten words of our past to lend them new application and new life. This explains the primary figure of the hieroglyphics that Goldbarth has elected in his title and his strategy. Who better to emulate than the Egyptians, with their remarkable successes of preservation—of the embalmed body as well as of the air-tight chamber painted over with language—in order to preserve the memory of one's loved ones:

> Also: *Hadnakhte,* "scribe of the treasury," proudfully left his name
> and time graffito'd on the wall of a chapel of Djoser's pyramid,
> 1244 B.C.—the need would seem to be built into us,
> to say, "I'm here."
>
> *(Ancient Stories: "Stop Me If You've Heard This One Before")*

Using whatever advice, technique, and folkloric remedy he can uncover, Goldbarth examines entombed bodies of the past and the "oncology sheets" of the present, alike. After all, "we don't need to tithe at the Temple of Unified Light / to find our own camcorderhead-linegossipdramafests / prefigured in the glory and horror of, say, / dynastic Egypt. I put my ear to the 10 o'clock news / and hear, from its pith, its magma." What the Mediterranean cultures—not only of the Egyptians but also of the Sumerians, Etruscans, and ancient Jews—provide him is a vast history of rituals, preservations, mummifications, and holy devotions, all to counter the erasures of death. In "Qebehseneuf" (which is, he reports, "the hawk, that spirit, your totem, night's lid") he examines one of many astonishing healing techniques: "An Indian medical text of the 15th century / discusses closing intestinal wounds by lining / black Bengali ants along the rupture. Really." The site of this wound, of course, suggests the mother's own. His desire is to find a way to heal her. "We *need* the dead," he urges in "Ancient Semitic Rituals for the Dead," as if to convince himself to look: "The dead are weird, man—*weird.*"

The mode of the elegy (as, indeed, this whole book is elegiac) is "about" death, but its desire is life, a poetic defeat or displacement of death and decay. This impulse is perhaps most overt and most effective in the sequence "Ancient Egypt / Fannie Goldbarth." Here the poet identifies the double desire of his whole book, mixing the ruined and historical with the personal.

Most directly, the mother's colon/intestinal disease and surgery become a trope for an entire excavation of history—from ancient and modern surgical methods to a sort of autopsy and reanimation of words nearly lost. It is, so to say, gut-wrenching, and "the man with his head in his hands like a flashlight / shining on her all night, afraid if it blinks off once" is a figure of Goldbarth himself, caretaker-son-poet, searching through the darkness, attending his loved ones (both mother and language). What the poet most believes in, finally, is his language. His "words with one foot over the precipice, / called back to bodies again" become his elixir for preservation.

As I said, I have never before seen Goldbarth so involved in the narrative of his own poems, so *willing* to be exposed:

> The grass the blanket the grass. . . .
> Livia was four—remember? We
> picnicked in Humboldt Park and a group
> of older girls asked if Livia could "go to the water"
> with them (meaning the swimming pool all afternoon)
> and you said Yes, sure (meaning the drinking fountain)
> —remember?

In another section from "Qebehseneuf," Goldbarth deploys memory as a device by which to cajole the mother back from the brink of her dying. He charms, he sweetens, he shows himself childish and cute. And as by magic, he brings the father back to life and restores the whole family to its health and youth:

> You young again. Livia four. Me
> squeezing the bark of a tree to study its grubs and
> sun is on my cheek in a wedge as heavy and gold and
> overhot as a slice of doublecheese pizza from Vito's
> where Daddy's going to meet us. Your husband,
> alive. Of course, alive, how crazy, 1956. . . .

But of course he knows now both the power and failure of his strategy, his faith in words. His bedside address to his mother, at first playful and nostalgic, finally bears the wisdom of his maturing sense of language:

Now 30

years later, what is it
except the words we remember it in? The words
are everything, Mother.

The words we save
are the words we save everything else in.

Really

what do we fear in looking at each other tonight
if not that every word we've said
so urgently between us all our lives
will herd at the edge of the memory record, stare
a moment into cloudiness, then step off . . .

love

being foreplay for loss.

Much of the power of Goldbarth's work is verbal. He is a contemporary
genius with the language itself, reminding me over and over of Suzanne K.
Langer's certainty that a language will die at the level of dead metaphor.
He is as gifted as any poet alive at invigorating the language; indeed, one
of his abiding investigations in this book centers around his locating ancient
words to revivify (Hadnakhte, rembaramp) and contemporary words to
coddle (noumenon, meringue, nsunnu). He is indeed a poet, self-defined
in "The Reliquary" as "one of those ditsy folk whose love is fixing *pixel,
lubber, rutch,* and *cresset* into the same line." What can't, and what won't,
this poet say or think of? He spins his massive sentences out like webs, but
perfectly so, and spins his hilarious and accurate metaphors and tropes with
equal portions of magic and grieving realism. He understands that the
impure—the muddled, contradictory, jammed-together, and nearly chaotic
—is the most accurate representation of our minds and our lives and deaths.

Another quality of Goldbarth's power stems from the massive effect of
his oppositions. The unrealness of mythology collides with the blunt facts of
history, pop culture with confessional intimacy, comedy with the lament and
the wail, his increasing formalism with a kind of brilliant improvisatory effect.
I am impressed to see a kind of formal restraint as well as variety in these

poems. Many are based on the structure of the sonnet, many others find regular stanzaic forms, while still others reach variously into further generic diversity. There are prose poems, short plays, long lyrics, scratched-out and rewritten lines, encyclopedic entries, blurts and curses. It's as if he wants to contain everything, as another passage from "Qebehseneuf" indicates:

> In some
> Medieval Hebrew manuscripts, the text
> is done so finely, with such supple twists, as to be given
> entirely over to forming the bodies of human beings,
> beasts, and birds. . . .
> A single "paragraph" might draw
> the picture of two grass-appraising oxen, a parrot their
> same size, fish, a huge central tree with a husband and wife
> enjoying supper under its reach, each leaf a word, each feather,
> scale, flex of flesh. . . .
> The whole of Creation, literally,
> from language. . . .

A text turned into human beings, precisely—this is the elegist's deepest wish, to make a language capable of enlivening the body of nature itself.

Goldbarth's grief in *Adventures* is all the more effective given his usual tendency to deferral, amusement, and disguise. All the various forces and subjects of his book come most fully together in the final "Deer" and do so with such force that Goldbarth must invent a suitable poetic form: an alternating double-stanza that is capable of dictating the figurative details of his mother's life and death while juxtaposing a kind of prayer or litany (in italics) that seems distant, grand, and deeply soulful:

> I saw Anubis walking the halls—Dr. Anubis, they called him here
> *He wrote his prescriptions: Death, take people as needed*
> Anubis walking the halls—the Devourer
> *His stethoscope drank up every heartbeat it listened to*
> I saw Horus, the Hawk, he was scrubbing up
> *The silhouette of his head on the wall: a medieval surgical scraper*

> I saw Nut, whose arching body is the sky
> *And as the stars came out, the shrieks of the world grew louder.* . . .

In this way, he says, both life and decay "go on," and the poet's occupation is to resist decay by reanimating our lost lives with the renewal of language.

Both in technique and theme, Goldbarth's hunger is for the extreme oppositions of clarity and inclusion. Even with all of the variety of forms and rhetorical strategies in *Adventures,* no poems, no sections, seem weak or out of place. The book reads like a single narrative, a life history of the poet, his family and mother, as well as a life history of language. Further, this is eminently readable poetry, original and educative. I *learn* things when I read him. I learn about ancient embalming techniques, I learn codes, I learn physics and astronomy, I learn new words (and old ones), and moreso I learn loss and great grief. Some of these poems are among the best Goldbarth has ever written: for example, "Ancient Stories (Stop Me If You've Heard This One Before)," "What the Poem is Actually About," and the whole sequence of "Ancient Egypt / Fannie Goldbarth." The final lines of this last piece show Goldbarth at his patient vigil:

> I think I've done
> what I wanted to do: they're out of the hospital,
> out of the limbo of cancellation in 1942, I see them
> turn a corner out of sight ("Scramola this way, kiddo,"
> says Bruce) and they're bringing their rollicking caper anew
> to the dangerous streets of America. I've given her a second chance.
> (It's easy: she's not "really" alive.) Now I turn back
> to my mother's bed on July 23rd, 1995.

In the story of the mother's death, this ultimate rhyme, pointing from "1995" back to the previous line's "alive," seems remarkably moving and final.

Albert Goldbarth is a distinct and prolific poet. At an exuberant forty-nine he's published sixteen books and nine chapbooks, mainly of poetry, and has won a wall full of awards. Yet he does not write in the current period styles, nor does he sound like a product of teachers, graduate schools, or any of his peers. *Adventures in Ancient Egypt* is a brilliant, harrowing, abundant book of poems and should serve as a landmark in the achievement of this truly original writer. There is simply no contemporary poet like him. If anything, I might compare him to the strange, energetic comic-book and sci-fi writers of the thirties and forties, or to Byron with his odd, majestic, abundant wit, or perhaps best, to Dr. Johnson. Goldbarth may just be the Johnson of our period—the documenter of our highest and lowest lives, our glories, goofs, miseries, and great losses. He's our cultural lexicographer, a reader and maker of the hieroglyphs of our temporary residence.

On Explication

"Still-Hildreth Sanatorium, 1936"

This really happened. The poet had just completed the evening's reading and eased shut his notebook with tangible relief, glancing first at the reception area, then at the host. But the host had swiveled to face the audience of about fifty. With eagerness, a solicitous smile, she said, "Does anyone have a question for our guest?"

A young student shot his hand into the air. It was still straight in the air when he asked, "Can you explain what your last poem was about? Why did you write it? I know what it says, but what is it supposed to mean?"

The jug wine and crackers and boxed cookies beckoned.

But the poet opened his book, and took a long breath, and read the poem once more, a little slower.

> When she wasn't on rounds she was counting
> the silver and bedpans, the pills in white cups,
> heads in their beds, or she was scrubbing down
>
> walls streaked with feces and food on a white-
> wash of hours past midnight and morning, down
> corridors quickened with shadows, with screaming,
>
> the laminate of cheap disinfectant . . .
> what madness to seal them together, infirm
> and insane, whom the state had deemed mad.

He woke up on his sleeper sofa again, at half past four in the morning, and realized he'd been sick for nearly three months.

He woke up abruptly, as if to an explosion, his heartbeat pounding in his ears, fever running down his arms like fire. His testicles were so swollen that the bedcovers hurt. Snow was falling in the frozen backwoods, and a hard north wind whipped sleet through the tall pines like rocks. He lay there. He had not written anything for more than a year. He could hardly read. Magazines were too much. The usual shows on the television upset him, set him grieving or shaking with anxiety. "Nick at Night" was salvation in the early evenings—Lucy, Dick Van Dyke—as was the local paper's easy crossword in the morning.

He went back to sleep, and woke, and went back to sleep.

The first time I saw them strapped in those beds,
caked with sores, some of them crying
or coughing up coal, some held in place

with cast-iron weights . . . I would waken again.
Her hands fluttered blue by my digital clock,
and I lay shaking, exhausted, soaked cold

in soiled bedclothes or draft. I choked on my pulse.
I ached from the weight of her stairstep quilt.
Each night was a door slipping open in the dark.

I want poems where the narrative line is bent, subverted, altered, multiplied, its ends splayed out like a broken rope. Or, another metaphor: where there is something like a photographer's error, a double exposure of story. Or triple. An overlay of times, actions, images, impulses.

In this way I hope to locate a kind of speculative dis-ease with the simple linear imagination. I want to trouble our thinking, to make it self-aware, at odds with our more typical analytic paradigms. Too often we read—if we read at all—with laziness, inattention, satisfied by the clichéd and familiar, soothed by the conventional, the facile: the sloth of the newspaper, the despicable formula of the popular novel, the mere condescension of most daily discourse. We want answers without understanding the questions. We want clarity, pure and simple, without dealing with the more natural disorders.

I want a poem that resists the tyranny of order, of easy clarity, of single-mindedness. Consider the possible rhetorical paradigms of the hallucination, the dream, and all the circular, associative workings of memory. These are the mind's most accurate and natural methods in its search for meaning. To give voice and appropriate form to these less orderly, these messier conditions is to attempt to depict the mind in its fundamental environs.

The real creative question is: How can I best compose or recreate the reality of my poetic occasion and subject—by pursuing an answer or by establishing the questions? By solving the problem or by representing the depths of its mystery?

> *Imagine, a white suit for gimlets at noon.*
> *This was my Hollywood star, come to be lost*
> *among dirt farmers and tubercular poor.*
>
> *He'd been forgotten when the talkies took hold.*
> *He saw toads in webs drooping over his bed.*
> O noiseless, patient, *his voice would quake.*
>
> *He took to sawing his cuticles with butter knives*
> *down to the bone and raw blood in the dark.*
> *Then, he would lie back and wait for more drug.*

The doctors refused to name his illness for many months. This was partly because the tests kept coming back normal: for HIV/AIDS, Hodgkin's disease, lupus, a variety of heart disorders, lung ailments, Lyme disease, liver failure, multiple sclerosis, and more. It turned out, in fact, that they couldn't call it chronic fatigue syndrome until after six months of symptoms.

To call this disease chronic fatigue syndrome is like calling blindness "chronic running-into-walls syndrome" or polio "chronic can't-walk syndrome." It is an insulting name that merely nominates one rather trivial-sounding symptom of a disease whose characteristics are bizarre and devastating and whose fuller symptoms are cruel, long-lasting, evolving, and slightly different for each victim.

Here is what happened to him first. He caught a cold. It lingered and turned into a bronchial infection that wouldn't relent, even with antibiotics. Indeed, antibiotics weakened his immune system by substituting for it. The bronchitis grew acute. He coughed constantly; his throat swelled, burned; the headaches became long nails driven in. He got sicker, run down, stopped sleeping, gradually became depressed. The original infection gave way to a battery of other infectious "opportunistic viruses," which were latent in his blood: the Epstein-Barr virus (the mono virus), cytomegalovirus, others. This took about four months.

Then, all hell broke loose.

He lay on the fold-out sofa, because his sleep disturbances were so radical that his wife couldn't sleep. Besides, it hurt every time she slightly shifted. For weeks he ran a savage fever of 102 to 104. It began to abate and hovered for another month or two at 100 to 102, then finally gave way, plunging to 97 for several more weeks. Months of burning, months of freezing. Days and nights of being not quite asleep, never quite awake. He had nightmares in the afternoons, violent hallucinations at night, shaking of the hands so bad he couldn't hold a cup, vision and hearing failures, drenching night sweats, a blazingly painful lymph system (especially under the arms, in the groin, running down the leg, under the jaw), tachycardia, an inflamed heart lining, blue fingernails, swollen testicles, frightening memory loss, liver swelling and pain, recurring anxiety attacks, chronic diarrhea, worsening insomnia, arthritis-like symptoms that moved from bone to bone, tissue inflammations, allergies (to milk; most weeds and grasses—and therefore corn, peanuts, wheat; most meats; shellfish; some fruits and vegetables; pesticides; carbonated drinks). He could not read. He could talk clearly but not always sensibly. He might say to his young daughter, "Bling me some cover that bangs tooly." He forgot his phone number. He was often unable to sit up without drooping back down. He suffered from persistent stupidity. Brushing his teeth took planning, a mustering of strength. He might waken at night to find his heart racing, slamming in his ears, or his whole gut convulsing, shaking up and down in spastic rhythm. He couldn't make it stop.

There is no actual treatment for chronic fatigue/immune deficiency syndrome. Or there are many treatments—meditation, herbal therapy, blood transfusions, radical vitamin infusion, psychoanalysis, dietary adjustments—none of which is particularly effective. Doctors don't often treat viral imbalances with medicines; there is no treatment for the flu nor for mono, for instance, other than symptomatic relief. But sometimes, after months or many years, CF/IDS just begins to go away. Sometimes it fades, with infrequent or milder recurrences. Sometimes it simply stays, worsening perhaps, or merely always the same.

In the later stages of this disease, after months or years of illness, victims may exhibit lesions on the brain; radical memory loss; liver, pancreas, and/or spleen failure; violent nightmares (if sleep comes at all); chronic depression; debilitating bone calcification; as well as all the earlier abiding symptoms. Many must quit or change jobs. Many divorce. The effects of long-term immune deficiency are perilous regarding the potential onset of cancers and other diseases.

Some still don't believe this is a real disease. Doctors may tell patients to get more rest or not to take things so hard. More than a few old hacks still assert, "It's all in your head." Brant Wenegrat, a psychiatrist, in his book *Illness and Power:* "Insofar as chronic fatigue serves some of the same functions as somatization disorder, it is likely that it too will appeal to persons who believe, often rightly, that they lack social power to meet their needs more directly."

He really wrote that.

"Of course, I am solely responsible for any errors, whether in fact or in reasoning, found in the following pages."

> And this was my illness, constant, insomnolent,
> a burning of nerve-hairs just under the eyelids,
> corneal, limbic, under the skin, arterial,
>
> osteal, scrotal, until each node of the four hundred
> was a pinpoint of lymphatic fire and anguish
> as she rocked beside me in the family dark.

Dr. Jack Kevorkian assisted just last week, mid-August, 1996, in his first CF/IDS–related suicide.

> In another year she would unspool fabrics
> and match threads at Penney's, handling finery
> among friends just a few blocks from the mansion-
>
> turned-sickhouse. She would sing through the war
> *a nickel back   a greenback   a sawbuck   a penny*
> and, forty years later, die with her only daughter,

The poet's purpose is to establish, represent, and articulate mystery. The critic's purpose is to analyze and interpret—and sometimes deepen—such mysteries. This is their fundamental difference and the locus of their mutually dependent natures. There are qualifications to make regarding the critical act. The deconstructive critic, for instance, has presumed to continue and extend the mystery of the creative act, rarely resolving but "playfully" deferring the explanatory urge. This makes most poets, who feel their status usurped, nervous. There are three good reasons why poets may have a point here. First, many current critics fail to exhibit an ounce of imaginative or creative talent, merely shoveling on tons of overbearing "discourse." Second, much contemporary literary criticism seems uninterested in actual literature. This perhaps explains the over-fondness many poets demonstrate for trying to enact a critical project within their own poems, creating as well as self-explicating their work, since many critics are no longer interested in or capable of doing so. Third, the hypocrisy of deconstruction seems obvious: this critical stance, which purports to represent victimization, marginalization, the decentered, is the result of a highly advantaged education, speaks in a radically rarified, codified language, and remains aloof as the discourse of privilege.

Another failure of criticism occurs when it seeks to explain a poem's mystery by attempting to trace the details of the poet's life. As if biography is exegesis. As if the imaginative is reducible to mere fact.

Even analytic criticism can be dulling or pointless when it is satisfied to be a plodding explication, like a fancy book report.

In my poem I have wanted, variously, to fuse and diffuse the elements of story, location, emotion, and thought. The details of any one part become the details of any other. Some of it is true to the facts of my life, and some is imagined. I hope you can't tell which is which. I want this poem to be a real experience rather than a true account.

> my mother, to hold her, who washed her face,
> who changed her bedgowns and suffers to this day
> over the dementia of the old woman weeping
>
> *mama, mama,* curled like cut hair from the pain
> of her own cells birthing in splinters of glass.
> What madness to be driven so deep into self.

My mother came to see me when I was at my most sick. This poem is really for her. Or, rather, it is for the abiding figure of the women I remember for months saving my life. I remember my two-year-old daughter touching my face with one finger, soft as a breath, mornings as I tried to sleep on the fold-out couch, her leaning face like warmth, part of the early light in our wide window. And as befuddled as I was, I knew even then that my wife was doing virtually everything to keep me alive, protected, safe, as comfortable as possible. Unhesitating support, selfless care. She became and remains one of my life's real heroes. My wife did everything for months and months.

I remember one early evening, as I drifted in and out, listening to my mother tell a story. She sat in the soft chair next to my bed on the couch, unworried, attentive. Was I six again? Was I already dead? I listened.

When I was about fifteen, my mother's mother came to live with us after she retired from J. C. Penney's in Macon, Missouri, and stayed for the remaining fifteen years of her life. I think now the arrangement must have been hard at times for her and for my parents, but it seemed entirely natural and wonderful to my brother and me. When she died, she died at home, and my mother took care of her to the end. I knew little about it then, living far away.

That evening eight years later, my mother leaned toward me and explained the death, its weeks-long marathon of great pain, dementia, the body's relinquishment of all its habits. My mother was an only child, doted over as much as a poor single mother could dote on her daughter, and perhaps this was part of my mother's great sadness, her disbelief, when my grandmother died. The old woman moaned, she curled like an infant, and she kept asking, or crying, for her mother. Not for my mother. For *her* mother. And so my mother took on the role. It is, it seems to me, entirely natural in a state of near-infancy to cry out for the maternal.

My grandmother worked for a while in the thirties and forties at a sanatorium in Macon run by a nearby osteopathic hospital. It must have been a zoo, for they treated the mentally unbalanced as well as the physically disabled, addicts from Hollywood alongside the poorest of farmers and miners in northern Missouri. The building still stands, huge, institutional, relic.

One night I woke up, in pitch dark, and spoke a long and lovely while with my grandmother, who sat beside me in my high fever. It was a late spring night. I was very happy.

To this day I swear it was her.

To this day I have no words to describe clearly my gratitude and love and amazement for the figure of the woman waiting with me while I tried to live.

If I can tell you anything useful, and critical, and explanatory about the poem, I can tell you that it takes place in several locations and in a single place, at several times but in just one instant, that it is about memory as well as the imagined. It is about strength and sheer helplessness, the support of others but the isolation, the absolute loneliness, of us all.

It is a love poem.

> I would waken and find her there, waiting
> with me through the bad nights when my heart
> trembled clear through my skin, when my fat gut
>
> shivered and wouldn't stop, when my liver swelled,
> when piss burned through me like rope against rock.
> She never knew it was me, my mother still says.

Disease: an illness; a chronic health disorder. *Dis-ease:* lack of comfort; a disturbance of the familiar.

> Yet what did I know in the chronic room where I died
> each night and didn't die, where the evening news
> and simple sitcoms set me weeping and broken?
>
> *I never got used to it. I think of them often,*
> *down on my knees in the dark, cleaning up blood*
> *or trying to feed them—who lost eight children to the Flu,*
>
> *who murdered her sisters, who was broken in two*
> *by a rogue tractor, who cast off his name . . .*
> *Sometimes there was nothing the doctor could do.*

The student's question after the reading was good enough. It was earnest, honest, and curious. We aspire to capture or contain mystery by means of rational explanation. But whose job is it to explain?

Deconstruction and its pretense that "the author is dead" notwith-standing, I wrote this poem. I planned it, constructed it, changed it, loved it, fought it, thought and thought about it. I am its author. But who holds the responsibility for the poem's interpretation and meaning? The "I" is the author, but who is the authority? Not me. I gave that to you.

> What more can we know in our madness than this?
> Someone slipped through my door to be there
> —though I knew she was a decade gone—
>
> whispering stories and cooling my forehead,
> and all I could do in the heritable darkness was
> lift like a good child my face to be kissed.

INDEX